Critical Acclaim for *Got, Not G*

The A-Z of Lost Football Culture, Treasures

The British SportsBook Awards 12

Runner-up, Best Football Book, British Sports Book Awards 2012

"A veritable Dundee cake of a book."
Danny Kelly, talkSport

"Recalling a more innocent time before Sky Sports and millionaire players, *Got, Not Got* is like a long soak in a warm bath of football nostalgia: an A-Z of memorabilia, ephemera and ill-advised haircuts."
In Demand, *Mail on Sunday Live magazine*

"The real magic is the collection and display of the illustrative material of stickers, badges, programme covers, Subbuteo figures and other ephemera. It is astonishingly thorough, well-presented, inspired and indeed had me going, 'yes, got, got, not got, forgot, never seen'."
When Saturday Comes

"A cracking book which whisks you back to a different footballing era."
Brian Reade, Mirror Football

"This memorabilia fest is a delightful reminder of what's gone from the game: 'magic sponges', Subbuteo and, er, magazines for shinpads. Such innocent times, eh?"
FourFourTwo

"The book's great fun. It's an essential if you grew up watching football in the 60s, 70s or 80s. It's a kind of football fan's catnip. Nobody can quite walk past it. They start looking at it and then realise they've got something else they should be doing 10 or 15 minutes later."
Paul Hawksbee, talkSport

"The best book about football written in the last 20 years."
Bill Borrows, *Esquire*

"A body of work that transcends being 'just a book' by a considerable distance."
In Bed With Maradona blog

"Obviously, everybody over the age of 40 is going to absolutely love this. There's something for every fan of every club."
Andy Jacobs, talkSport

"Browsable for hours, even days, preferably with your favourite records from the 1970s in the background, this is the Christmas present that every football fan of a certain age yearns to peruse while their neglected partner's busy basting the turkey and getting quietly pickled on cooking sherry... Sit back and be blissfully reminded of adverts, food products, players, toys, kits, magazines, stickers and trends you'd long since confined to your mental attic."
Ian Plenderleith, Stay-at-Home Indie Pop blog

"I've had this for a month but haven't got round to reviewing it because it keeps disappearing. It's the sign of a good book that people repeatedly pick it up and walk away with it. A hardback collection of vintage football memorabilia that you need in your life... It's like finding your old football stickers."
James Brown, SabotageTimes.com

"It's a real table thumper with some weight to it, great pictures and some terrific writing. Bathe in a sea of nostalgia and rail against the fact that these things aren't there anymore."
Nick Godwin, BBC Radio London

"A fantastic book, there's just so much in it. You really should get it."
Steve Anglesey, Mirror Football podcast

"This exquisite book is a homage to the game of 40 years ago – not just the mudheaps and the mavericks but a celebration of its wider culture [which] rises above lazy, modern-life-is-rubbish nostalgia... The design is so sumptuous and the stories so well chosen and written that it's hard to resist the authors' conclusion that much – call it charm, character or even romance – has been lost in the rush for cash. Regardless of whether it really was a golden age, this is a golden volume, as much a social history as a sports book. If you've not got Got, Not Got, you've got to get it."
Backpass

"It is a work of genius, I cannot state this too highly. The most brilliant book I've opened in a long, long time."
Monica Winfield, BBC Radio Leicester

"Wallow in the days of your youth until your heart is content, as the days when you were a football mad youngster come flooding back. If someone wants to buy you a Christmas present, then ask for this. You will not be disappointed."
United Review Collectors Club Newsletter

"Those were indeed the days"
Those Were The Days: The Independent Ipswich Town website

"It focuses on the 1960s, 70s and 80s, and anyone who had anything to do with English football during this period will instantly relate to just about every page. I'm sure that you will both laugh and cry as the memories come flooding back."
Nigel Mercer, Football Card Webspace

"No. 339: The book Got, Not Got."
500 Reasons To Love Football blog

"An excellent and unusual new football book."
Fly Me To The Moon, Middlesboro fanzine

"Got, Not Got is an affectionate and humorous celebration of football's pre-sanitised era: when players clutched their cuffs, Derby County won the league and dads did the pools. A timely, and welcome, exercise in nostalgia."
ShortList

"I can guarantee that virtually anybody who flicks open this magnificent book will immediately want to have it. Whatever you have loved about our game, it will almost certainly be buried within this lavish trove of treasure."
Winger: The Review of British Football

"Got, Not Got is wonderful. I'm feeling quite emotional leafing through it!"
Nick Alatti, The Bridge 102.5FM in the Black Country

"A great read with fantastic visuals, the book reflects on how football used to be before the sanitisation of the Premier League. Amusing and quirky, this book captures the spirit of football from the terraces. This book is an absolute must for any footballing household."
King of the Kippax

FULLY PROGRAMMED

The Lost World of Football Programmes

FULLY PROGRAMMED

The Lost World of Football Programmes

Derek Hammond
& Gary Silke

pitch

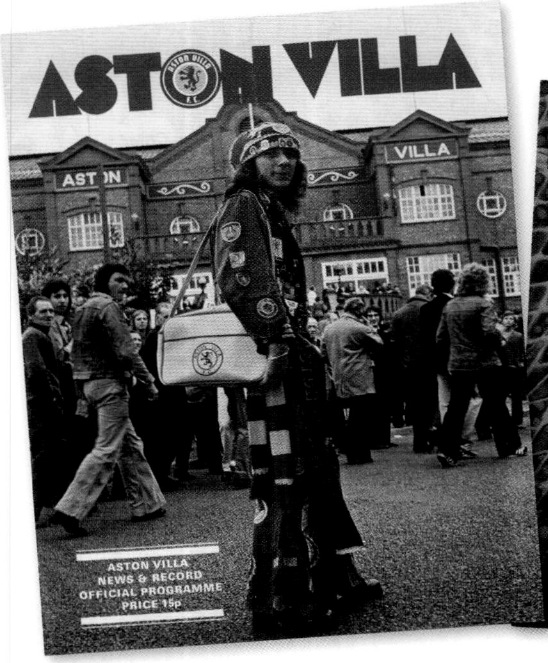

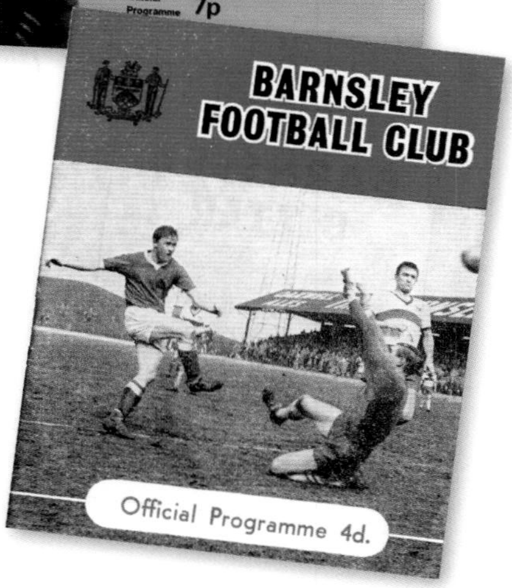

Pitch Publishing Ltd
A2 Yeoman Gate
Yeoman Way
Durrington
BN13 3QZ

Email: info@pitchpublishing.co.uk
Web: www.pitchpublishing.co.uk

First published by Pitch Publishing 2015

A CIP catalogue record for this book is available from the British Library.

13-digit ISBN: 9781785310768
Design and typesetting by Olner Pro Sport Media.
Printed in the UK by CPI Group (UK), Croydon CR0 4YY

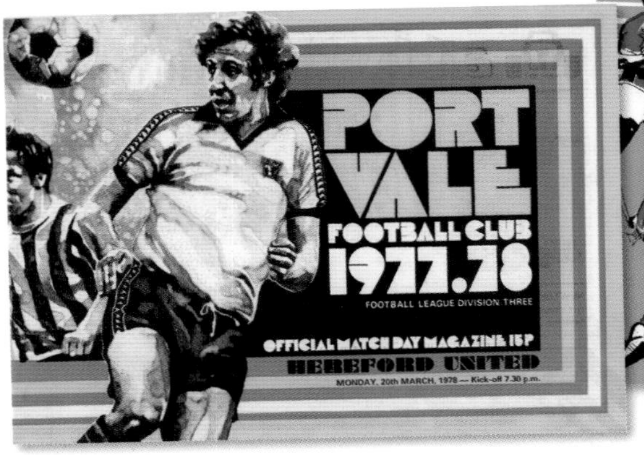

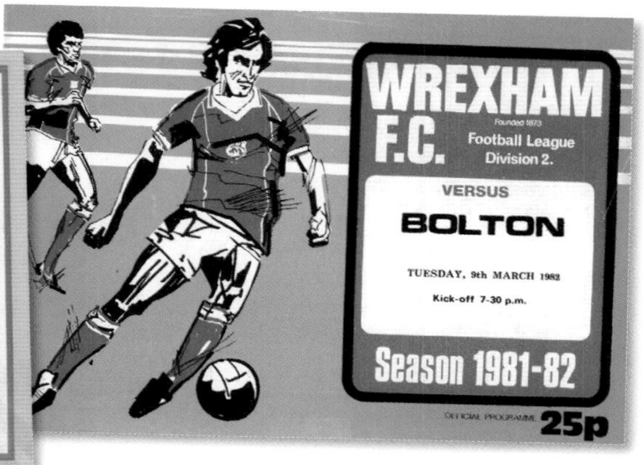

"When I was first asked to write this article my initial reaction was to say 'No', because a football manager's job is not about writing notes for a match programme.

But it is the first opportunity I have had to introduce myself to you, so here I am for the first – and last – time this season. If you want wild promises of First Division football, big signings and glamour in the near future... forget it!"

600 words later...

"After Manchester United, Forest's hot heads have one of the worst reputations in football and I aim to end that. My message to trouble makers is simply: 'Get lost!' To the well behaved majority, I hope we have a successful time together and it is my intention to get to know you a lot better over the coming months.

I am not a manager who sits in his ivory tower all day long. I am a 'half a beer and fish and chips man.'

I know I have got the name as soccer's 'big mouth' but, deep down, I am an ordinary bloke doing a job of work!"

Brian Clough's home-debut programme notes at Forest, January 1975

Introduction

The first football programmes were simple printed teamsheets, produced back in the game's formative Victorian era. Their function was simple: to let supporters know who was playing, and where. Names were presented in formation, ranked in tactical waves from the goalkeeper and back line to the mob-handed forward line – enabling an onlooker to match positions with hard-won reputations, and maybe faces drawn in newspapers or on cigarette cards.

Between the wars, the introduction of shirt numbers made things easier on the identification front. By now, a programme would constitute one or two folded sheets of paper emblazoned with the home club's name and badge on the cover. Content had ballooned to include ghost-written welcoming notes, a fixture list and league tables, and occasional, brief 'pen pictures' of the opposition team. Photographs came later. The A-Z half-time scoreboard decoder became a staple before the age of the Tannoy. And of course there were adverts for local breweries, fags and flat caps.

And so things remained up until the 1960s, and the gradual arrival of the football programme as we know it.

From the mid 60s to the early 70s, Britain's sudden evolution from a grey, self-important place entombed by social strictures, low income and lack of choice saw a joyful exploration of possibilities in the fields of design, photography, art, fashion, media, music, film, sex, drugs, food and satire. Expectations changed along with attitudes. Football changed, too – and the changes were mirrored, gradually but unerringly, in the content and especially the covers of our clubs' official programmes.

We've said before that the 'Golden Age of Football' is in fact a movable feast equating roughly to whenever you were, say, 9 to 16 – at your most receptive to new influences and images, soaking up ideas like a sponge. However, as luck would have it, the Golden Age of the Football Programme really did correspond with our own, which took in 60s hand-me-downs from cousins and work colleagues along with the burgeoning boldness of the 70s which we experienced ourselves.

At last, the football programme was developing a personality. That's why practically every supporter queued to buy one from a bloke in a white coat. Led by Jimmy Hill at Coventry City, managers' notes became more arsey, chatty, off-the-wall. Content was upped to include cartoons, action photos, awayday directions, player posters, optimistic Cup Final coupons and glimpses behind the scenes at the new celebrities. Covers began to turn full-colour. Most importantly, designers were unleashed to reflect their own ideas and individuality. Sometimes their work was groundbreaking – all hail Sportsgraphic for West Brom and Cov's greatest moments – but even the less ambitious and more idiosyncratic efforts were unique, a mirror to the soul of the club and creator.

Unfortunately, the development of the programme would not continue skyward. In the 80s, football's grim reputation was met by falling budgets, production values and cheap DIY design. Financially at least, football recovered; but the Premier League's cash injection coincided with the standardising effect of digital printing and the bland demands of sponsorship. The art form stalled forever, overevolving into a glossy half-inch-thick slab of marketing messages from the club and its business partners.

Ironically, the modern matchday magazine may take up a metre per season on your bookshelf, but it fails to

provide the key information that was on an original single-sheet programme. In the days of rotating 30-man squads, it's impossible for the prog ed or the manager to predict who's playing, while squad numbers ensure you don't have a clue where.

We hope you enjoy this timewarp trip through our own prog piles and various far-flung boxes and binders, where we went in search of programme covers that are full of personality, memories and signs of lost times.

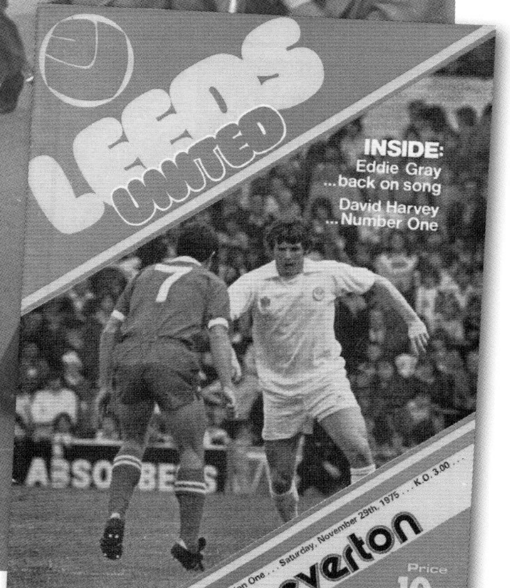

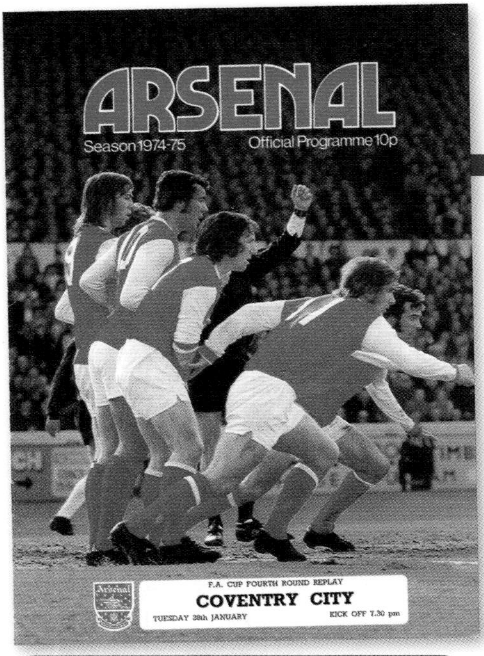

1974/75 – Storey and Kelly fast out of the blocks back at Highbury, pre-shaving foam, when free-kick walls lined up exactly 8 yards from the ball.

1983/84 – Tony Adams' rookie programme. Mr Arsenal's 669th and final match didn't come until the last game of the season in 2001/02.

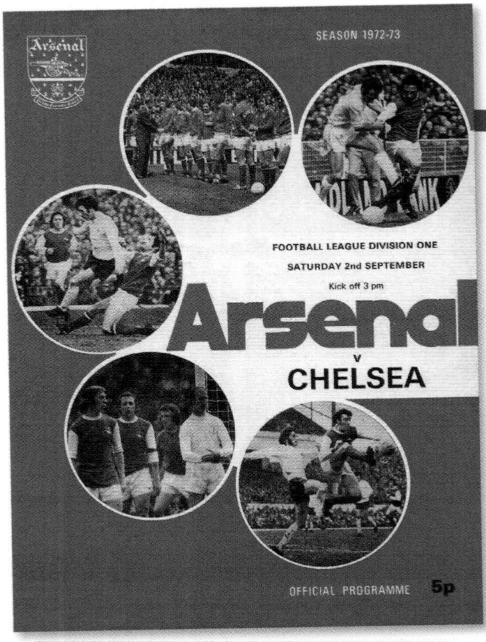

1972/73 – Dial A for Art in Action: Arsenal get it spot-on again.

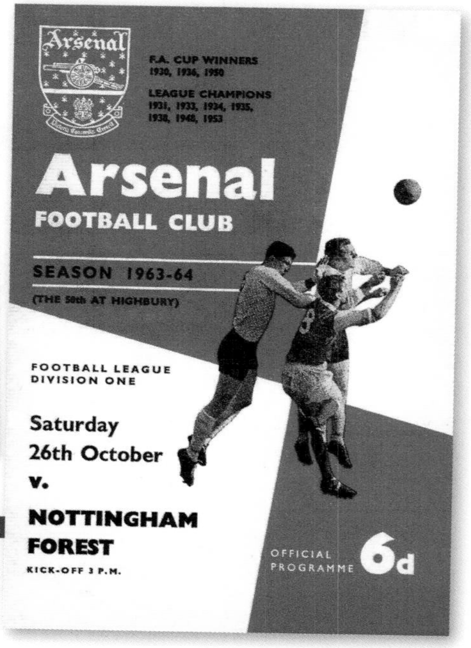

1963/64 – A beautiful quartered composition from the Lost World of Typographical Alacrity.

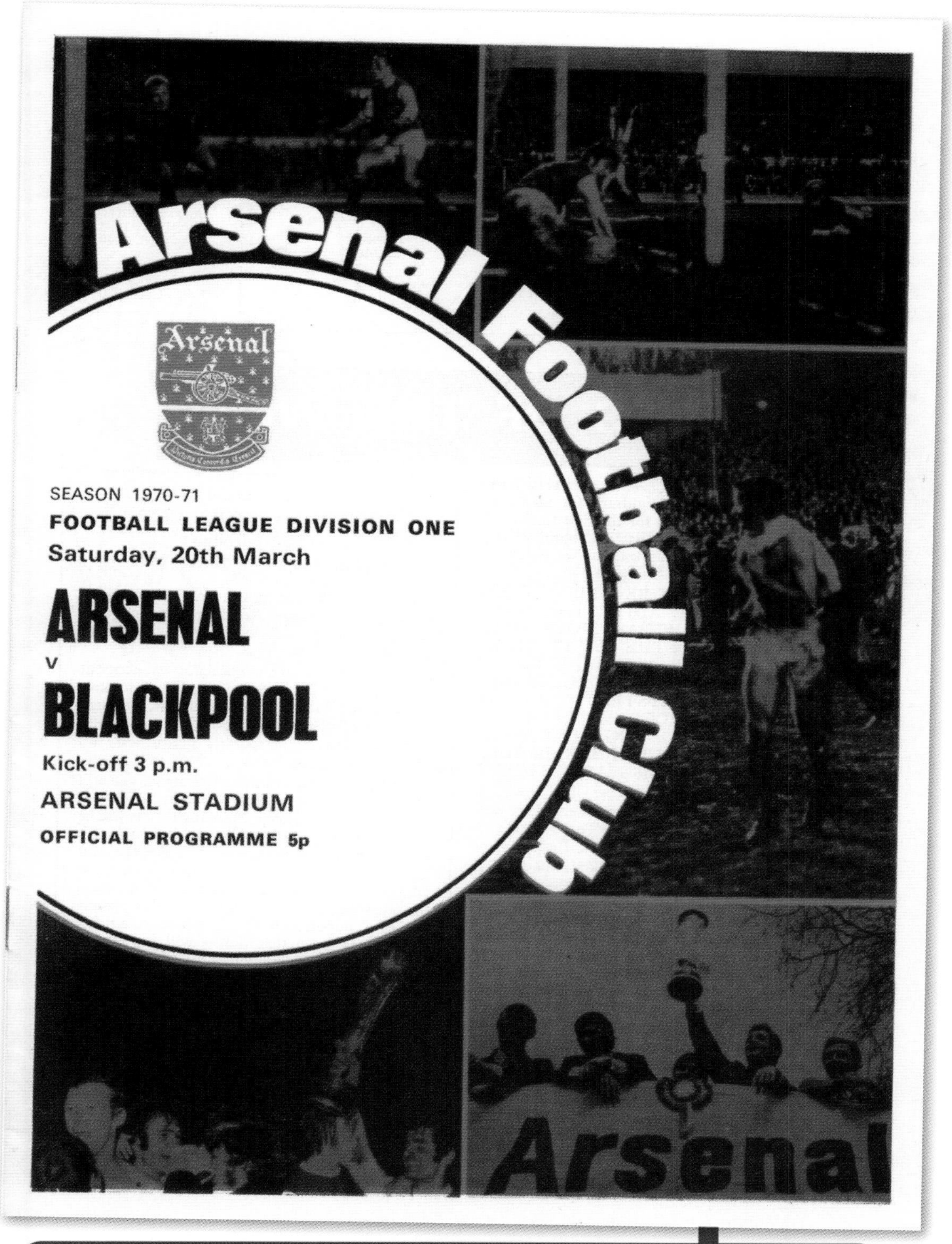

1970/71 – A classic programme design was required for Arsenal's historic Double season, and the designers hit paydirt when they gave the previous season's effort the subtlest of tweaks, introducing a subconscious suggestion of success in the form of dingy, dreamlike images from the 69/70 Fairs Cup triumph. We like mod-ish 'football' circles, autosuggestion and daring white space: Charlie George would have approved, too.

Aston Villa

1967/68 – Deceptively clever design here, incorporating a pennant shape and a V for 'Villa' in a cheapskate double issue that covered two home games (badly).

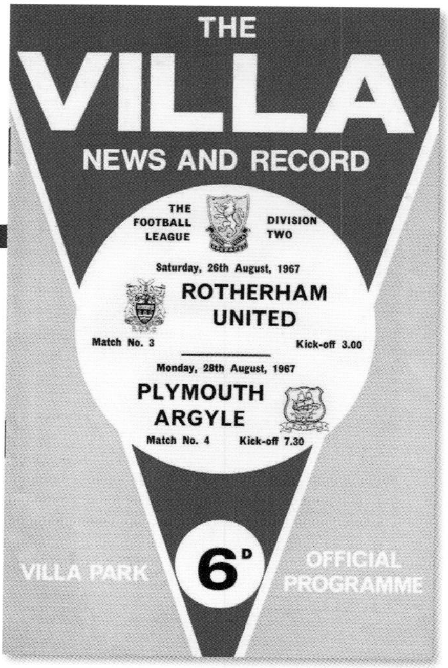

1974/75 – Villa go all Edwardian, as befitting the strict schoolmasterly style of boss Ron Saunders. Ron is positively beaming here, because he's Bell's Manager of the Month.

1962/63 – This design was used across many seasons, each pinpointed in time by the steady evolution of Villa Park – the new roof over the Holte End, here.

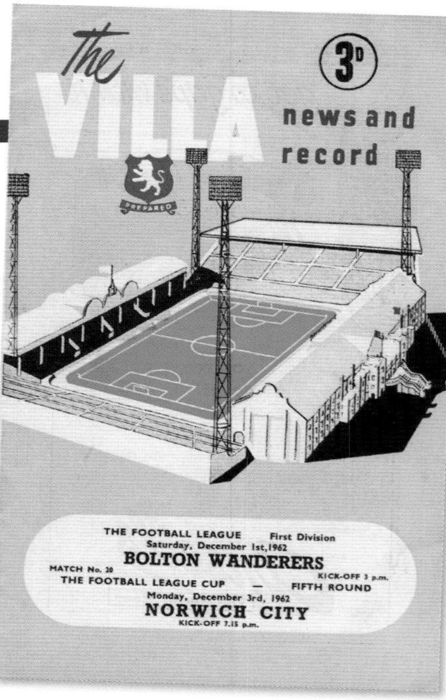

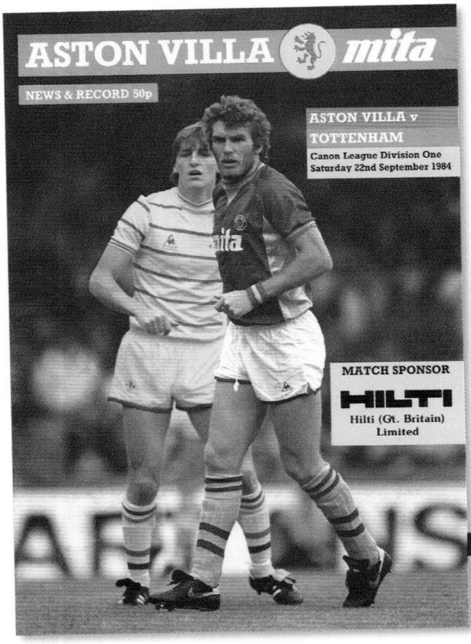

1984/85 – The age of sponsorship elbows in, Mita and Hilti handed real estate rights on the cover. Terrific twin Le Coq Sportif kits save the day.

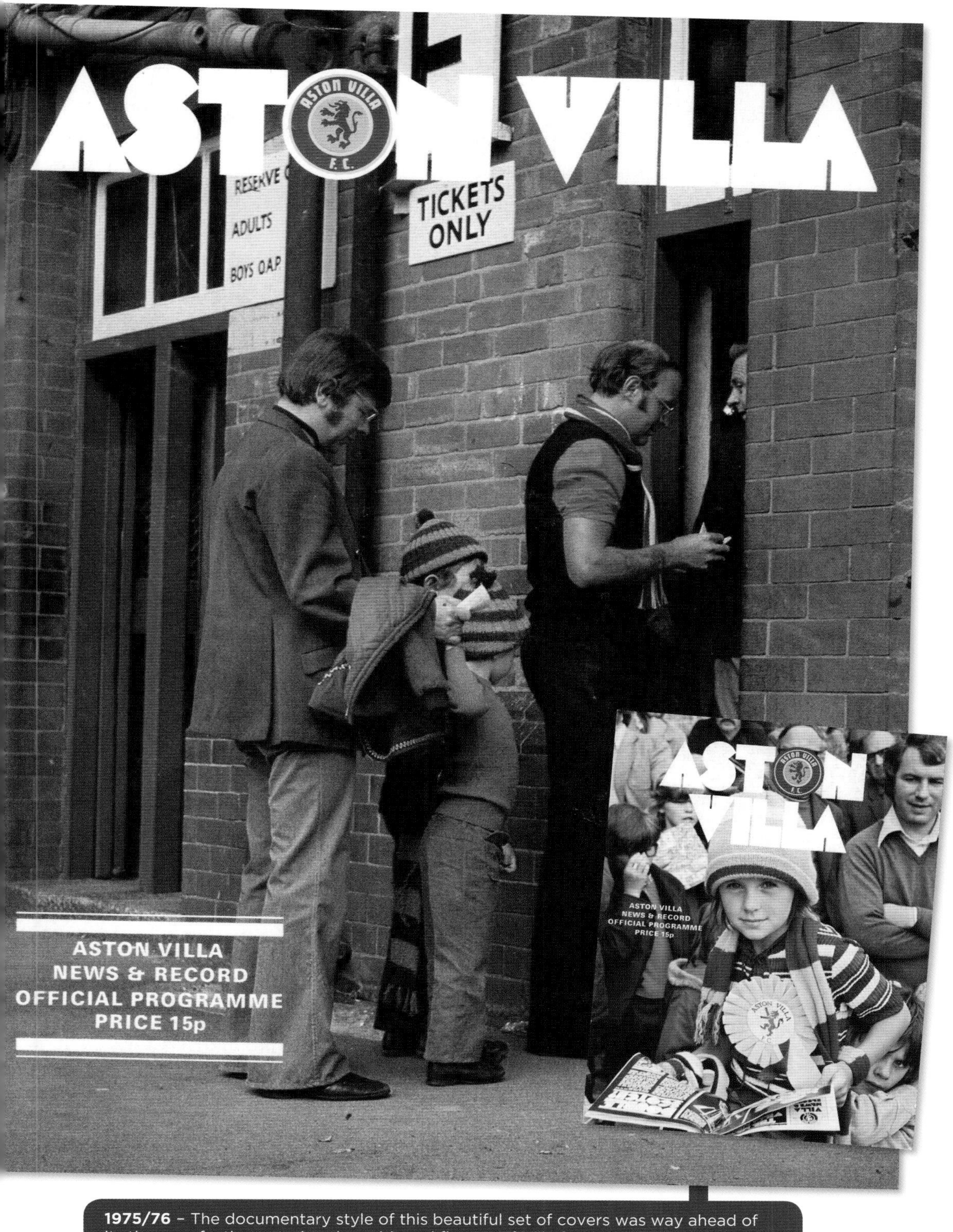

1975/76 – The documentary style of this beautiful set of covers was way ahead of its time, perfectly capturing the spirit and flavour of Villa fandom. Big Ron Atkinson is caught here on a day off from bossing Cambridge United, minus his big suit and detachable hair, dreaming of the day he'd take charge of a Division One giant.

Barnsley

1971/72 – We love cartoon mascots in general and Toby Tyke in particular. Any relation to England's Bulldog Bobby or Blues' Beau Brummie is strictly coincidental.

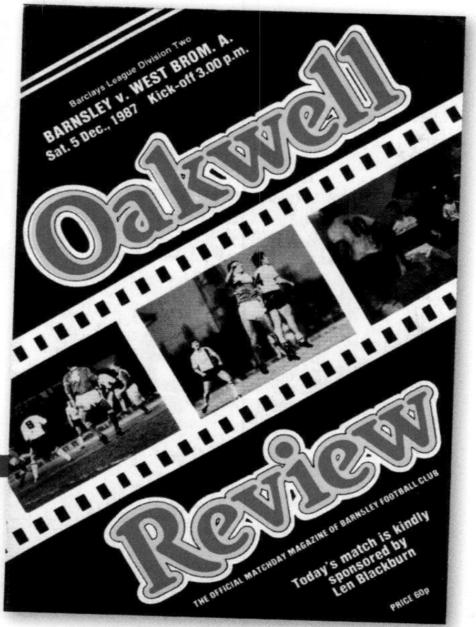

1987/88 – We also hold 'filmstrip'-style photos in high regard. There really was no better way for a prog editor to use up all his distinctly average stock.

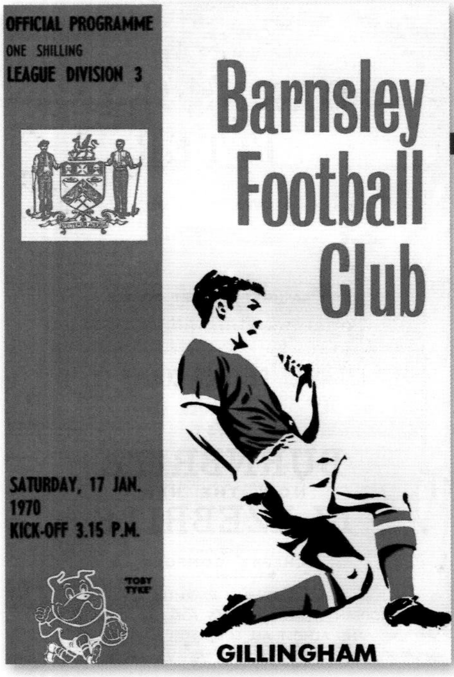

1969/70 – An early Banksy centre stage. The miner and glassblower look strictly past tense, while Toby waits in the wings for his big moment.

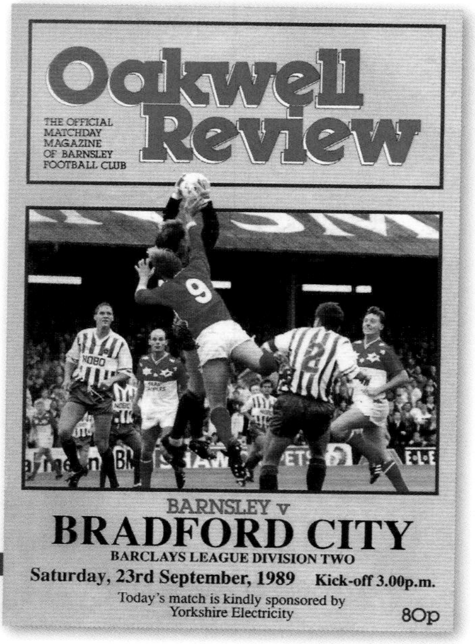

1989/90 – The Beaver Inc. sheriff-star kit and a pink programme weren't good looks for the visit of Yorkshire rivals.

Psychedelic Progs

There must have been something slipped into the Midlands' water supply in 1972, when no less than five of the region's clubs started to vibe up their club programme with some frankly disturbing psychedelic effects.

Could it be that a single hippy mastermind was behind the adoption of the far-out ink-blot look at Blues, Leicester, West Brom, Wolves and Walsall – possibly attempting to saturate the programme market in patchouli oil and clouds of incense?

More importantly, were any of the clubs aware that the others had bought into the same prog-rock look, or did their programme editors independently happen across the tie-dye technique at the summer's free festivals?

Questions, questions. But none so obvious or as unfathomable as 'how?' – or 'why?'

Birmingham City

1970/71 – Hmm, it's that oversize effort which used to stick out of your neat box, getting all dirty and creased. Groovy rattle graphic, mind – featuring young Gordon Taylor.

1979/80 – What a happy, stylish slice of the late 70s. Smashing Adidas kit. Archie Gemmill, Alan Curbishley, Mark Dennis. Big hugs all round.

1984/85 – *Blues. News.* The shorts. The carpet. The bodged mascot graphic. The 80s.

1966/67 – Beau Brummie – Deputy Dawg meets Droopy and Huckleberry Hound – greets an off-the-shelf wolf. Half-hearted lower-case conceit.

1976/77 – One of the greatest prog covers of all time – not just for the chance for Blues fans to scour the crowd for their own fair fizzog, but primarily for the mardy Villa fan who's sneaked in to the away end for a scowl, all centre-parting and scarfs tied round his wrists. Respect due.

Blackburn Rovers

1965/66 – An out-of-shape ball rumples an unconvincing net. But that's a neat little goal graphic at the bottom.

1967/68 – Rovers' blue-and-white halves reflected with a hint of the cool reversed collar and cuffs.

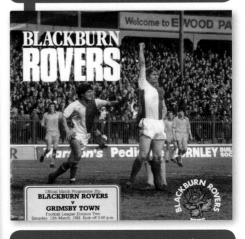

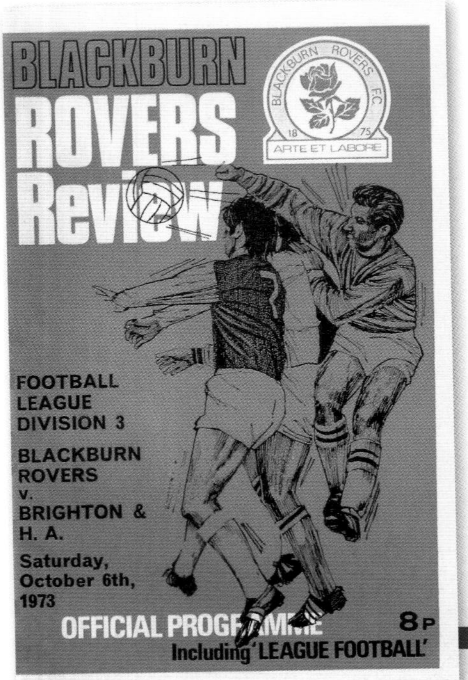

1973/74 – A cover ad for the *FLR/ League Football* was always a giveaway sign of thin prog content.

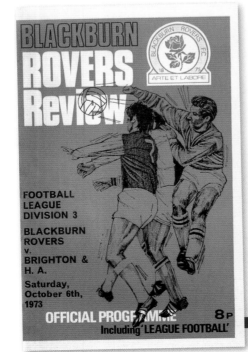

1981/82 – Rovers triumphant in front of Ewood's grand old Archibald Leitch stand.

1978/79 – Now this is what you might call a prime example of a Blackburn Rovers programme. Good old Ewood Park shot from the skies and emblazoned with the proud red rose badge. The local-derby match against Burnley sponsored by Walker Steel – Uncle Jack waiting in the wings to transform the ground along with Rovers' fortunes. Hmm, shame Burnley won the match 2-1.

Blackpool

1967/68 – The Tower runs through BFC covers as consistently as the 'Blackpool' in a stick of rock. Ace Golden Mile graphic, uncannily evocative of the 'Kiss Me Kwick' era.

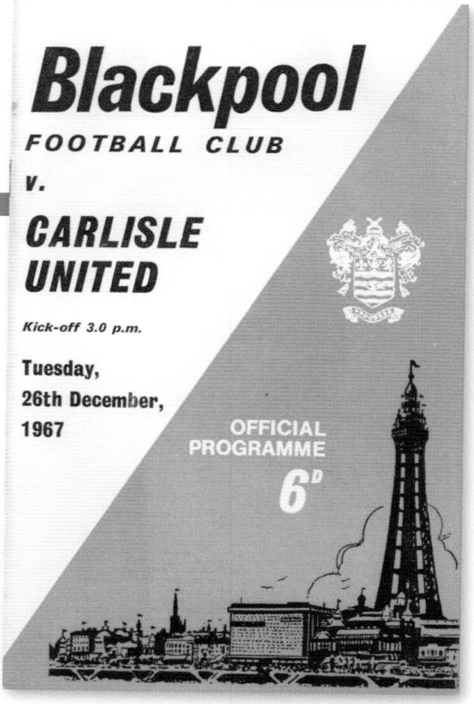

1990/91 – The odd time they leave the Tower out of the mix, it's still there in everyone's mind, lurking in that big Tower-shaped gap in the sky.

1970/71 – *The Scorcher* artist lets his hair down on a full-page graphic from the *Summer Special*. Love those hooped socks.

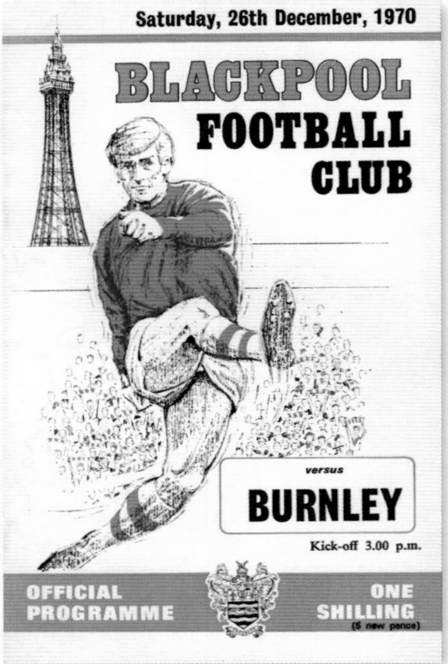

1984/85 – Seaside Special: Summertime city ain't got the summertime blues...

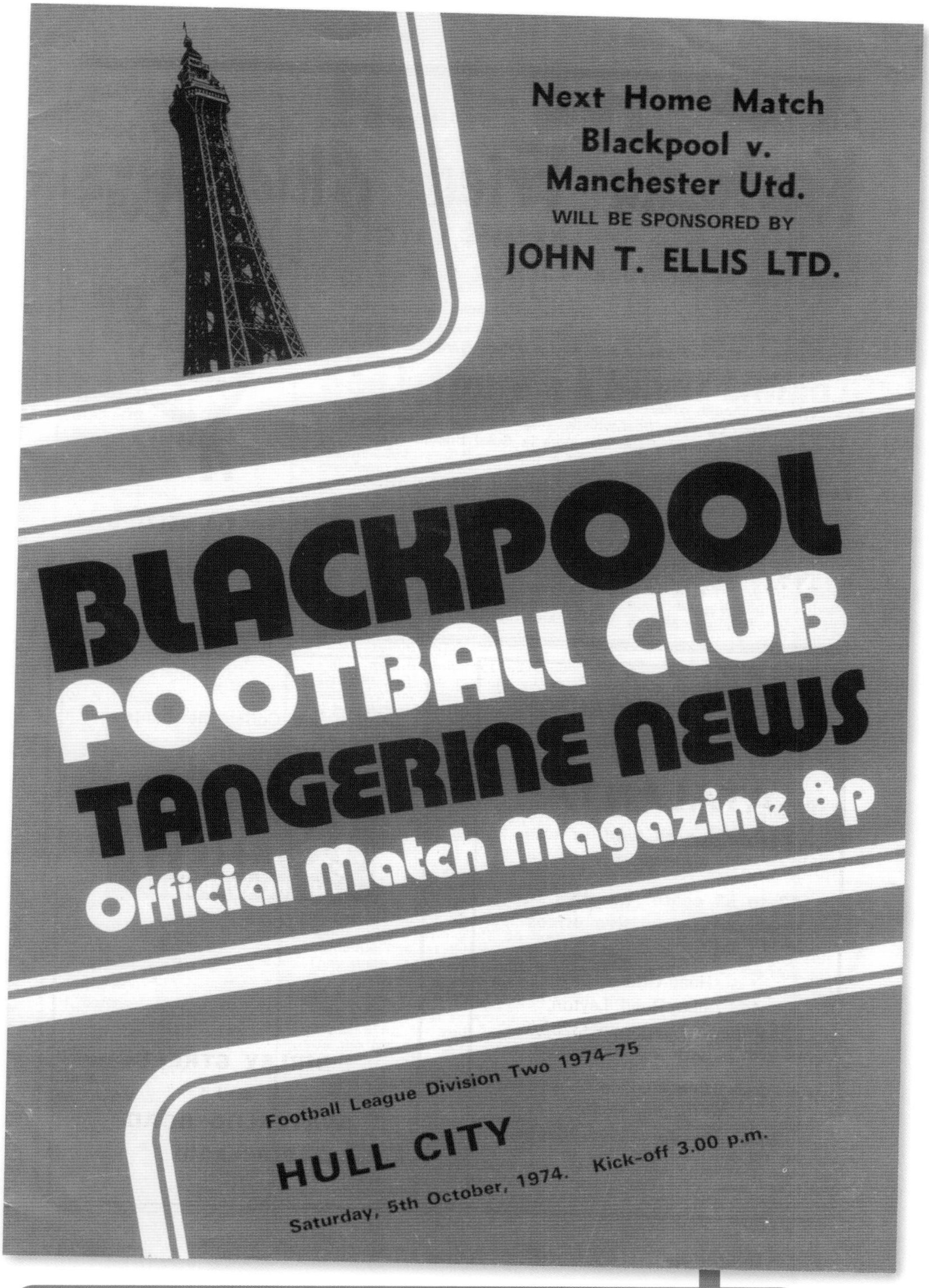

1974/75 – How very forward-looking, adding the sponsor of next week's match to the prog cover: great idea, provided you weren't the sponsor of this week's match. And how progressive of the Tangerines to foresee the trendy Fully Programmed font no less than 40 years into the future. Who needs seafront fortune tellers when you've got a Blackpool programme?

Bolton Wanderers

1968/69 – The first home match of the season. An elephant and a storm of spy-movie fonts nestle in unseasonal arctic tableau.

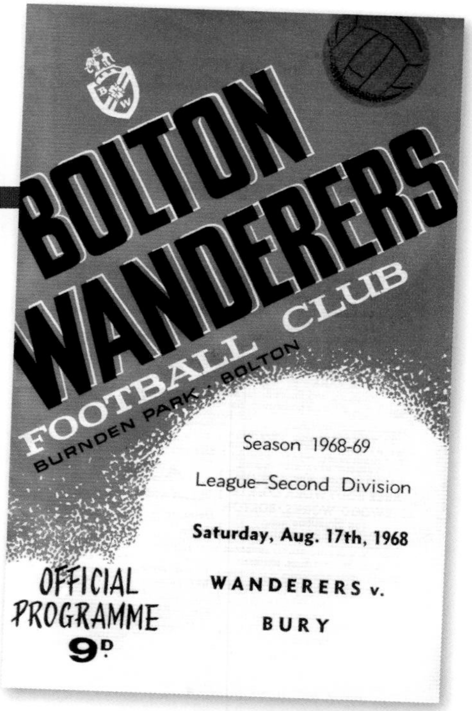

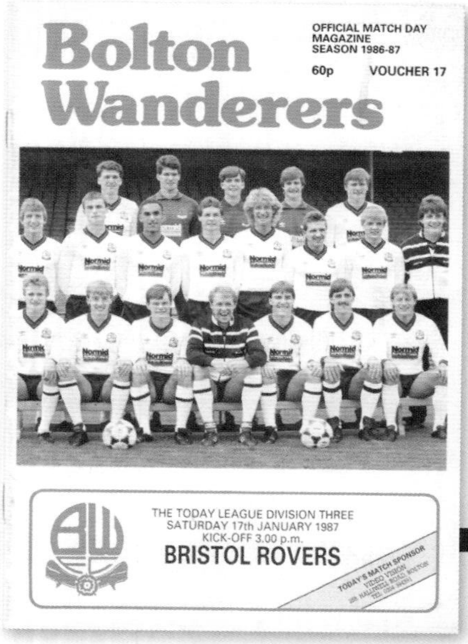

1986/87 – Normid sponsor the shirts (and get to build a supermarket across half the Railway End terrace).

1980/81 – Kiddology. And welcome to the unfathomable logo of the century.

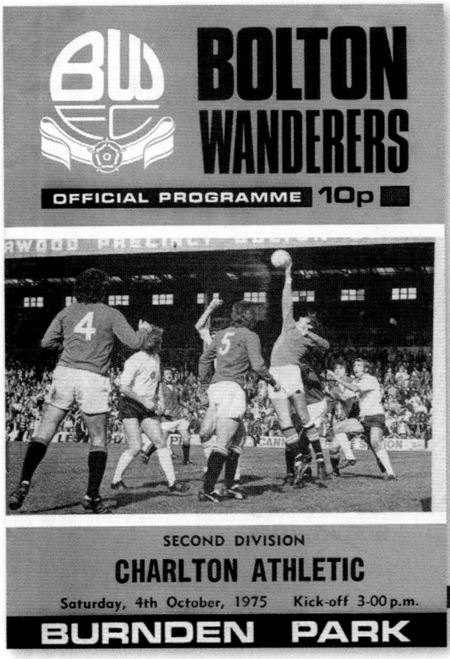

1975/76 – Letters in a circle: this one will run and run.

1963/64 – Collectors will tell you that a penned-in scoreline, team changes and substitutes' names ruin a programme and detract from its value. Doesn't anybody else think these little personal touches add uniqueness and value, providing evidence that somebody, sometime – maybe infant you – really cared? This was filled in by a Prestonite, who was at Deepdale for the replay two days later. Bolton won 2-1.

AFC Bournemouth

1971/72 – My first ever away match. Got there a bit late, left a bit early. Imagine our surprise when the Sunday paper said it was Cherries 3-1 Rotherham, not 1-1!

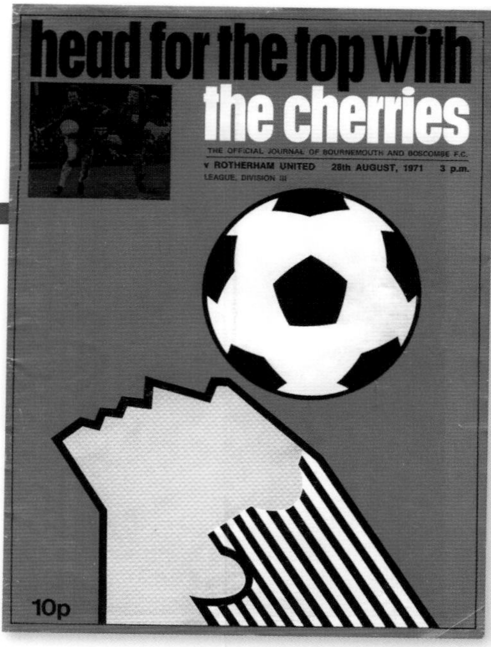

1974/75 – After Go(al)ing Along and Heading for the Top, where else for the Cherries to head except sexual innuendo, and a chance to Score in a frenzy of hot action.

1960/61 – From 1955 to 1968, B&BAFC persevered with this postcard design, its font reminiscent of a seaside guesthouse sign. No, not the one that says VACANCIES.

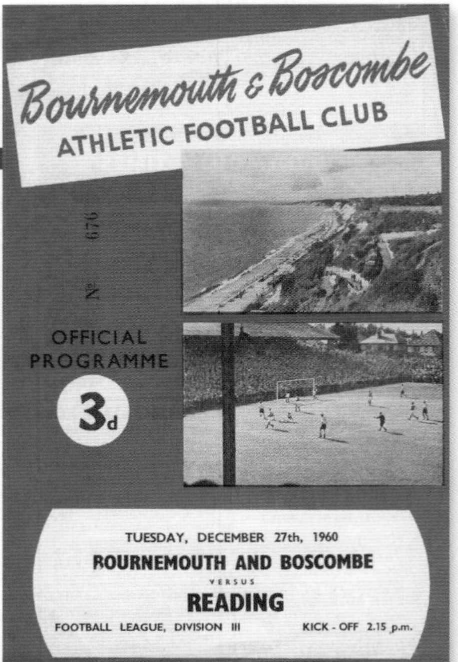

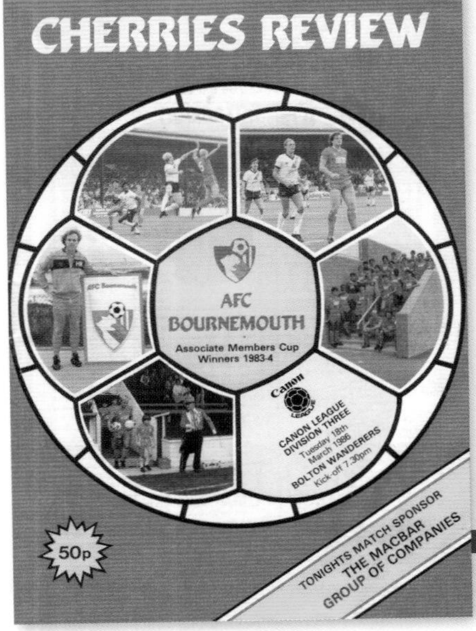

1985/86 – Famous residents: England & Bomo mascot Ken Baily; Harry Redknapp and giant postcard home. Yes, it's pink.

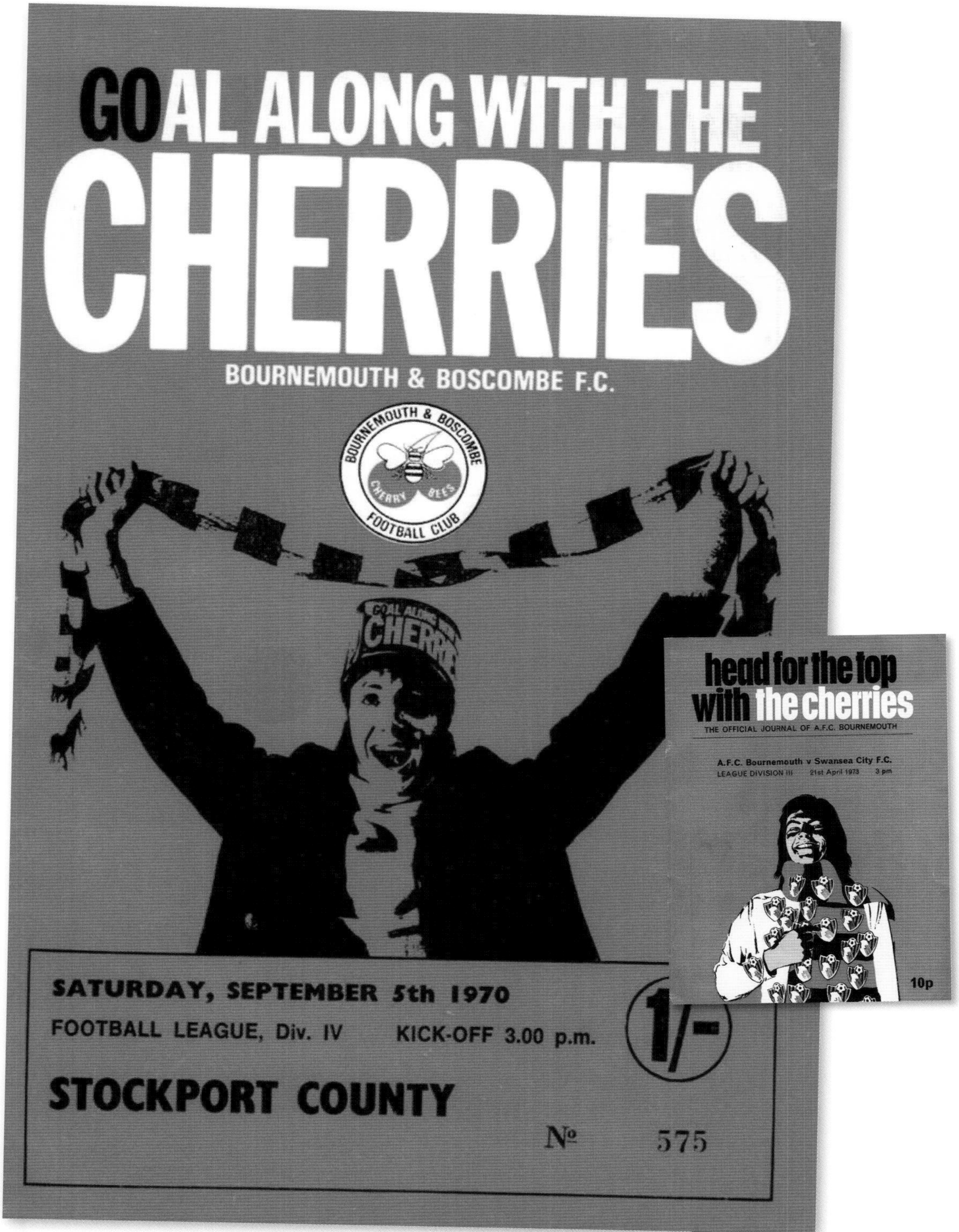

1970/71 – After a brief 60s flirtation with groovy graphics, Bomo went overboard with some of the wildest pop-art design of the early 70s. Not so sure about the punful (ie not punful) title or the bee with massive bollocks on the soon-to-be restyled badge, but love the Andy Warhol posterised look.

Bradford City

1987/88 – It's painfully 80s, but we like programmes based around kit design and we like architectural drawings – these in the aftermath of the Valley Parade fire.

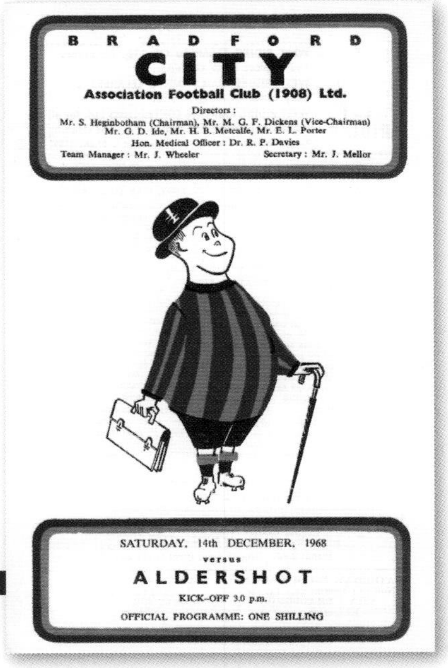

1968/69 – A classic in the field of cartoon mascots – the 'City Gent' later adopted by the early, long-running fanzine of the same name.

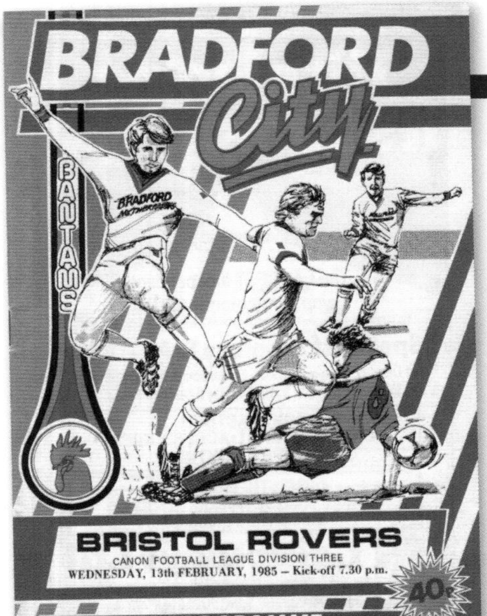

1984/85 – It's painfully 80s. Period. An avalanche of garish pink 'n' amber, clipart action and downwards writing. Ooh, and that 'special offer' explosion sticker...

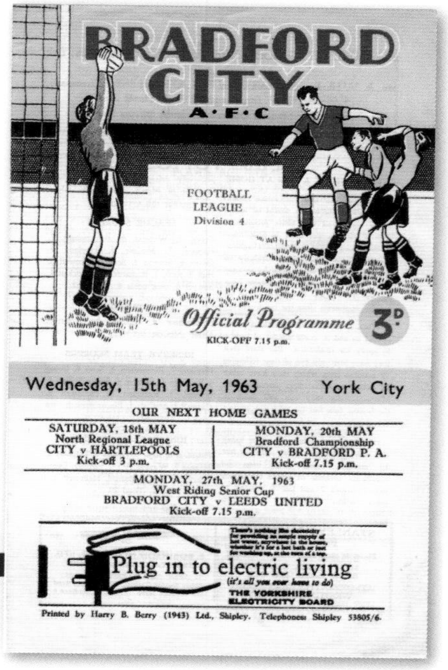

1962/63 – The sheer elegance of post-war design, just before it fizzled out in the mid 60s. Whatever happened to futuristic ads for the Yorkshire Electricity Board?

Brentford

1982/83 – There's no doubt why this posed skill-shot cover makes the cut. It's Chris Kamara, looking suspiciously young. And that's one hell of a supportive cartoon bee.

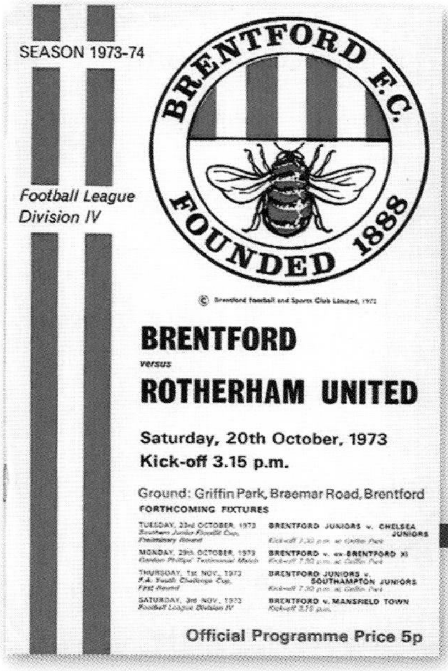

1973/74 – Old-school: The bees were more realistic down in the Fourth Division.

1979/80 – We wonder how many away fans failed to spot the arch honeycomb reference here? Meanwhile, fake posed home crowd claims Brentford Are Magic!

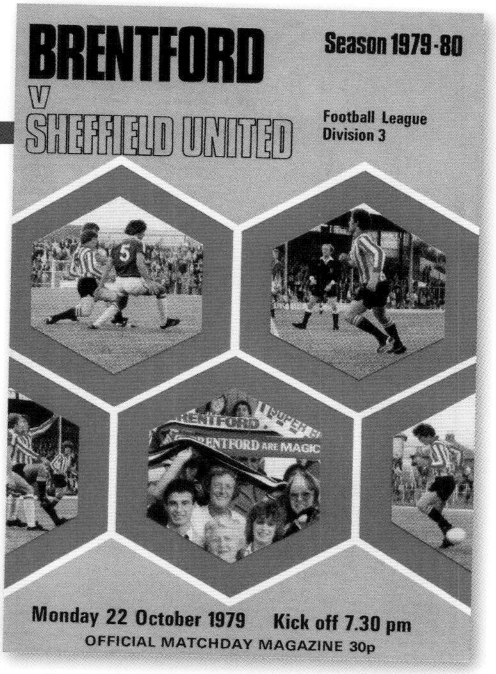

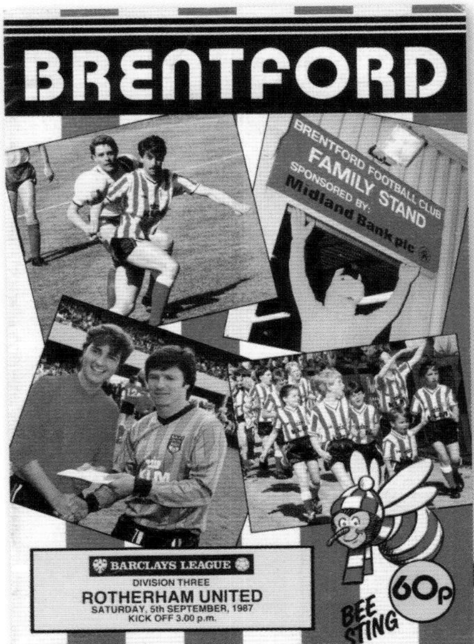

1987/88 – It's Wicksy out of *EastEnders*! And a disturbing griffin mascot hostage situation! All this for a 60p 'Bee sting'!

Aerial Shots

It's strange to think nowadays that the oh-so-familiar aerial shot of your club's football ground was once associated with hi-tech glamour and taste. Lordie, imagine a football club that knew someone with a plane and a camera. Or, failing that, imagine a club that could afford to hire a draughtsman to imagine what Goodison Park or Turf Moor might look like from a pigeon's eye view.

The aerial drawing of the ground was still a programme-cover staple in the early 60s, usually prinked up ever-so-slightly to even up the level of the stadium roofs. This trend was then gradually superseded by the bona-fide black-and-white photograph, which made away fans gasp with envy every Saturday afternoon, imagining the denizens of Norwich, Swansea and

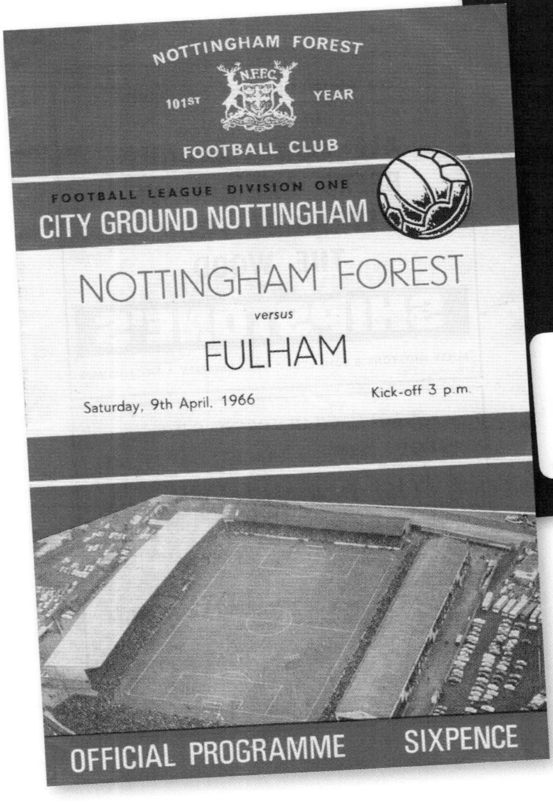

Tottenham soaring off to the Riviera on one of those new-fangled Pontinental holidays.

It was the addition of extra-thick pitch markings that always seemed extra impressive. Did you know the centre-spot at Portman Road, Ipswich, was apparently the first to be visible from space?

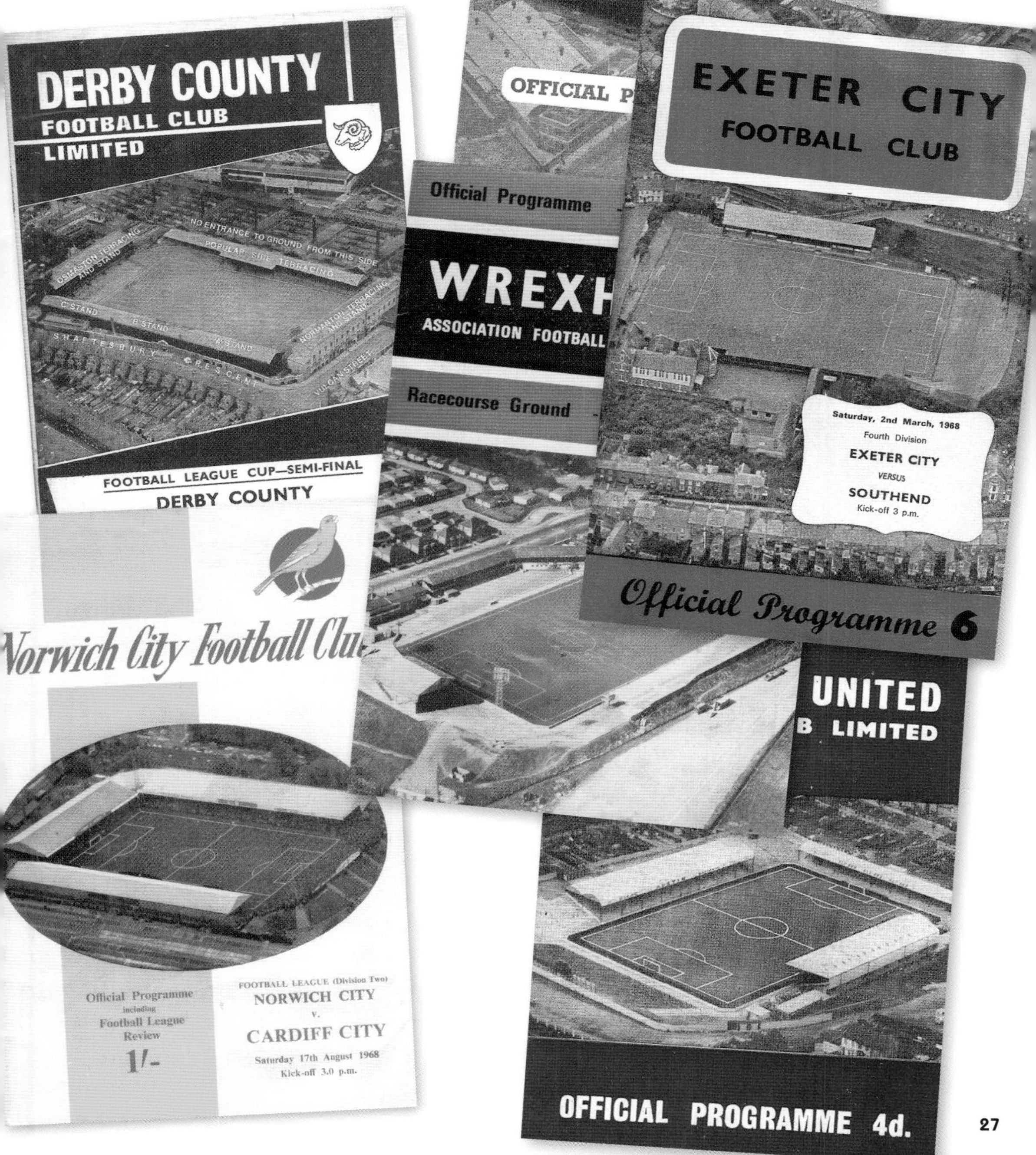

Brighton & Hove Albion

1978/79 – It's the Battle of the Seasides: Blackpool, home of the Labour Conference, vs Brighton, the Tories' choice. Oop North vs Dahn Sarf. Peter Ward on the case.

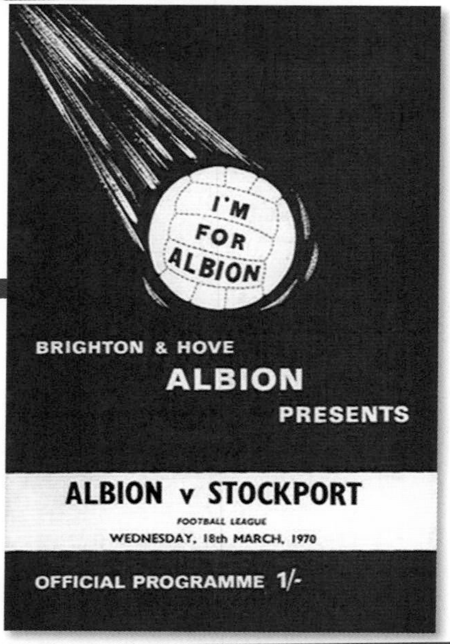

1969/70 – BHA to the future: Hard to believe *I'm For Albion* is more modern than the trio below.

1980/81 – Going Goldstone gone: You don't get pylons on the terraces at the Amex.

1967/68 – Seaside civic pride at large. After the match, why not do a show on the end of the pier? Visit our Regency Royal Pavilion? Or this outstanding modern precinct?

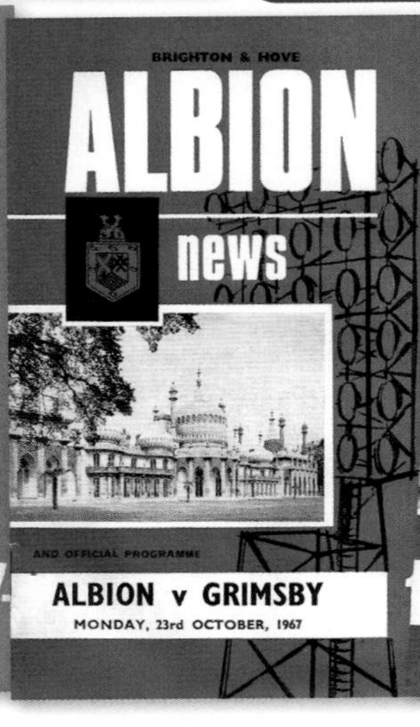

1987/88 – This *Seagull Review* serves up a perfect storm of attractions. The cartoon animal mascot is present in the form of a seagull swooping down to steal a Nobo corporate sponsor scarf. There's more gritty realism in the view in through the windows of two B&Bs. To top it all, we love the two blokes watching the match over their garden fence.

Bristol City

1983/84 – The very nerve. The Bristol City prog team were so bereft of inspiration, they only went and lifted wholesale the cover of Leicester City's 77/78 offering.

1974/75 – Ah yes, we like round shapes with writing in. They're easy but effective, even picking up a reference to Leeds United's cool 'Smiley' badge, on the cheap.

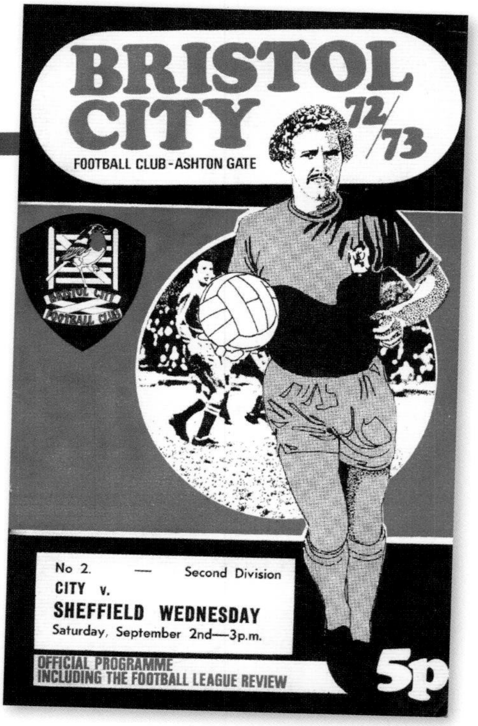

1972/73 – City break with the prog tradition of anonymity to feature an actual cartoon player, Robins lifer Geoff Merrick.

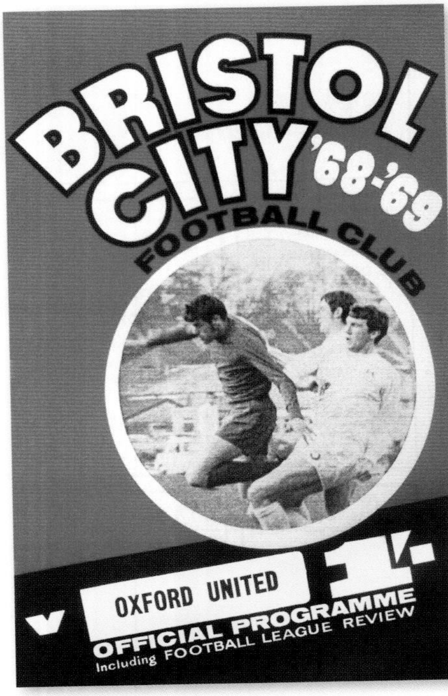

1968/69 – A crisp one shilling postal order to the first reader who can tell us where this mysterious Robins-Millwall match in the cover pic was played.

1979/80 – We like cartoon mascots, and even bemoan the fact that they don't make 'em like this apparently infant-targeted robin any more. We also like programmes with definite-article names like *The Robin.* And Division One terraces with room for just one front row of fans. And wingers jumping to compete for headers 40 yards from the action.

Bristol Rovers

1968/69 – When Rovers were champs at making wobbly text 'bend' around a ball. In 67/68, they'd had their name running right up a player's arms. Impressive.

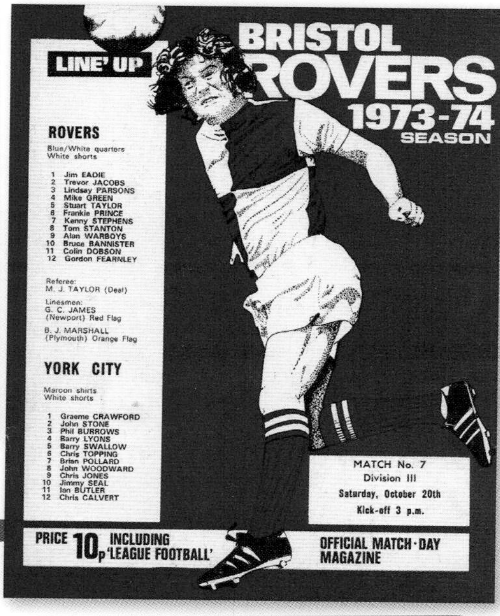

1973/74 – Rovers break with the prog tradition of anonymity to feature an actual cartoon player, Gas goalbanger Bruce Bannister. (See previous spread).

1989/90 – Shiver me timbers, Rovers have gone all piratical. Resembles an advert for a disappointing seaside theme park, complete with sponsor's name on a scroll.

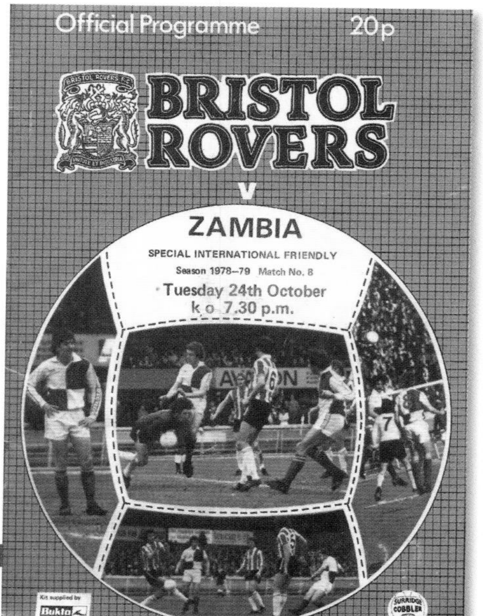

1978/79 – The Pirates take on landlocked Zambia in a sea of graph-paper squares. Ours is not to reason why.

Face in the Crowd

Match the Face

A photo of the Plainmoor crowd, the magic box is there again.

Is that your face inside the box? If it is then bring your programme to me, Martyn Goulding, and claim your prize.

HEADS YOU WIN

Lucky Face

Each home game, our photographer will take a shot of a section of the crowd. If you see your face circled in the published photograph, take it to BEN SULLIVAN at the Development Association offices and he will give you a crisp £5 note.

Tonight's Lucky Face is from the Newcastle v West Bromwich Albion match on Saturday 10th September, 1977

Face in the Crowd

SECTION OF THE CROWD TAKEN FRIDAY, 26th DECEMBER, 1969

Preston North End v. Bolton Wanderers

Supporters who have been ringed will receive the following prizes:

ADULTS: Two Complimentary Tickets for the Next Home Game.

JUNIORS: An invitation to meet the players in the dressing-room and see the game from the Trainer's Bench at the next home game.

Winning supporters to call at the Secretary's Office after the game.

'FACE IN THE CROWD WINNER'

Are you the face ringed in the photo above? If it's your face that's ringed, you've won two tickets for an Arsenal home game this season.

Back in the day, it wasn't only the promise of discovering the identity of the opposition left-back that drove the tide of fans in the terraced backstreets toward the man in the white coat, 5p's at the ready.

There was also an element of naked self-interest involved. Buying a programme was part leap of faith, part wild gamble.

True, it was only a one-in-a-thousand chance, but what it your team happened to make it through to the Cup Final at Wembley this May… and you couldn't get a ticket to go? Buying the programme every week furninshed you – and every other fan – with a full set of Cup Final coupons, which could be clipped, stuck on a sheet (thus decimating the future value of said vintage collectable on the memorabilia market) and traded in for a spot just by the Royal Box.

Those odds were made to look relatively attractive by the second strictly selfish reason for a purchase: the one-in-20,000 chance that your face might magically appear inside a white bubble on the inside back page. Imagine the glorious honour of being this week's Face in the Crowd. More to the point, imagine the crushing ignominy of people in your row all telling you that you're the Face in the Crowd… and it being too late to buy a prog to claim your 5 bob prize…

Burnley

1963/64 – Burnley product oozes quality and confidence, guiding the unsuspecting visitor's eye to a roll call of recent League title triumphs.

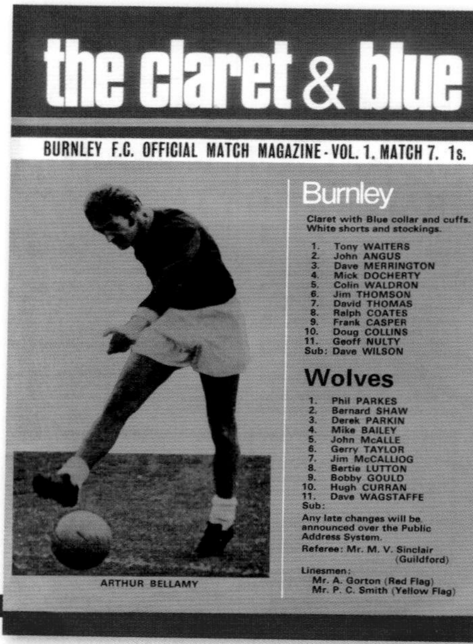

1970/71 – The blue wash on this cover could theoretetically have made us think of bright skies and sunny days, but it came out gloomy instead.

1979/80 – A festival of pinkish Clarets action with curiously exaggerated club crests and Umbro logos. Scores high for subtle product placement on the stand.

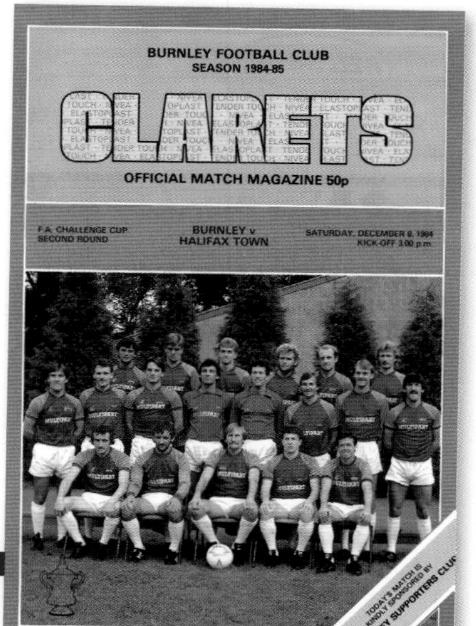

1984/85 – A festival of unfettered, bright pink Clarets action. Scores even higher for subliminal product placement within the title of the prog.

1975/76 – More gloom at Turf Moor, in an age when a night match was like firework night, cocooned in the dark while floodlights flooded down. There's not even a single 30W bulb illuminating the back of this stand. Fab Umbro shirt with 'V' front shirt and central badge, mind – matched on the night by Stoke's exotic sash.

Bury

1968/69 – Cracking name for a prog, *The Shakers*, its impact multiplied a hundred times with that DIY shaky font effect (and a 200-yard long pitch).

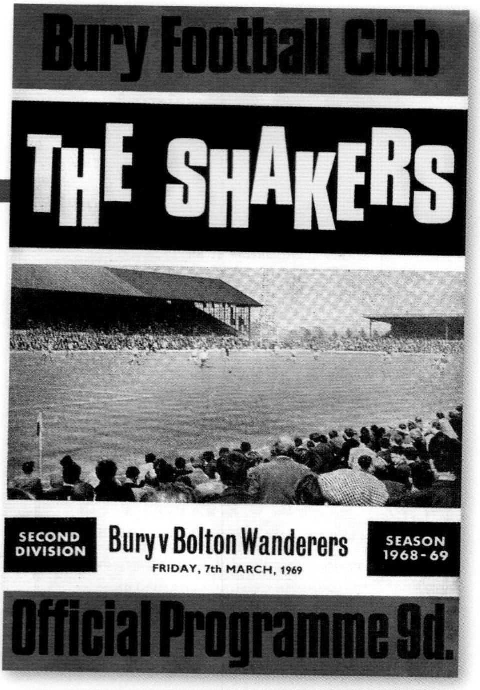

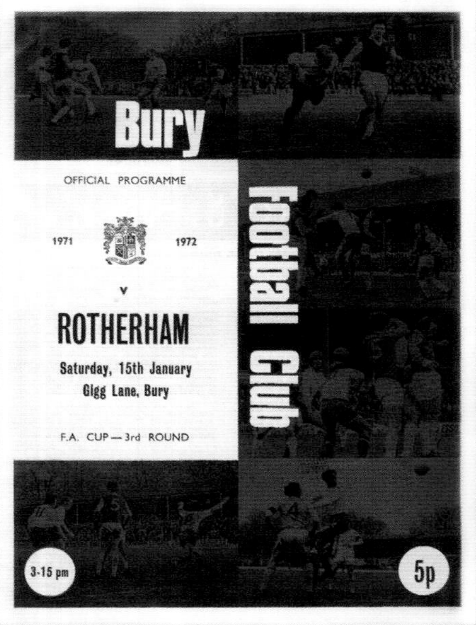

1971/72 – Compare and contrast with our featured Arsenal programme. Close, but no cigar.

1986/87 – Jesus, what a mess. This looks like a whole pile of crap pogrammes, with nasty red text overlaying horrible 80s pinstripes. Evolution in reverse.

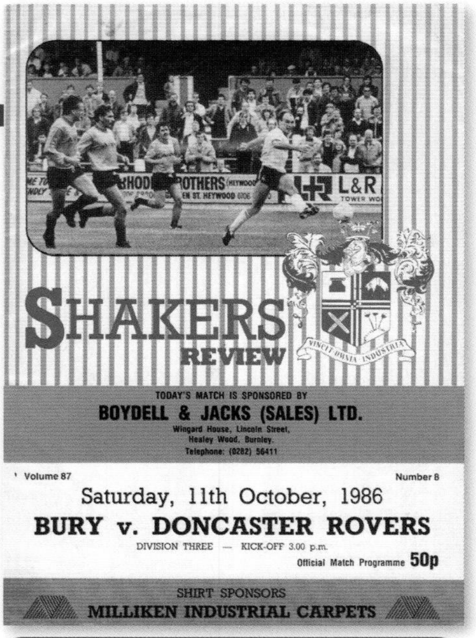

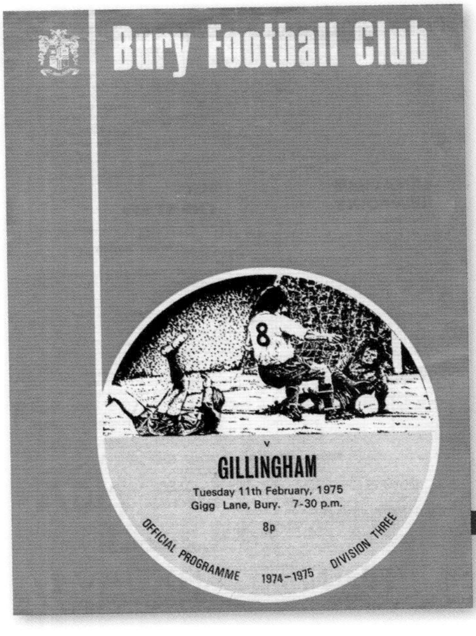

1974/75 – Hands up who clocked the fact that the mysterious yoyo motif here is in fact a lower-case 'b' for Bury? And what a curious choice of cartoon action.

1970/71 – How cruel for Cambridge to be celebrating their arrival in the big league while the spectre of the league's last failed re-election hangs over Southport.

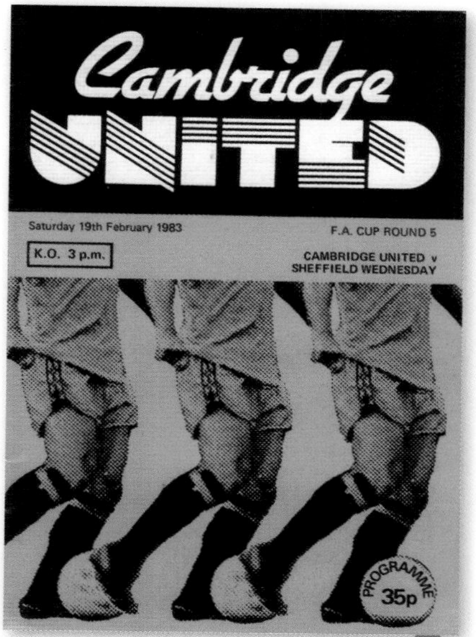

1979/80 – On second thoughts, who needs art at all when you can get a talentless 10-year-old to make with the felt pens? A low point in prog-cover history.

1982/83 – Who needs Andy Warhol when your prog is pop art? On reflection, Andy might have helped match up the cosy 'Cambridge' and edgy 'UNITED' fonts.

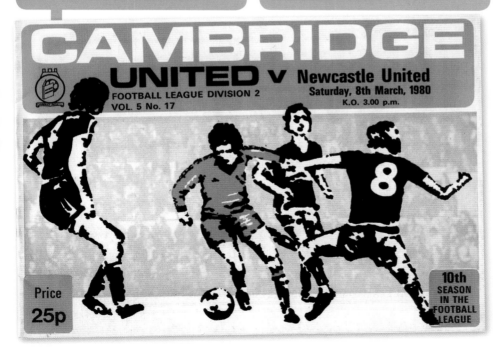

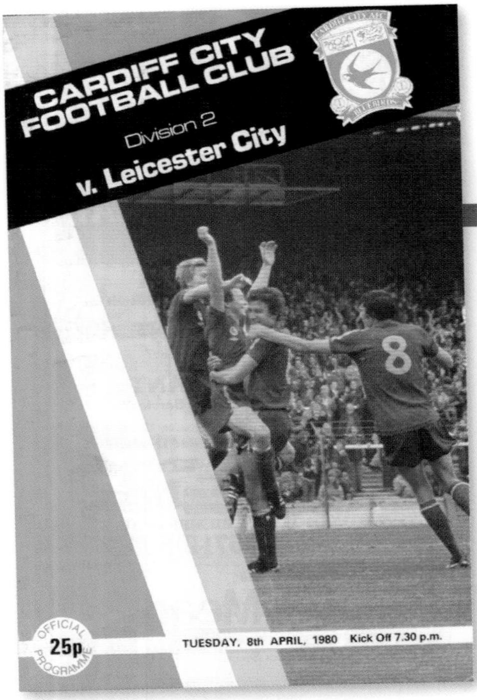

1979/80 – The yellow-and-white slash from the classic Umbro shirt echoed in the cover, if curiously out of sight out on the pitch.

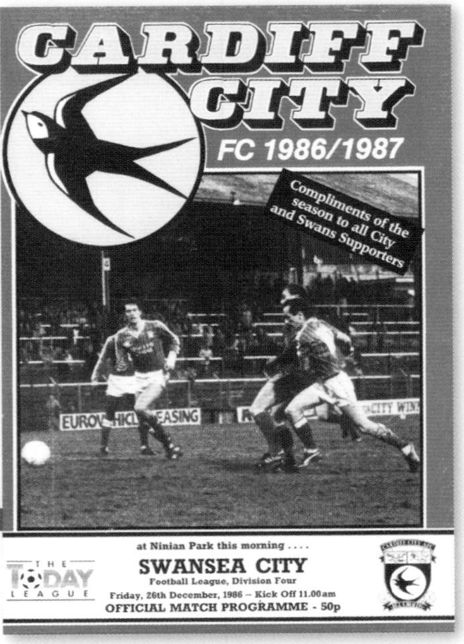

1986/87 – A prog that was inferior to the average fanzine of the time. The Today League era was miserable in the lower divisions, starved of cash and inspiration.

1971/72 – Perfectly balanced, resplendent with colour, creativity and care. Cardiff take on Watford under Captain Morgan's all-seeing gaze.

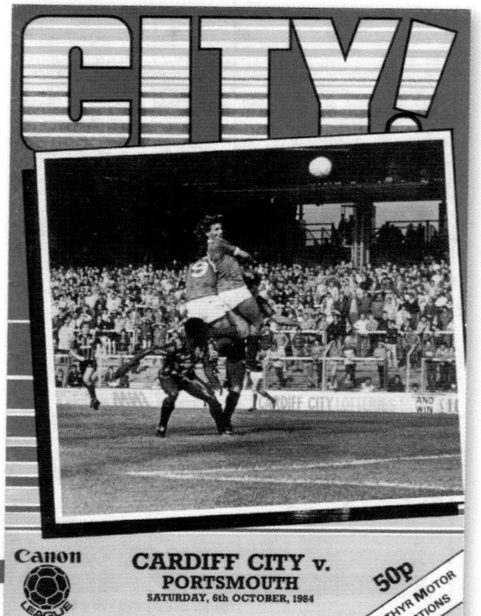

1984/85 – The desperate use of an exclamation mark attempts to lift a dismal offering; but no one was fooled.

1968/69 - Smart Cooperish font, tidy fox-head badge, the squad all spic and span on the first day of term. Many a modest delight.

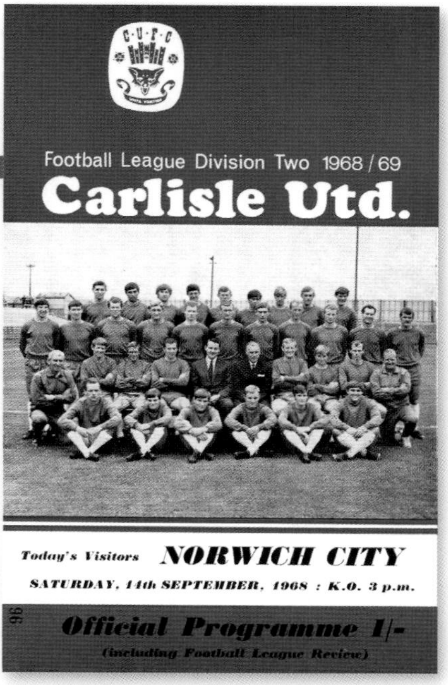

1977/78 - Ah yes, you can't beat a programme cover that echoes the colours and design of the club shirt. There's a certain elegance about this. Perhaps accidental.

1982/83 - A timewarp special, at first glance surely a programme from the 60s with its mod 'swoosh' text and 'flying' ball incorporating a black-and-white non-action shot.

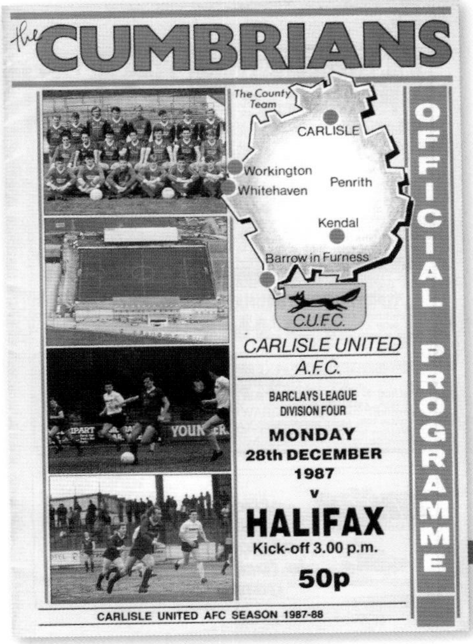

1987/88 - *The Cumbrians* is a decent name for a prog, and a map is a handy touch to help fans find their way home.

Football League Review

Run from the back bedroom of secretary Alan Hardaker's Blackpool bungalow, the Football League was devoted to showing everyone what a big, happy family their 92-member club was. *The Football League Review* was a feelgood customer mag, given away free inside club programmes, where it bolstered many four- or eight-page lower-league efforts. The *FLR* was conspicuous in its absence from several larger League grounds, where power brokers were already wary of growing League influence.

However, in stark comparison to the petty politicking backstabbing golf-clubbing small-minded scrap-metal merchant football-club owners of the 1970s, fans dug the freebies to bits.

The *Review* was 5 pence 'when bought separately'; which is to say never. It was full of behind-the-scenes peeks at the day-to-day running of all the League clubs, an article on the bootroom at Barrow being just as likely as a visit to the Arsenal trophy room. Then and now, its allure was almost entirely down to staff photographer Peter Robinson, who spent whole seasons travelling around snapping mascots at Mansfield and tea-

ladies in Tranmere, thinking up ever more unusual formations for his teamgroups.

"I was conscious that I was different when I talked with other photographers at games," he told *When Saturday Comes*. Robinson never missed an angle, an expression, an oddity or a location, showing more interest in football culture than the game itself. "I felt that you didn't just have to start photographing when the ref blew his whistle. I was interested in the whole build-up to the game."

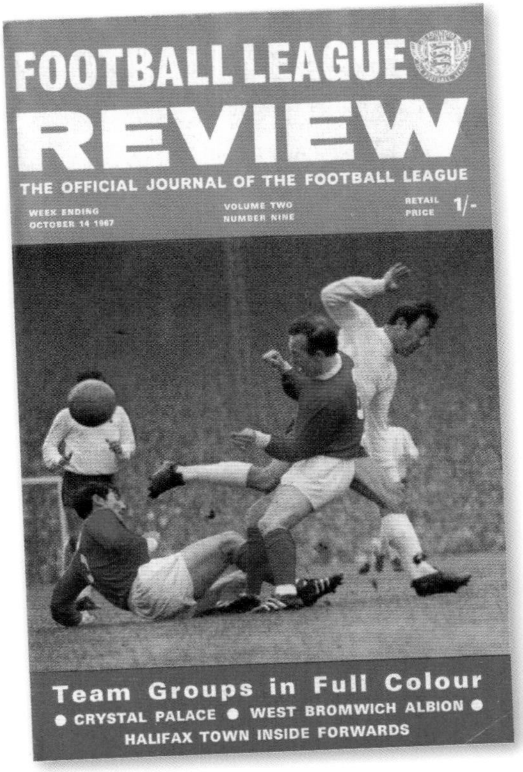
FOOTBALL LEAGUE
REVIEW
THE OFFICIAL JOURNAL OF THE FOOTBALL LEAGUE
WEEK ENDING OCTOBER 14 1967
VOLUME TWO NUMBER NINE
RETAIL PRICE 1/-
Team Groups in Full Colour
● CRYSTAL PALACE ● WEST BROMWICH ALBION ●
HALIFAX TOWN INSIDE FORWARDS

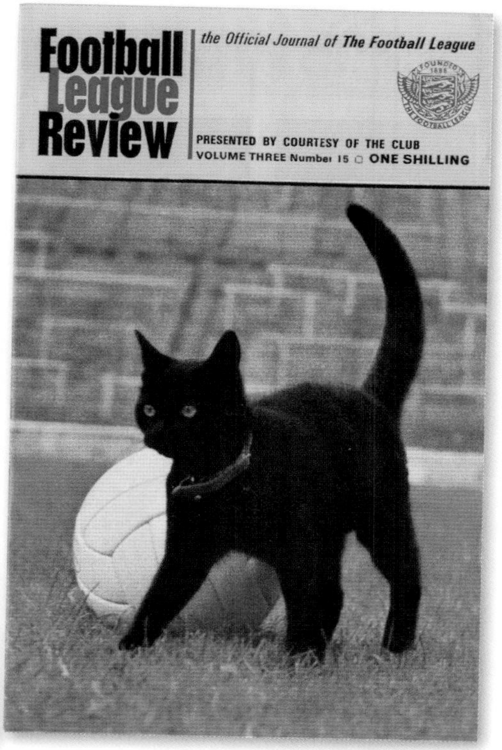
Football League Review
the Official Journal of The Football League
PRESENTED BY COURTESY OF THE CLUB
VOLUME THREE Number 15 ONE SHILLING

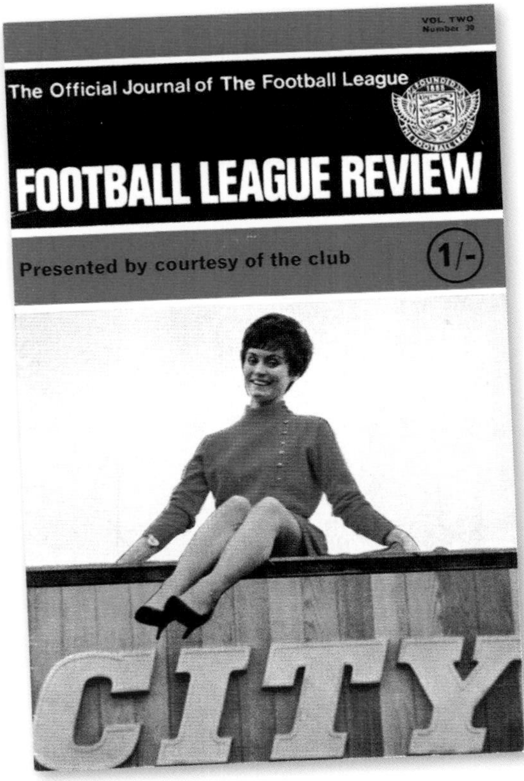
VOL. TWO
Number 30
The Official Journal of The Football League
FOOTBALL LEAGUE REVIEW
Presented by courtesy of the club
1/-
CITY

FOOTBALL LEAGUE
REVIEW
THE OFFICIAL JOURNAL OF THE FOOTBALL LEAGUE
WEEK ENDING SEPTEMBER 9 1967
VOLUME TWO NUMBER FOUR
RETAIL PRICE 1/-
8
BLIND BOYS LIVE FOR SOCCER
—Special feature inside
8,000 MILES OF SHOE LEATHER — page 8

Charlton Athletic

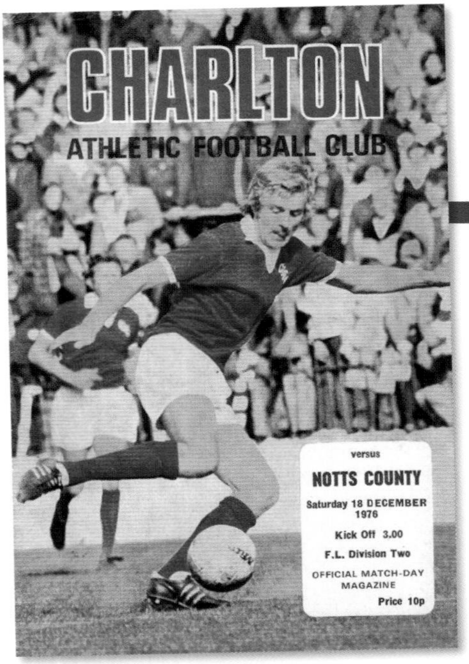

1976/77 – Having flicked through a million dog's-breakfast programmes over the past months, it leaves you wishing for more clean minimalism – the Charlton way.

1967/68 – There's a certain elegant simplicity here, a balance of composition that works apparently effortlessly. Swimming duck syndrome.

1975/76 – If it ain't bust...

1978/79 – And so years of staid, understated design came to an end in an orgy of cascading yellow and orange text, dingy action and Tangoed fans. Wahey.

1979/80 – Years before the landmark signing of, ahem, the 'Great Dane' Allan Simonsen, the Addicks signed up these lesser Danish bods with the sole intention of creating the reddest full-colour programme cover in League history. We don't know who they were, but it was a job well done. And great to see that 3-D font again for the first time since the Lower Sixth.

1974/75 – Every home programme produced by Chesea this season featured Bill Garner's aerial battle vs. Wolves, one lonely copper and zero ad hoardings.

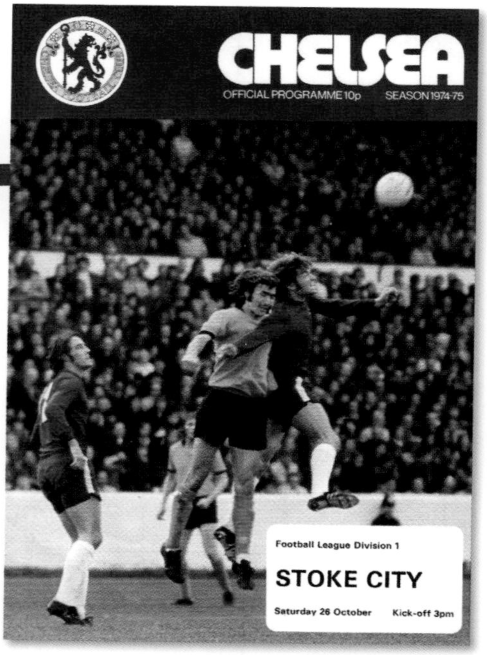
CHELSEA
OFFICIAL PROGRAMME 10p SEASON 1974-75
Football League Division 1
STOKE CITY
Saturday 26 October Kick-off 3pm

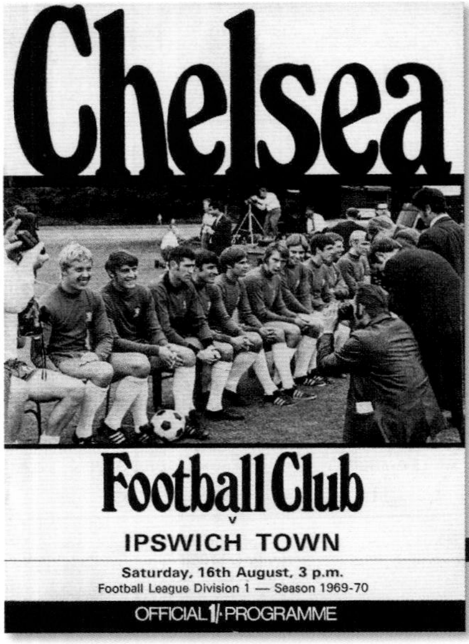
Chelsea
Football Club
v
IPSWICH TOWN
Saturday, 16th August, 3 p.m.
Football League Division 1 — Season 1969-70
OFFICIAL 1/- PROGRAMME

1969/70 – We know now what the 60s down the King's Road signified. So it's easy to pick up on jaunty typography, a casual behind-the-scenes vibe – and to extrapolate.

1981/82 – Ken Bates strikes back against the CFC hoolies.

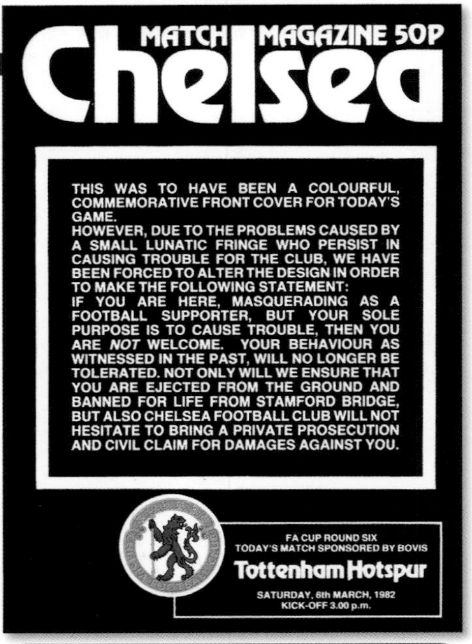
MATCH MAGAZINE 50P
Chelsea
THIS WAS TO HAVE BEEN A COLOURFUL, COMMEMORATIVE FRONT COVER FOR TODAY'S GAME.
HOWEVER, DUE TO THE PROBLEMS CAUSED BY A SMALL LUNATIC FRINGE WHO PERSIST IN CAUSING TROUBLE FOR THE CLUB, WE HAVE BEEN FORCED TO ALTER THE DESIGN IN ORDER TO MAKE THE FOLLOWING STATEMENT:
IF YOU ARE HERE, MASQUERADING AS A FOOTBALL SUPPORTER, BUT YOUR SOLE PURPOSE IS TO CAUSE TROUBLE, THEN YOU ARE NOT WELCOME. YOUR BEHAVIOUR AS WITNESSED IN THE PAST, WILL NO LONGER BE TOLERATED. NOT ONLY WILL WE ENSURE THAT YOU ARE EJECTED FROM THE GROUND AND BANNED FOR LIFE FROM STAMFORD BRIDGE, BUT ALSO CHELSEA FOOTBALL CLUB WILL NOT HESITATE TO BRING A PRIVATE PROSECUTION AND CIVIL CLAIM FOR DAMAGES AGAINST YOU.
FA CUP ROUND SIX
TODAY'S MATCH SPONSORED BY BOVIS
Tottenham Hotspur
SATURDAY, 6th MARCH, 1982
KICK-OFF 3.00 p.m.

CHELSEA
OFFICIAL PROGRAMME £1.
TOTTENHAM HOTSPUR
SATURDAY, 27th APRIL 1985
KICK-OFF 11.30 a.m.
Canon
DIVISION ONE
RH
PRESIDENT'S DAY
CHELSEA 80th
ANNIVERSARY SPECIAL
EDITION

1984/85 – Two uniforms that made fans mighty proud to be Chelsea: Le Coq Sportif's finest hour and the bright red of the 'Pensioners' Royal Hospital.

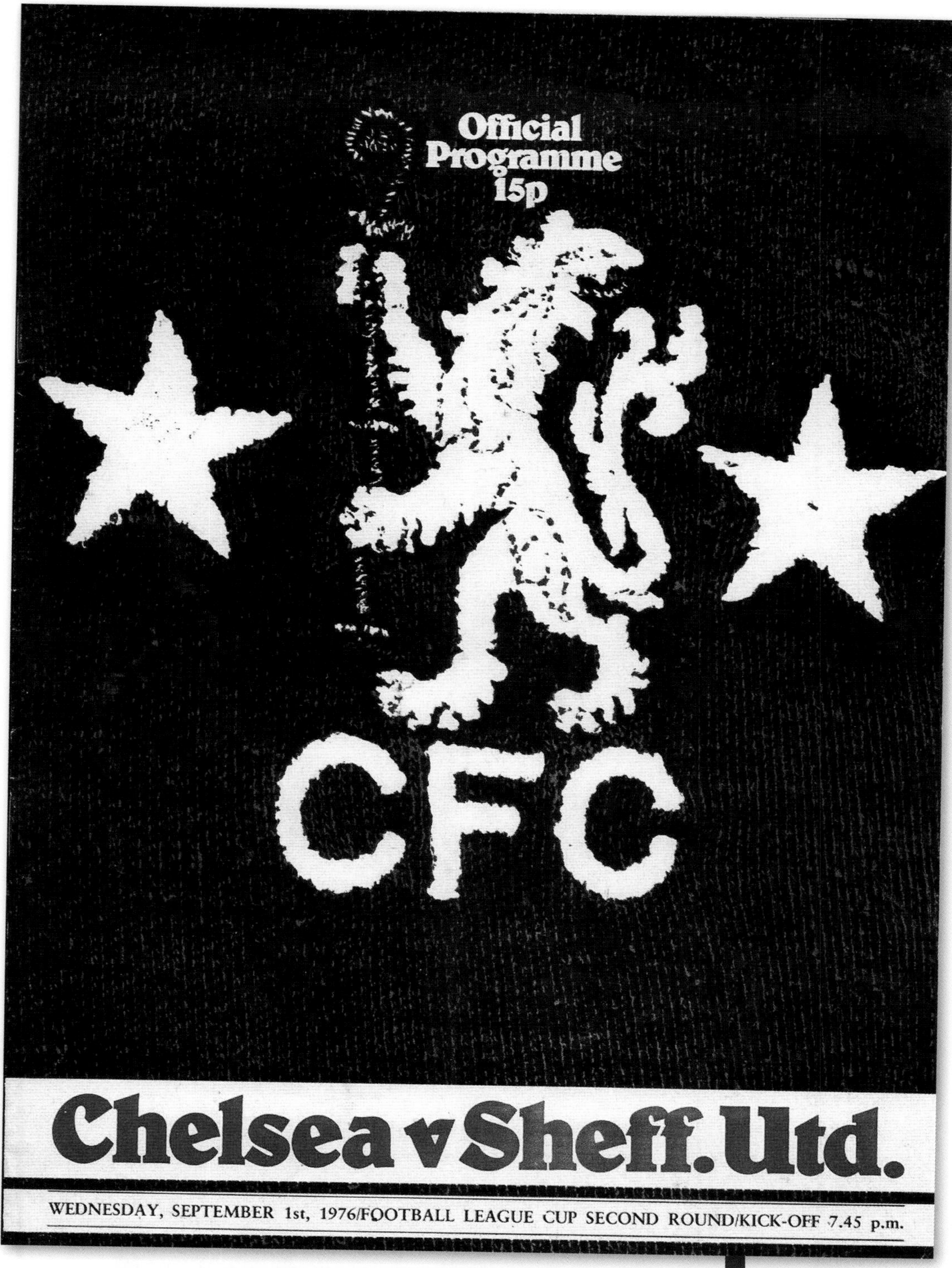

1976/77 – When punk was born in a World's End clothes shop, and Chelsea FC were also experimenting with a striking new iconography based around the power and meaning of uniforms and logos.

Chesterfield

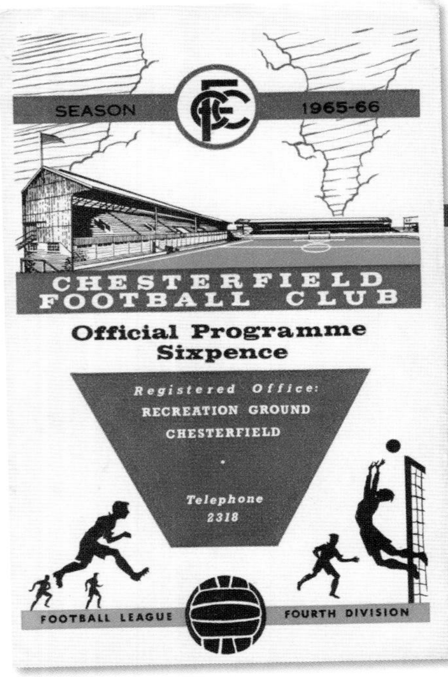

1965/66 – An absolute beauty. Look at that stadium perspective, those banks of fluffy clouds, the innocence almost worthy of a Famous Five illustration by Eileen Soper.

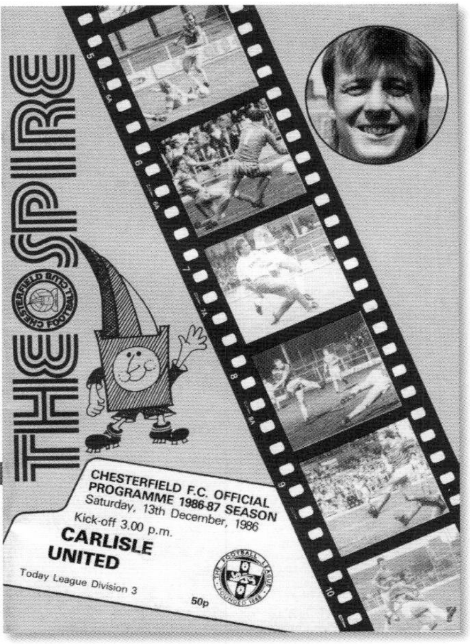

1986/87 – We probably already said that we like filmstrip photos. And progs with 'The' in the title. And iffy cartoon mascots – eg an anthropomorphised church spire.

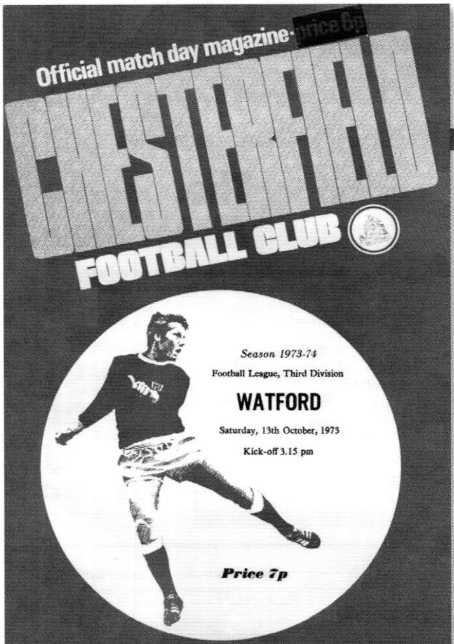

1973/74 – Dungly-dung-dung. James Bond title-sequence chic.

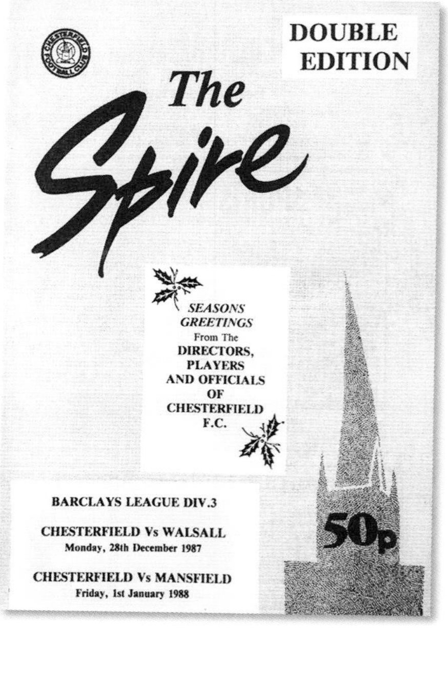

1987/88 – The absolute nadir of prog production values. A grim church spire. The title written in blood. A half-value double edition. A miserable Xmas to you.

1974/75 – No need to put the year on this one. Just one glance at those suits, that hair, those ties, those trees, that shed – and you know it's the pinnacle of the 70s.

1987/88 – There aren't many clubs or progs that leverage their history as effectively as Colchester – the Roman capital of Britain, no less. Roll the titles of *Gladiator*...

1979/80 – That's more like it. Ditch the iconography two millennia old for a cartoon bloke giving a thumbs-up. Meet Layer Road Larry.

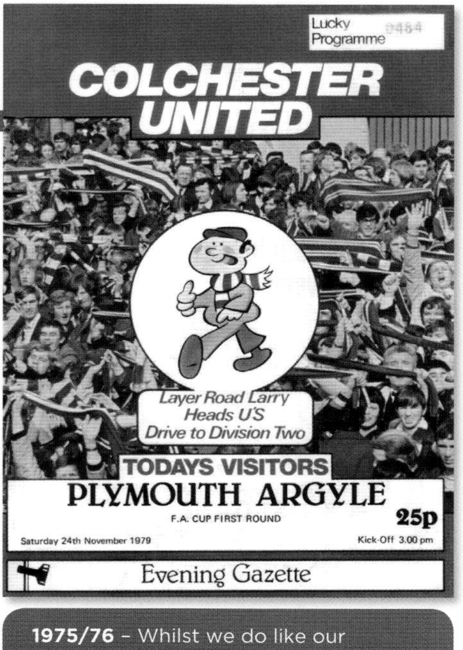

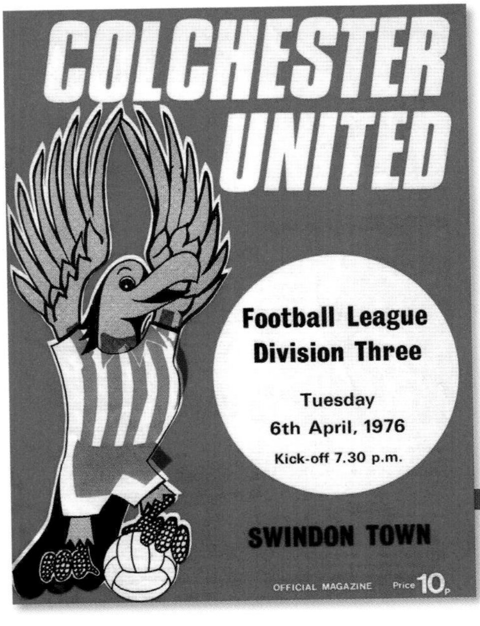

1975/76 – Whilst we do like our cartoon mascots to err on the side of amusing and weird, we have to draw the line (ahem) at downright disturbing.

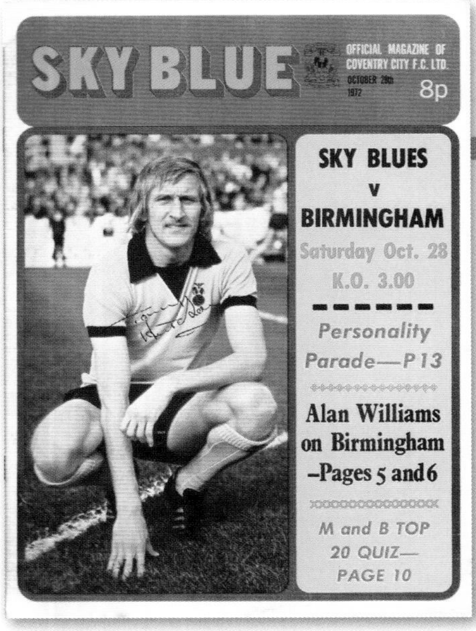

1972/73 - The greatest programme of all time? Put it down to the lavish design and format, the player recipes, the cool 'at home' slot. And - sigh - Girl of the Match.

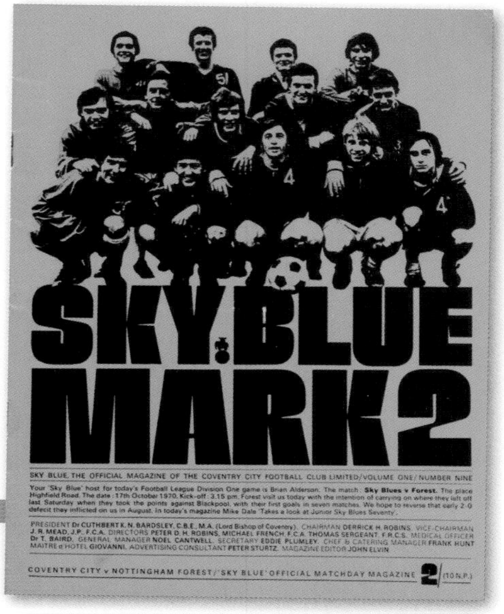

1970/71 - After stealing a march on every other club with the content-packed *Sky Blue*, Sportsgraphic's stylised 'Mark 2' was a bit self-important; but still a big production.

1962/63 - Cov soon found themselves way ahead of their time thanks to Jimmy Hill's fan-friendly revolution. Play Up Sky Blues!

1979/80 - A Sky Blue red rose for the luvverly ladeez.

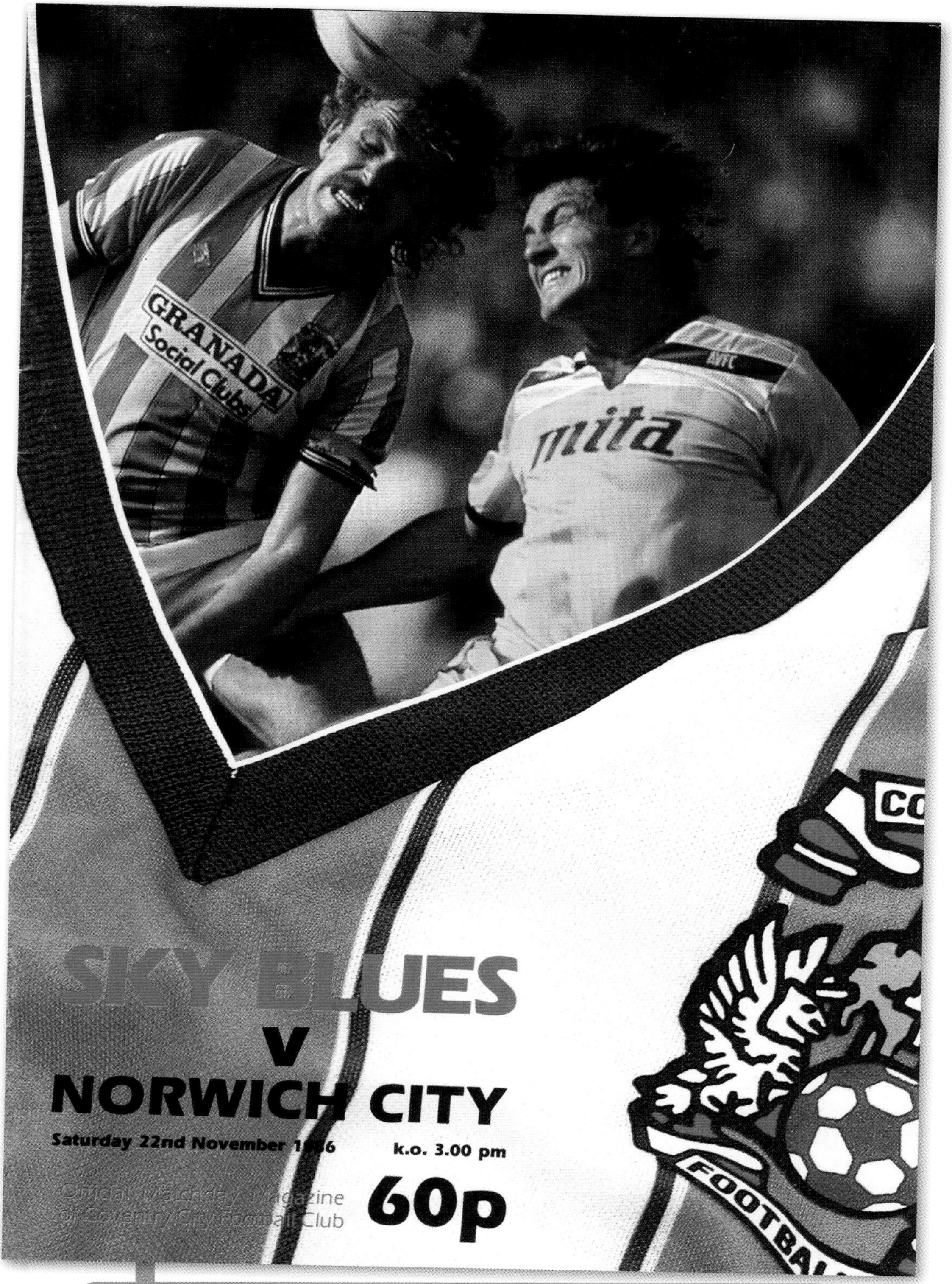

1986/87 – Here's a unique way to incoporate the shirt into a programme's front cover, which represents great work for the late 80s when production values and ideas were generally on the slide. It's a great shot of 'Killer' Kilcline, too, on his way to FA Cup final glory in Cov's greatest ever season.

Progs by Post

If, like us, you spent an indecent chunk of the 1970s putting self-addressed envelopes into bigger envelopes and then into the postbox, you probably sent at least one to Steve Earl Football Programmes, Earsham Street, Bungay, Suffolk.

Steve advertised in every issue of *Shoot!*, offering a FREE programme catalogue to anyone with the wherewithal to send a stamped, self-addressed envelope (or 4p in stamps) to Bungay's World Prog HQ.

Having done all that, and probably waited 28 days for delivery, I received a thrilling envelope containing a few roughly typed pages of folded A4, cataloguing thousands of available programmes... But what to order?

I trusted to fate and opted for a bargain bundle of '30 progs (many 1st Div)' for only £1.50 – or about three weeks' pocket money.

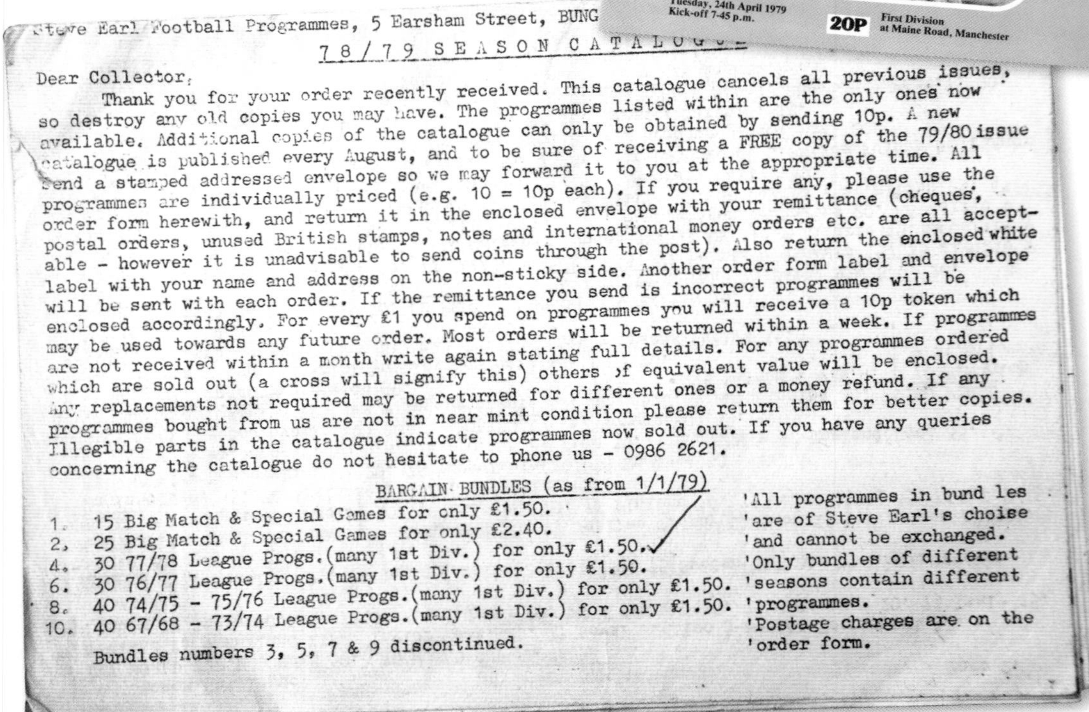
Steve Earl Football Programmes, 5 Earsham Street, BUNG

78/79 SEASON CATALOG

Dear Collector,

Thank you for your order recently received. This catalogue cancels all previous issues, so destroy any old copies you may have. The programmes listed within are the only ones now available. Additional copies of the catalogue can only be obtained by sending 10p. A new catalogue is published every August, and to be sure of receiving a FREE copy of the 79/80 issue send a stamped addressed envelope so we may forward it to you at the appropriate time. All programmes are individually priced (e.g. 10 = 10p each). If you require any, please use the order form herewith, and return it in the enclosed envelope with your remittance (cheques, postal orders, unused British stamps, notes and international money orders etc. are all acceptable - however it is unadvisable to send coins through the post). Also return the enclosed white label with your name and address on the non-sticky side. Another order form label and envelope will be sent with each order. If the remittance you send is incorrect programmes will be enclosed accordingly. For every £1 you spend on programmes you will receive a 10p token which may be used towards any future order. Most orders will be returned within a week. If programmes are not received within a month write again stating full details. For any programmes ordered which are sold out (a cross will signify this) others of equivalent value will be enclosed. Any replacements not required may be returned for different ones or a money refund. If any programmes bought from us are not in near mint condition please return them for better copies. Illegible parts in the catalogue indicate programmes now sold out. If you have any queries concerning the catalogue do not hesitate to phone us - 0986 2621.

BARGAIN BUNDLES (as from 1/1/79)

1. 15 Big Match & Special Games for only £1.50.
2. 25 Big Match & Special Games for only £2.40.
4. 30 77/78 League Progs. (many 1st Div.) for only £1.50. ✓
6. 30 76/77 League Progs. (many 1st Div.) for only £1.50.
8. 40 74/75 - 75/76 League Progs. (many 1st Div.) for only £1.50.
10. 40 67/68 - 73/74 League Progs. (many 1st Div.) for only £1.50.

Bundles numbers 3, 5, 7 & 9 discontinued.

'All programmes in bund les
'are of Steve Earl's choise
'and cannot be exchanged.
'Only bundles of different
'seasons contain different
'programmes.
'Postage charges are on the
'order form.

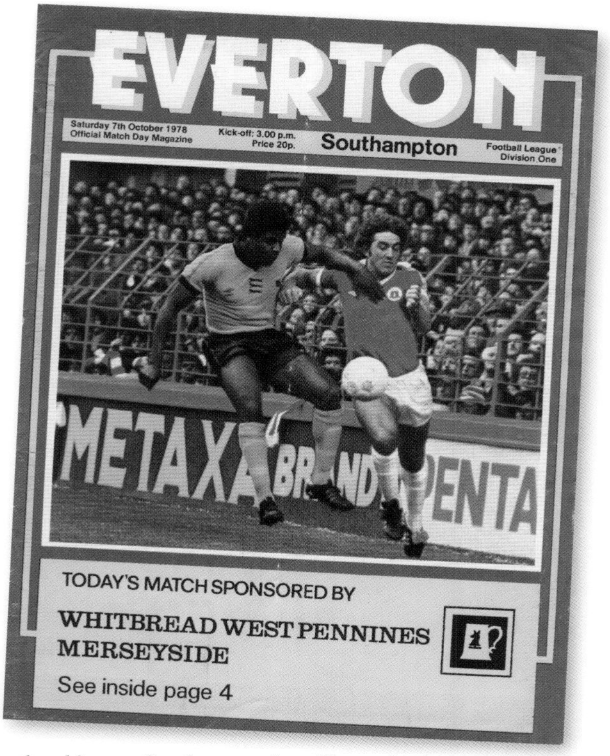

I recall the thick bundle arriving through the door, barely able to tear it open with the excitement of discovering which programmes Mr Earl had chosen for me.

There were a few Everton, a few Birmingham, a Villa, a West Ham, a Man City or two, a Bristol City and something from the Debenham's Cup Final – whatever that was.

I pored over them for hours, for this was the genesis of a programme collection which still takes up a lot of garage space to this day.

The long and the short and the tall, from a time before programmes all conformed to standard sizes, when they still had a stamp of originality and a local flavour about them.

When we featured 'Steve Earl Programmes' on the Got, Not Got: Lost World of Football blog we received many messages from fans who also fondly recalled receiving their catalogues and bundles with a Suffolk postmark...

And then we received a Christmas card and a mug mat from Steve himself, thanking us for the mention. If you don't already know, you'll be pleased to hear he's still trading, has a website, and is still using that same old cartoon logo that used to appear in his *Shoot!* advert.

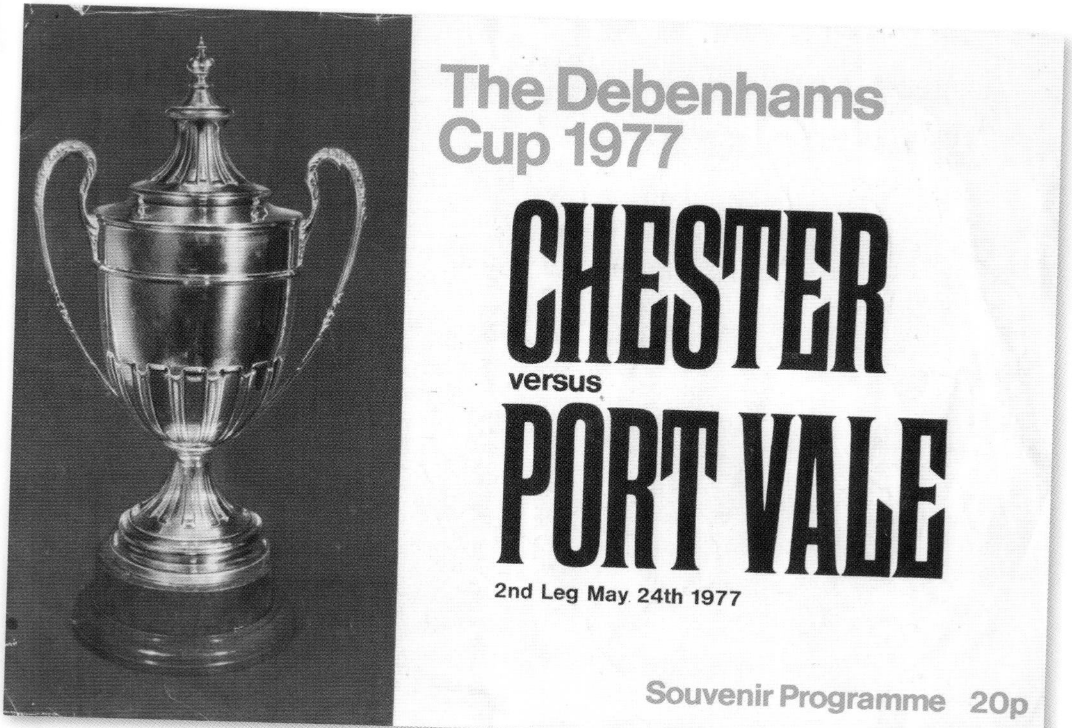

Crystal Palace

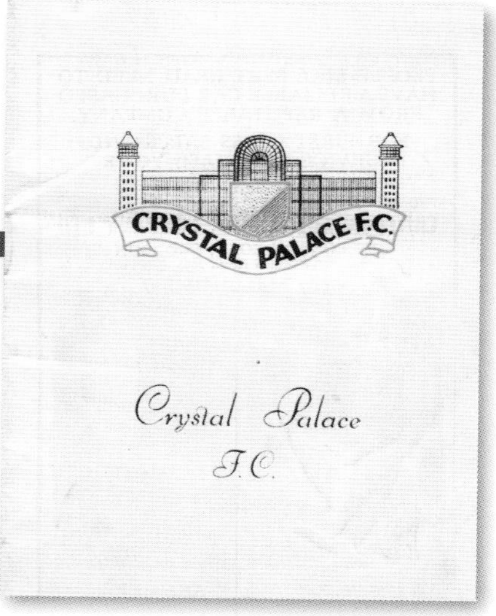

1966/67 – The classy 'wedding menu' look was first adopted for a Real Madrid friendly in 1962, then was used right through to 1967.

1969/70 – Neat incorporation of the shirt design is compromised by tagging on a letterbox reminder of the preceding prog cover. Fresh start time, lads.

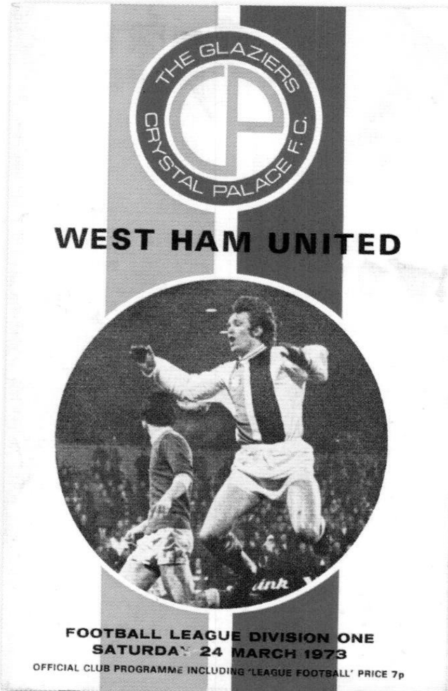

1972/73 – It's that shirt-design element again, augmented here by twin mod-ish circles, one containing a furiously 'now' CP logo. Up the Glaziers.

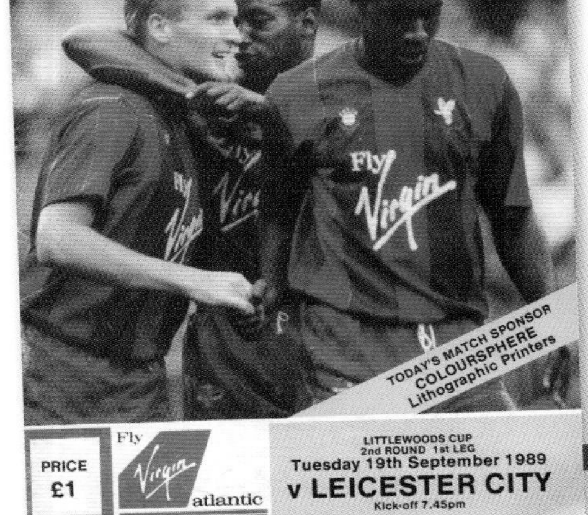

1989/90 – Geoff Thomas and Ian Wright attempt a private moment, foiled again by the Palace paps.

1981/82 – Ker-pow! A wildly enthusiastic prog for optimistic times at Selhurst Park. 'The Team of the 80s' is captured by a moderate felt-pen talent, who then follows up with a showcase of skills hard won in school TD lessons. Great how he incorporates 'O'-Level perspective into the title, and still finds a way to reference the classic sash shirt. A for effort.

Derby County

1964/65 – It's surprising how many clubs used the 'headless player' motif, one answer to the design requirement for player neutrality – and handy if you couldn't draw faces.

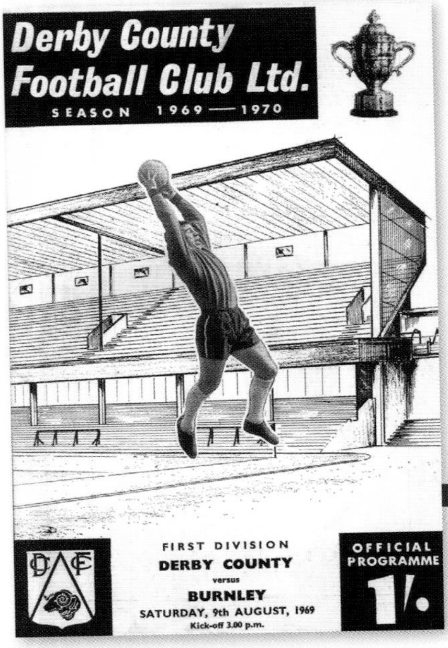

1969/70 – Now here's something you don't often see: Rams goalie Colin Boulton leaping for a cross, superimposed out on the left wing in an architectural drawing.

1985/86 – A rare example of humour on a programme cover, featuring Rammy the mascot in a quandary, caught between iconic and iconoclastic mode.

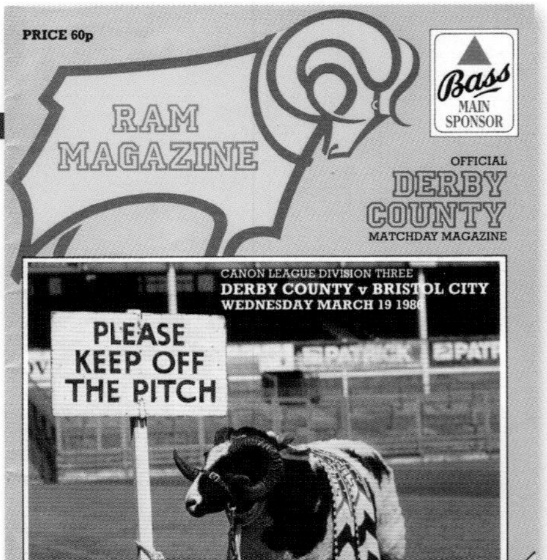

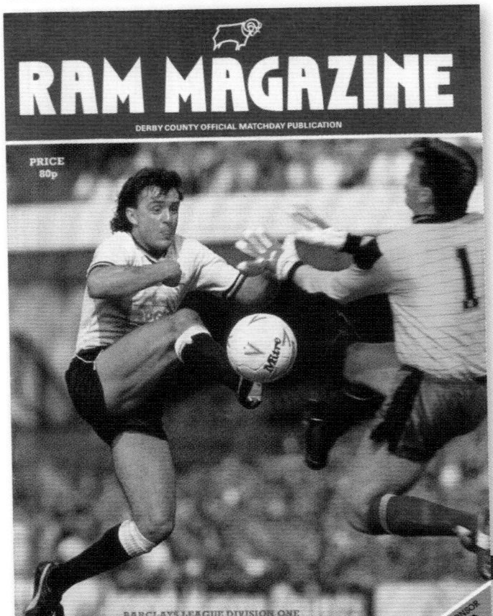

1987/88 – Heritage caption: 'Soccer ballet' was used 23 million times between 1960-79, but sadly not once in the 80s.

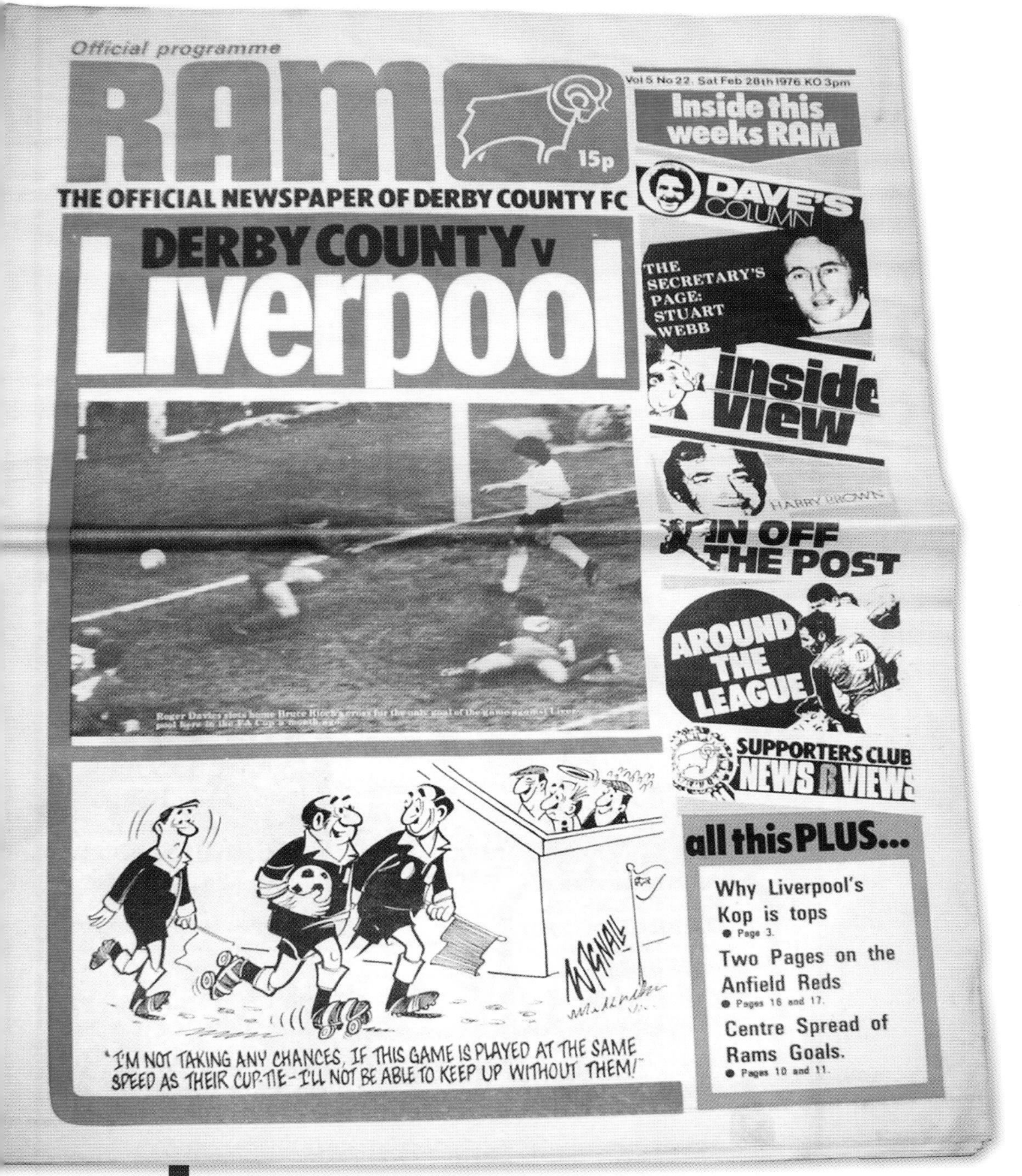

1975/76 – Derby were at the vanguard of the 'newspaper programme' format, with Rotherham, Tranmere and Shrewsbury following eventually, all signing up to publishers Sportscene. Unpopular with fans and an OCD collector's nightmare, they didn't fit boxes, were always folded, and quickly became foxed and torn. As a result, mint copies are now worth a pretty penny.

Everton

1970/71 – It's the old mod circle/football motif with black-and-white action. A simple trick, but so often bodged. This is how to pull it off to perfection.

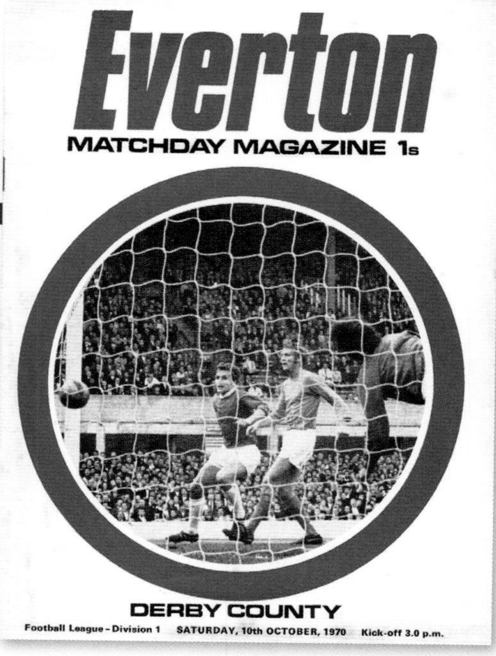

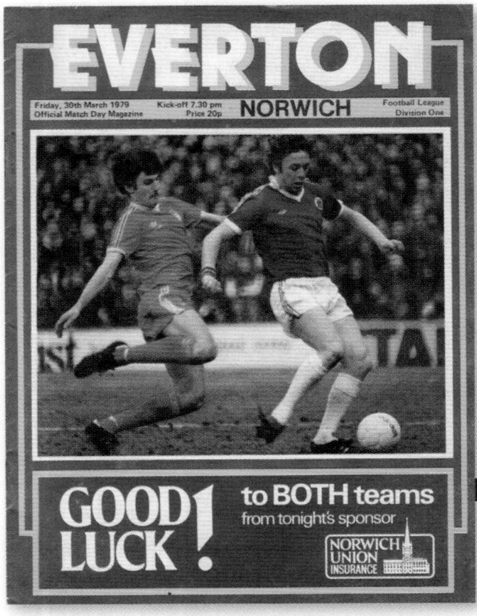

1978/79 – It was mighty big of Everton to allow Norwich Union insurance a cover ad for their match against Norwich. An awkward compromise, and shallow sentiment.

1974/75 – More magnanimity on Everton's part, here handing equal billing to their Merseyside rivals in a one-off derby design.

1962/63 – Two days after author Derek's birthday: Everton 2-2 Liverpool in front of 73,000 on an autumn afternoon at Goodison.

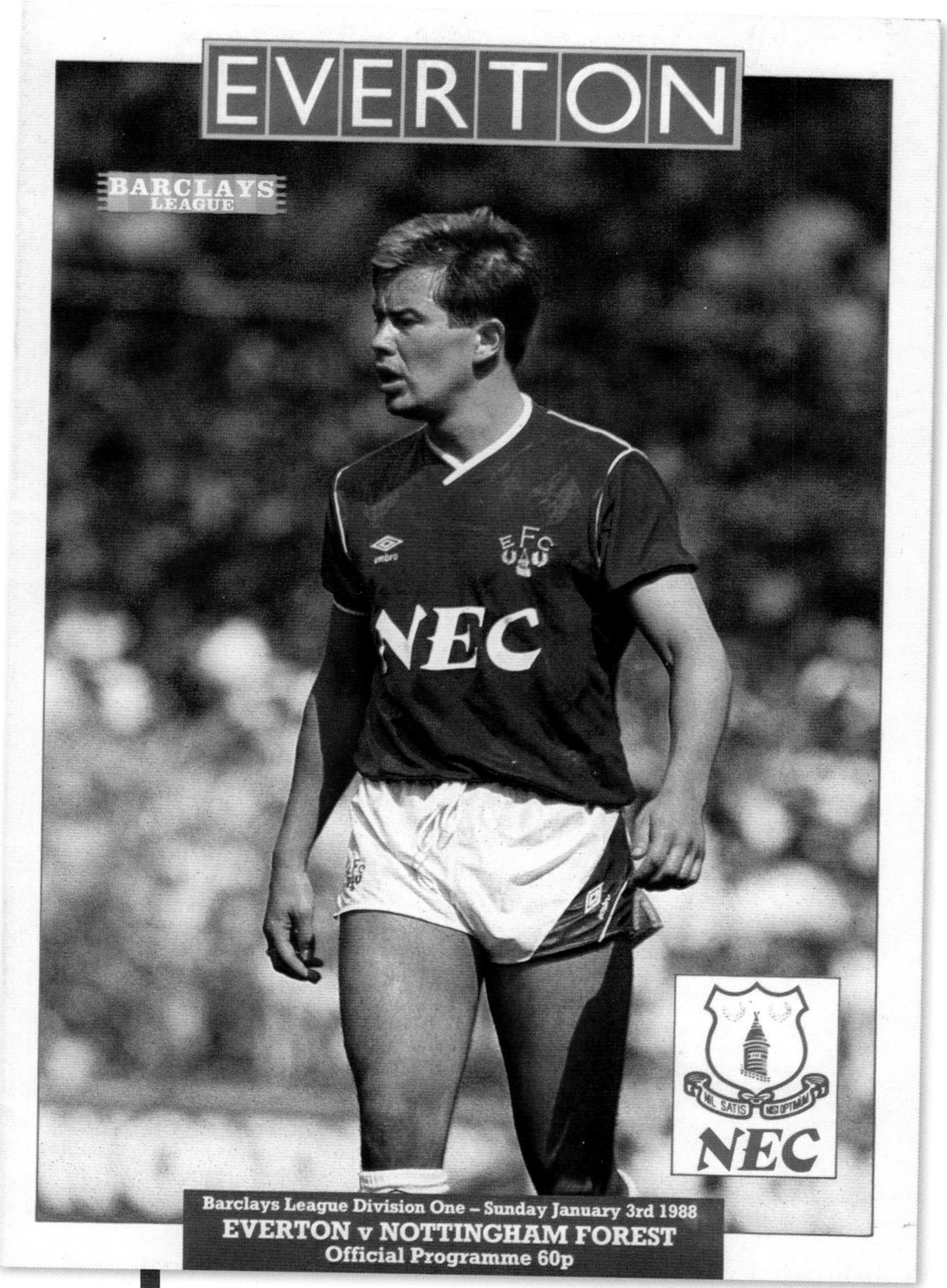

1987/88 – Clean, crisp design at any time, but a real rarity in the 80s. Less is more. Keep it simple, stupid. Everton are one of the few clubs whose programmes stuck to the basic rules in the DTP decade, and so stand up beautifully today.

Exeter City

1980/81 – The Duplex Litho revolution rolls into Exeter, offering an instant upgrade and an *On Target* middle section. Cover star: PoY Dave Pullar, smart in Adidas.

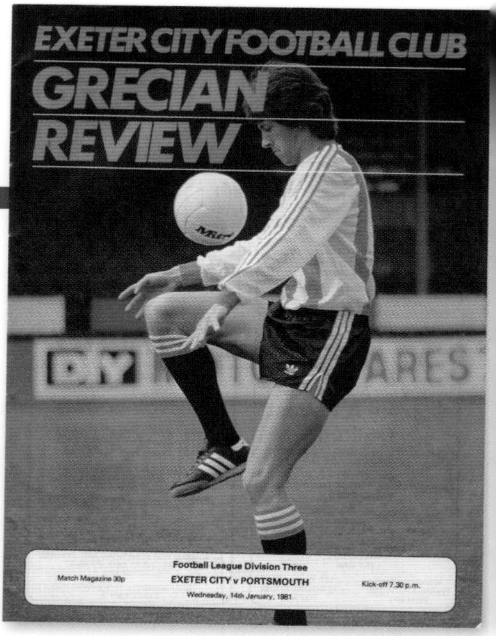

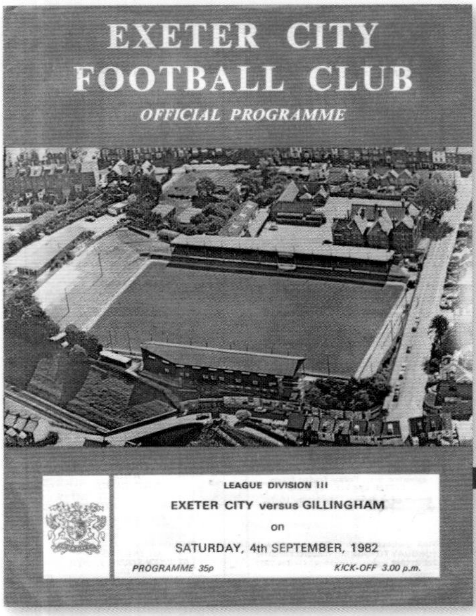

1982/83 – Cunning devils beneath the cream tea exterior, these Devonians. See how they ingeniously disguised this 80s prog as an archetypal 1966 job? We wonder why.

1986/87 – Lovely retro design harking back to a mid-50s issue, when jet planes meandered through the clouds over the Cathedral and all was tickety-boo.

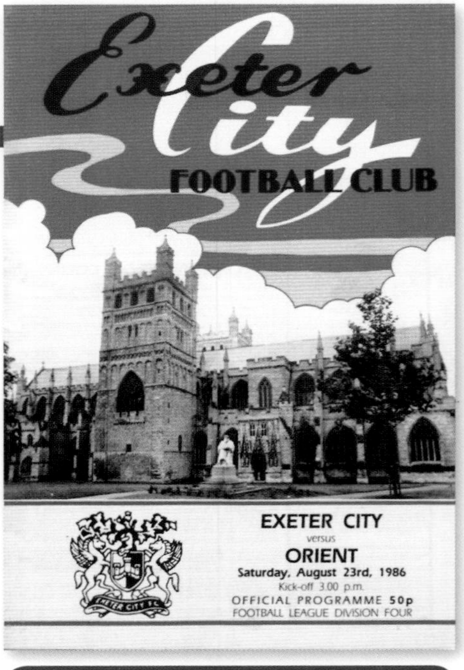

1974/75 – Exe Offender: the audacious theft of QPR's classic chequerboard design, right down to the range of different colours it came in.

Fulham

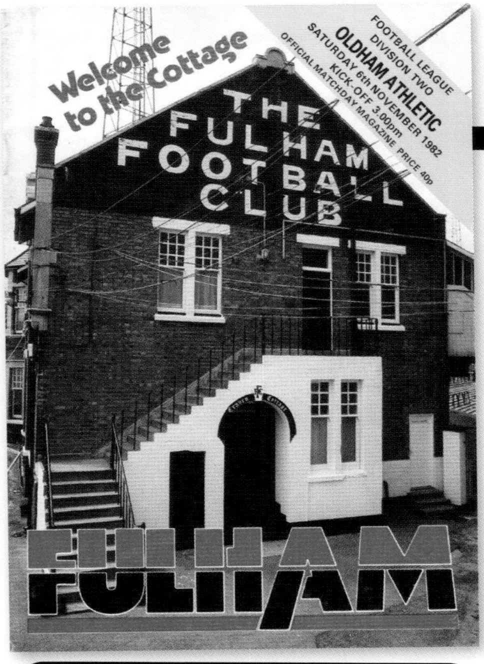

1982/83 – Nice contrast of old and new in the Cottage and the 80s tool company/Heavy Metal logo; clever use of the roof lines, too. A subtle smash.

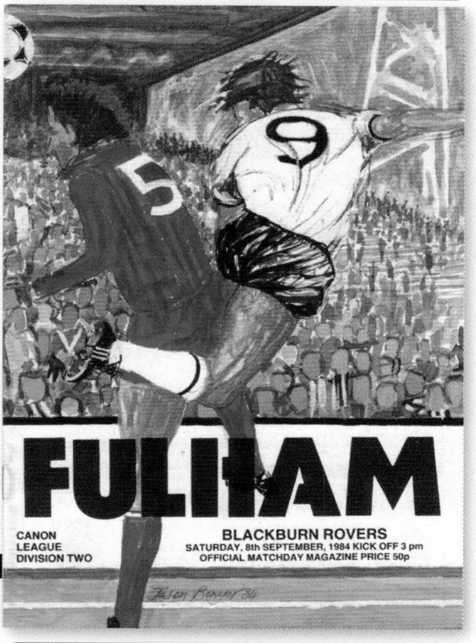

1984/85 – And yet within two short years, things had gone tits-up with pass-grade felt-pen art ('naïve', the dealers call it) partly obscured by a tidied-up tool logo.

1987/88 – What a plonker. It's FFC chairman Jimmy Hill flogging a noticeably inferior version of the matchday mag to unsuspecting fans.

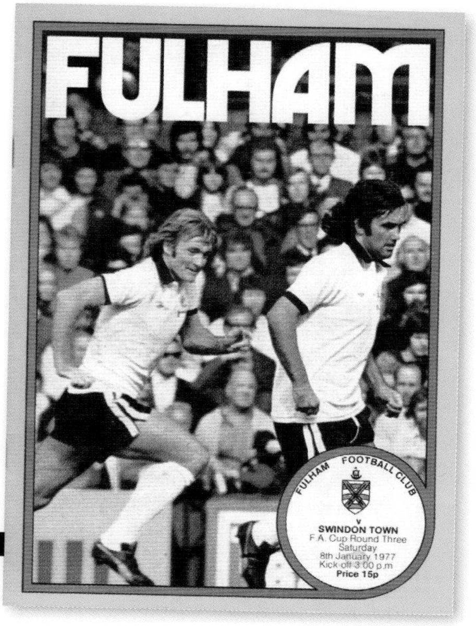

1976/77 – This was a bit more like it. If you've got it, flaunt it.

Creeping Commerce

When you look back at programme covers covering the whole span of football history, there have always been adverts for beer and fags, razor-blades and *Sports Final* newspapers cluttering up the corners in various degrees of irresistible style.

In retrospect, the incidental ads provide just the kind of period details which trigger a collection of brain cells to line up and fire neurons so you can make a great leap back in time, whether to 1962 or 1992.

Imagine a time when blokes at football wore suits, hats and mackintoshes. SCORE with Thompson's, The Man's Shop – for the very best in men's wear.

Remember when a state-of-the-art Nokia candybar had a stubby little aerial, coverage comparable to that of an average tablecloth, and still cost £234?

Some of these ads may even have sparked you into action in real time, for example suggesting a deep-seated requirement for post-match lubrication. Head in the RIGHT direction! IVOR THIRST for SHIPSTONE'S ALE.

It was back in the 1980s when advertisers and football clubs put their heads together and came up with a cunning plan to trawl greater revenues, cleverly integrating the bits of the programme we looked at voluntarily with the incidental ads destined to have the piss taken out of them 30 years hence.

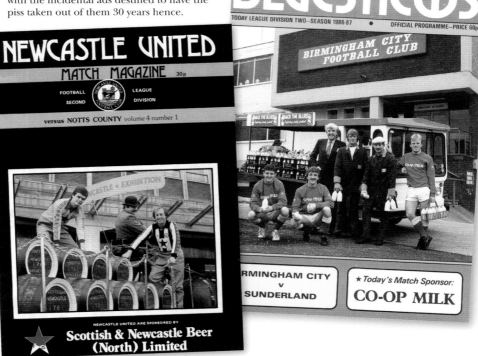

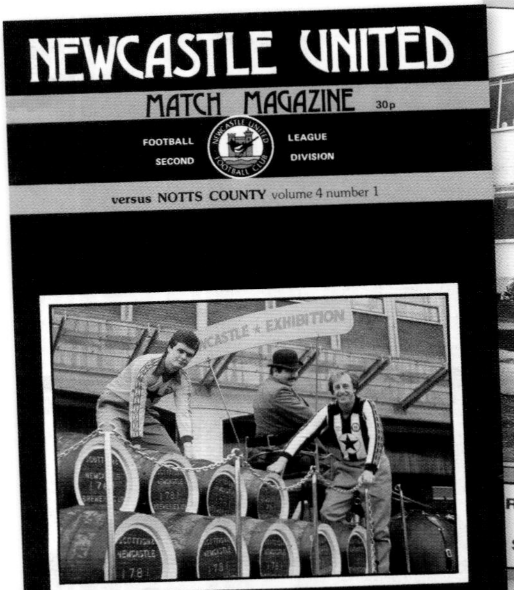

The previous clear delineation between football and advert became deliberately blurred. For the first time, it was now possible to lock eyes with cover stars such as Wayne Clarke and Des Bremner of Birmingham City – and then five minutes later, at the start of the second half, would come a creeping realisation. A subliminal message had been planted regarding the urgent necessity to order an extra pint off the milkman on Monday morning.

It seemed like science-fiction at the time; but, some day, all advertising would be carried out this way, with faintly familiar TV celebrities paid a small fortune to plant the idea of soup, pants and 3-D television sets in your unsuspecting noggin.

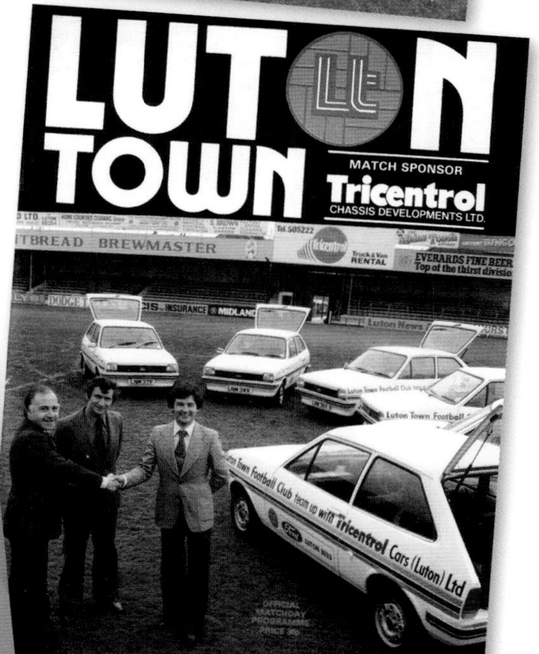

Gillingham

1970/71 – Note to artist: check relative lengths of legs, arms, etc. Maybe this was worth a bob, but we're not so sure about 5p.

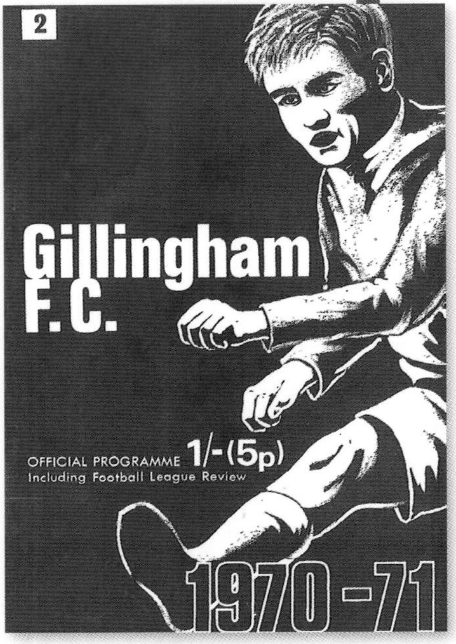

1986/87 – Centaur-forward gag alert! Gills boss Keith Peacock metamorphoses into a horse.

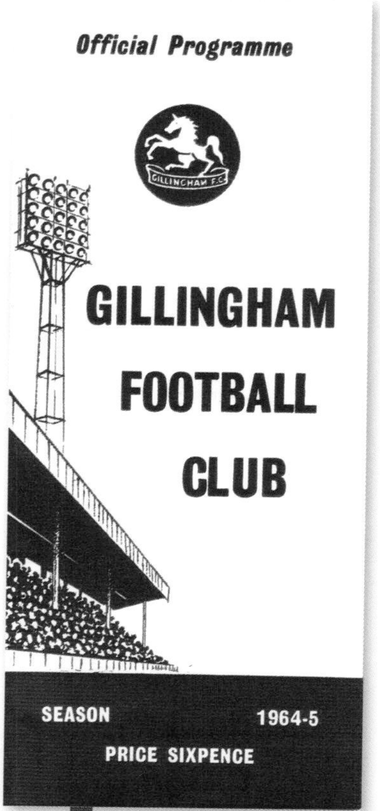

1964/65 – Not a bad idea, on the face of it: a programme that looks like a leaflet. Then you wake up and discover you really have gone to school wearing your slippers.

1988/89 – Suddenly the Gills are desperate for attention, with their zig-zag kit, their garish banner title and fully transmogrified Keith Peacock.

Grimsby Town

1966/67 – How many programme collectors grew up thinking Grimsby Dock Tower was Britain's second most popular landmark, behind the Blackpool Tower?

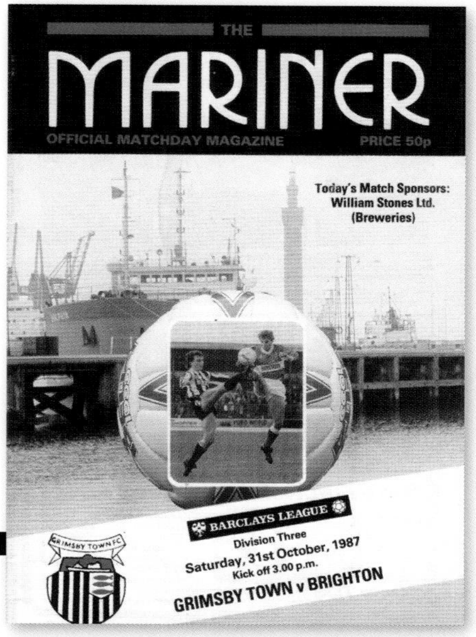

1987/88 – Local flavour: social realism down the docks, in stark contrast to the interchangeable Disneyland fantasy of today's Premier League clubs.

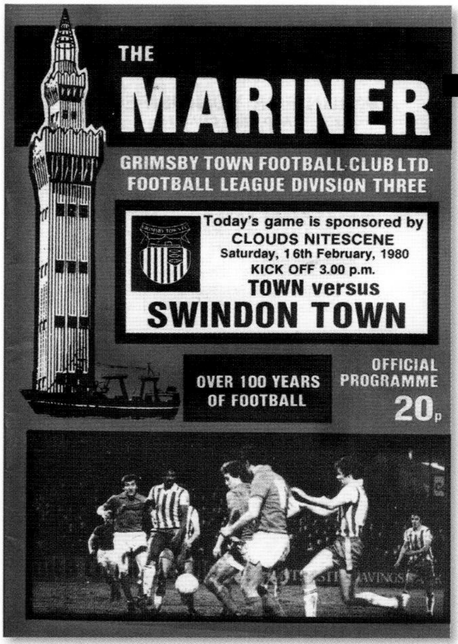

1979/80 – After sticking with our top-left prog cover for 33 years, it was at last time for a new Mariner makeover. Not exactly a sea change...

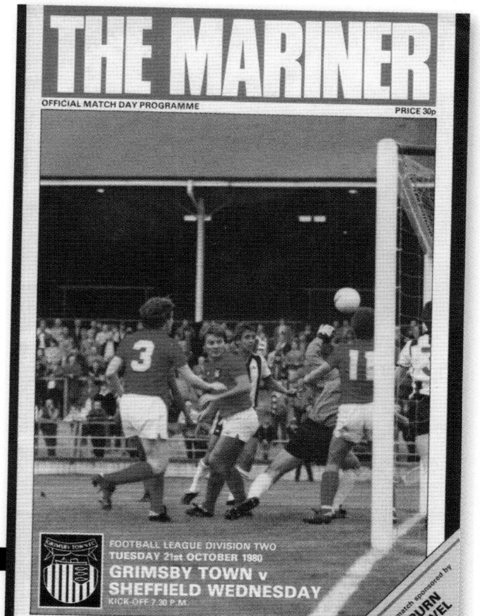

1980/81 – Tabloid times: the real shock horror here is that it's Notts County playing in the black-and-white stripes, and Grimsby in red.

Huddersfield Town

1972/73 – Just one problem, inviting comparison between Second Division football and goalbanging football-comic action. Especially in a relegation season.

1976/77 – Let's go retro: an Art Deco edition pines for the 1920s, for Herbert Chapman and three successive League championship successes.

1987/88 – We like *Talk of the Town* as a title, and aerial battles for clipart footballs.

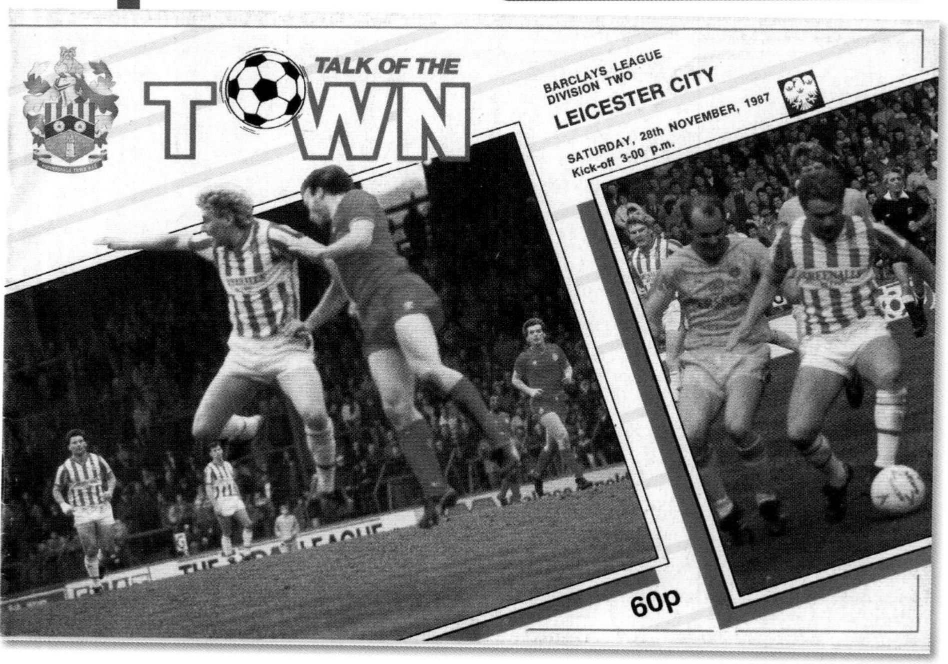

Clip Art

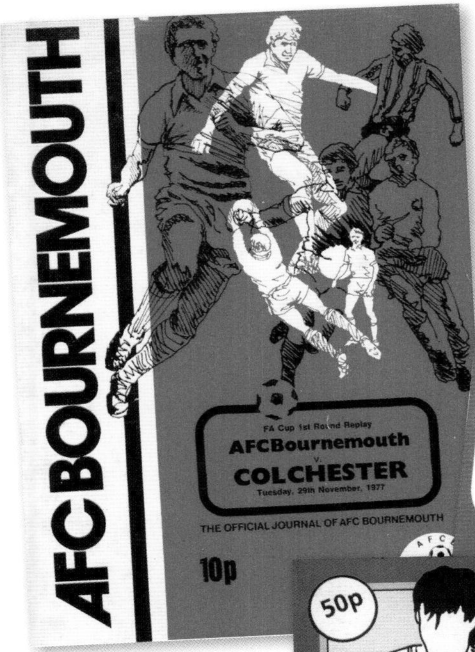

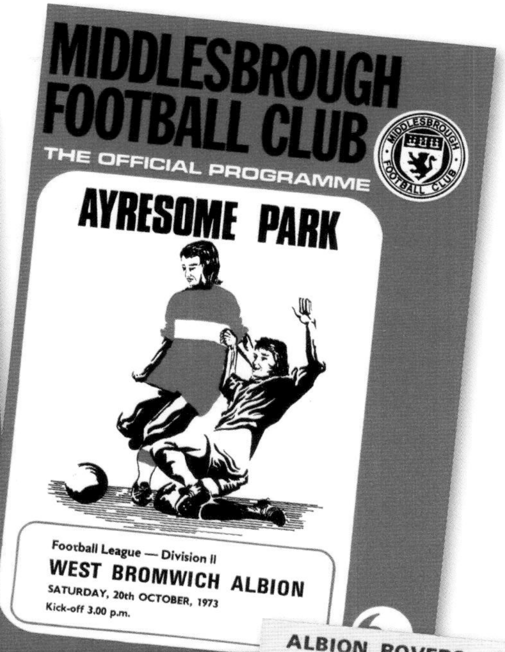

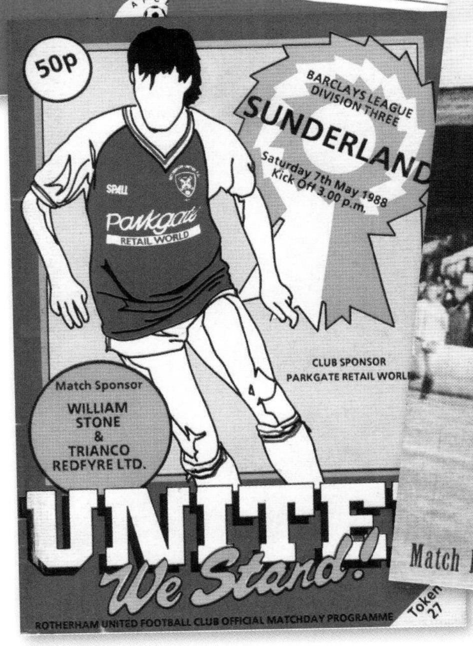

Long before the age of computer clipart cheapened the reputation of off-the-shelf, ready-to-use images, a hard-pressed programme or magazine designer used to reach for his stock footballer cartoons and action silhouettes without fear of letting the side down, or provoking sniffy disdain among fellow pros.

Almost every advert in every football magazine or comic was once emblazoned with little diving goalies, goalnets, goalmouth melees and thundering hotshots. Not to mention the lids of games, football annuals, toys and sticker books.

It's hard to believe now, but these little signifiers – shorthand for football – were actually capable of inspiring excitement in a small child; they brought the promise of a fix in a world where comics and games were relied upon to fill the terrible football void between Saturday afternoons and kickarounds up the park.

And, perhaps strangely, even in the age of overkill, they can still work their innocent magic.

I can feel another collection coming on.

Hull City

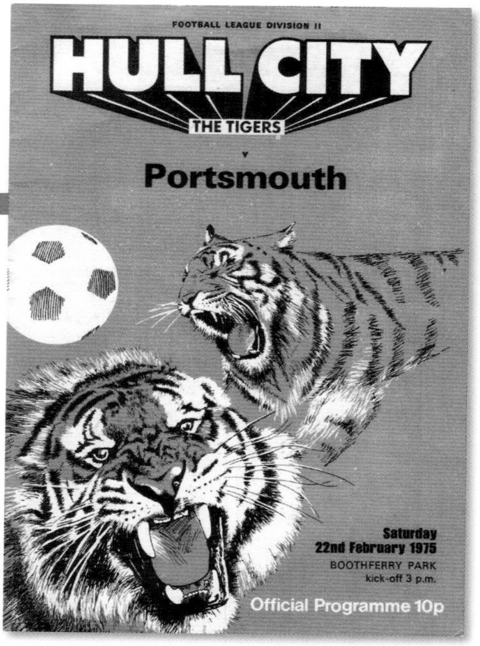

1974/75 – The Tigers. Literally. Two of 'em. It's plural, see? But what a shame there wasn't a picture of a football in the prog ed's *Bumper Book of African Wildlife.*

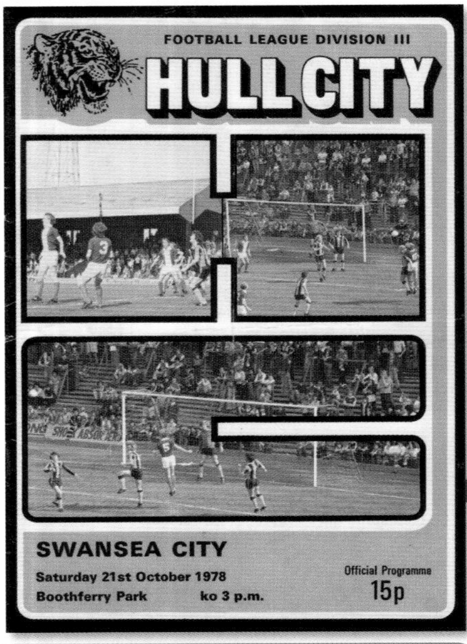

1978/79 – Prog eds used to think they'd had a great idea, dropping match action into big capital letters; but pic eds took some convincing...

1973/74 – The Tigers go a bit Shere Khan, out of *Jungle Book*. Watch out, Mowgli.

1989/90 – An intricate job was required to mimic City's notorious red-epaulette Matchwinner shirt, right down to the iffy self-coloured checks.

1980/81 – The absolute emptiness of the stand makes this programme cover a questionable advert for 80s football, as well as a perfect summary of its dwindling charms. Meanwhile, the tiger tail on the 'g' could easily have stood for 'genius'.

Ipswich Town

1973/74 – "Our new cover design shows some of the major trophies won by the Ipswich Town club last season"...?

1969/70 – If the BBC had made an oh-so-60s documentary behind the scenes at Portman Road, the titles would have looked just like this.

1981/82 – Mick Mills in splendid Adidas kit (wot, no Pioneer logo?) shows off the European silverware. A pitch-perfect Ipswich moment.

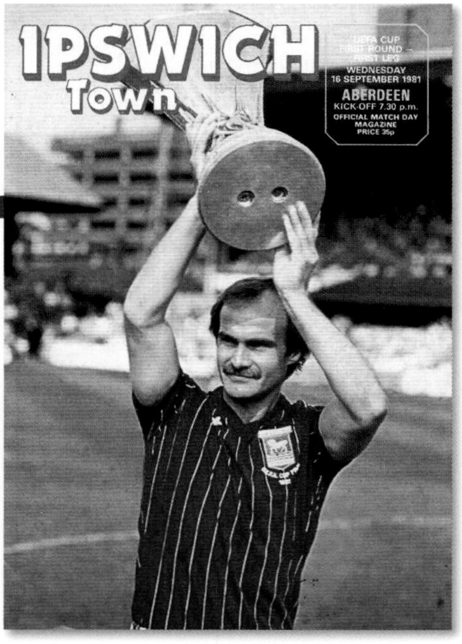

1975/76 – In the future, all programmes will be square, y'know. Hence the mass rush to squareness in the mid-70s. Just before the inevitable return of the oblong.

1985/86 – Things all went a bit weird when Ipswich's powers-that-be decided to adopt the French national side's colours, and rather overdid it on the red. Order was soon restored, but not until fans had put up with a couple of years of oddities such as this red-hooped prog, apparently a Doncaster Rovers cast-off. Allez les Bleus.

Leeds United

1972/73 – There's a stark chill about this old-school publication which recalls Norman Hunter's elbows and Don Revie's legendary carpet bowls sessions with his lads.

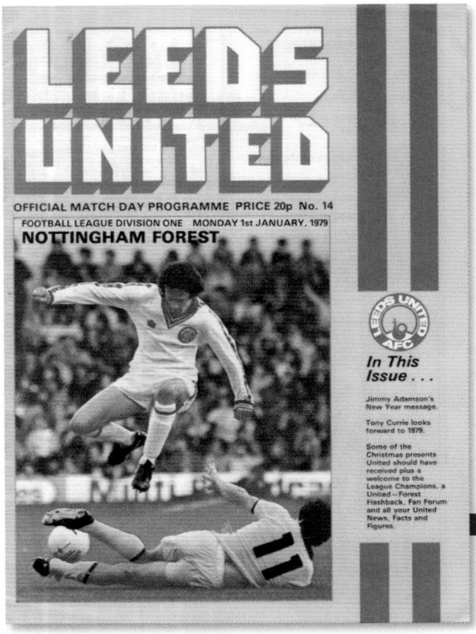

1978/79 – The programme picks up the traditional yellow-and-blue trim of the kit and the latest change of badge in an unnervingly cheerful number.

1984/85 – Another badge, another bodge. It's the 80s school jotter look, complete with learner's 'L'-plate.

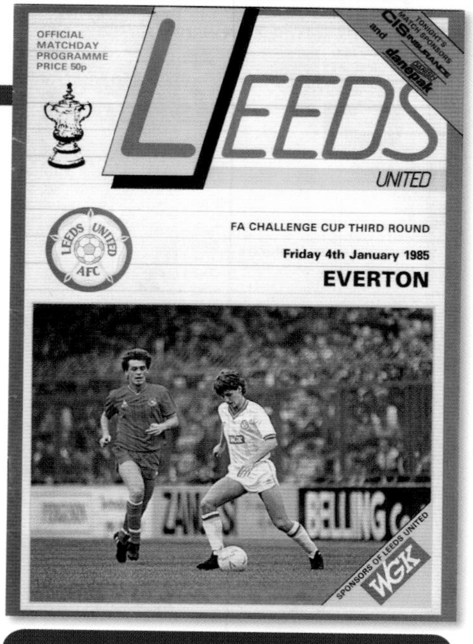

1967/68 – Leeds lost this Fairs Cup showdown but bounced back to beat Ferencváros and Juventus in the '68 and '71 finals. The rare use of gold hinted at class.

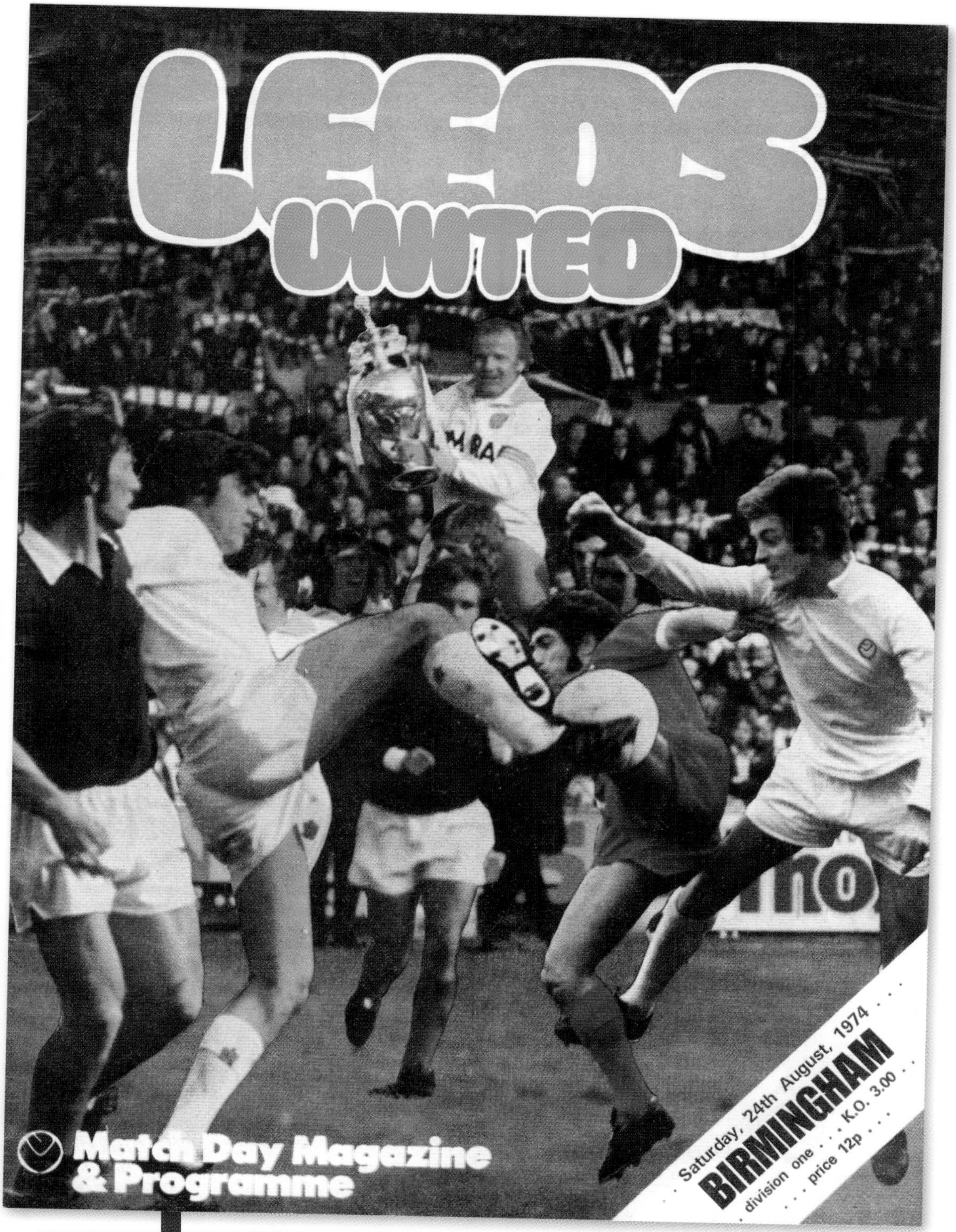

1974/75 – Although Yorkshire didn't seem an obvious origin for cutting-edge football design, Leeds apparently called in Peter Blake to create this terrific pop-art collage. Oh, for the groundbreaking 'Smiley' era of waving at fans, names on trackies and bubble writing like you used to do on your pencil case. This was Leeds' second home game under Cloughie: a 1-0 win after two opening defeats.

Leicester City

1979/80 – Jock Wallace was framed: sergeant major and father figure to a whole new generation of City kids.

1970/71 – Can it really be true that Leicester City were the first and only club to use this kind of simple, effective rosette graphic? Fit for a promotion season.

1968/69 – Waste not, want not. Spot the sticker with the rearranged date for a Cup match in the season City made it to Wembley for the fourth time since the war.

1976/77 – The sheer insanity of filling in letters with photographs is illustrated by the bottom-right element here: it's not an edit that really makes you think 'cover shot'.

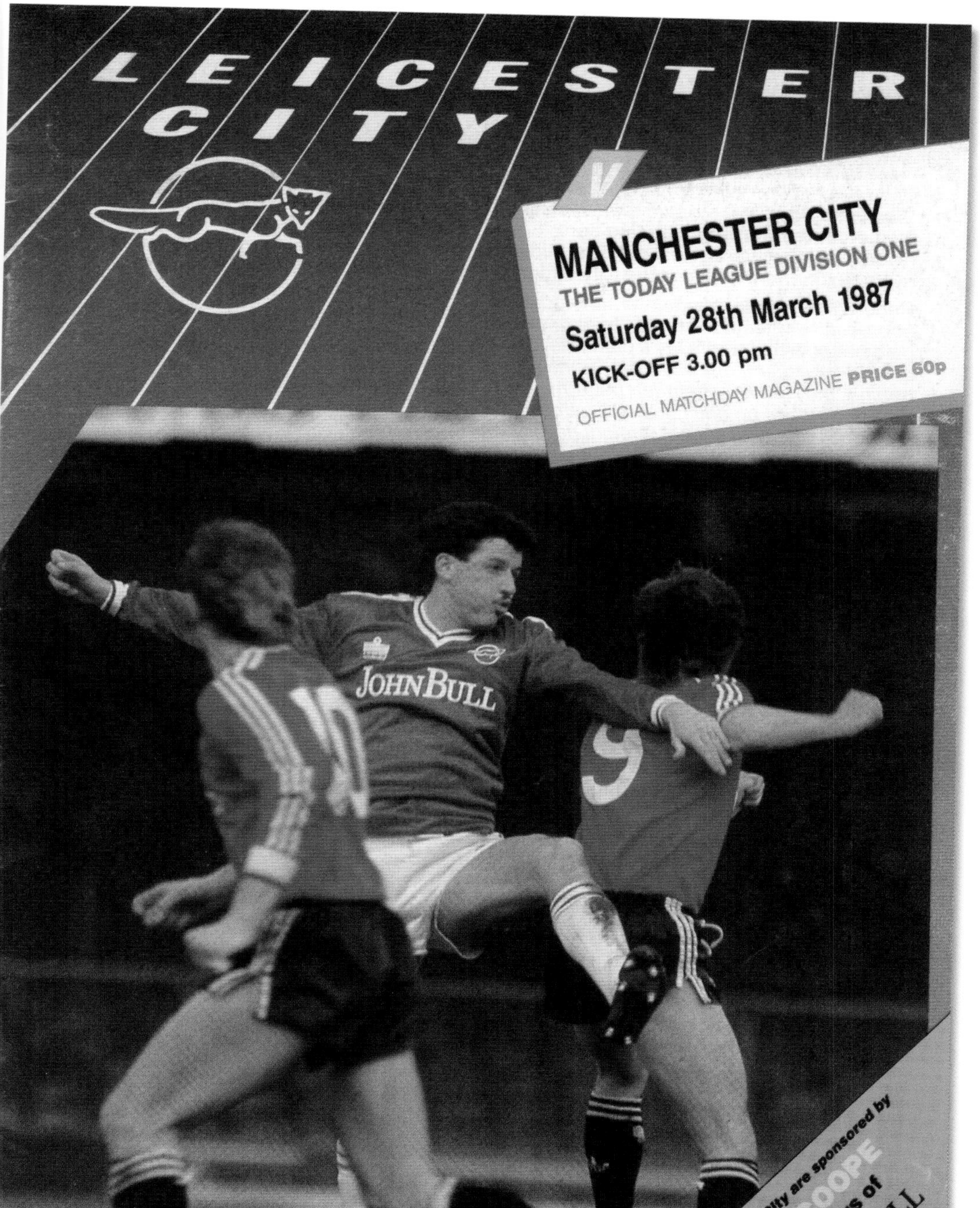

1986/87 – City were only pulling 8,000 or 9,000 punters in the top flight, so it's quite fitting that no one's home in this evocative shot of star battler Paul Ramsey. There are compensatory memories, but you had to be there. Relegation at the season's end meant an absence from Division One that lasted until Brian Little mastered the play-offs in 1993.

Lincoln City

1976/77 – Classy, to lift the boot 'n' bubble writing idea that launched a million enamel Coffer badges. Gotta love the multi-panel footy photoframe, too.

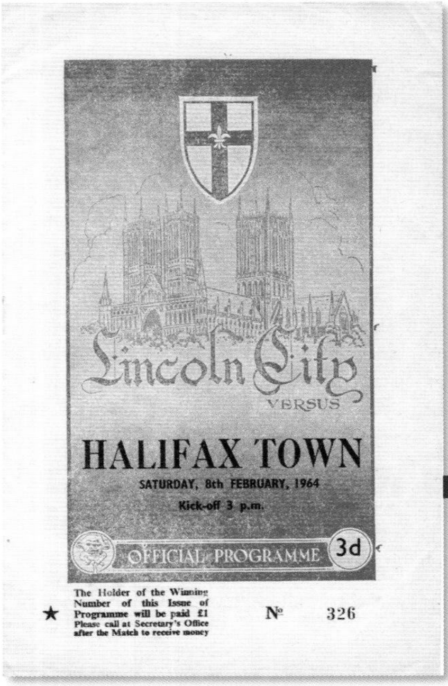

1963/64 – City go for the curlicued medieval hymnsheet look in a 63/64 edition – 1463/64, that is.

1971/72 – One of the few horror programmes to have slipped past the League authorities. Bizarre juxtaposition of cross-legged Devil and House of God.

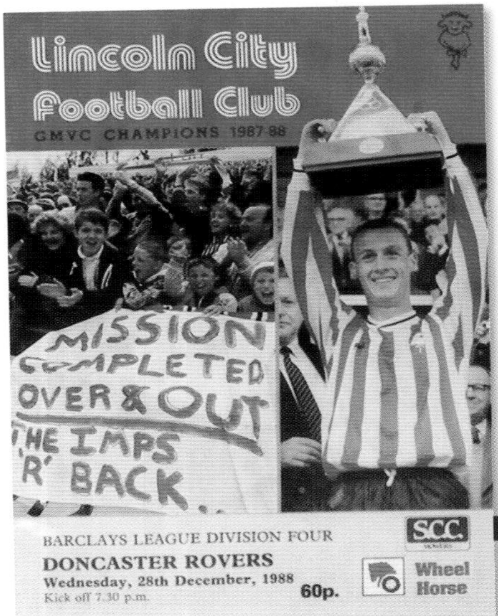

1988/89 – Having bounced back from the GM Vauxhall Conference, a whole season of festivities ensued. Especially at Christmas.

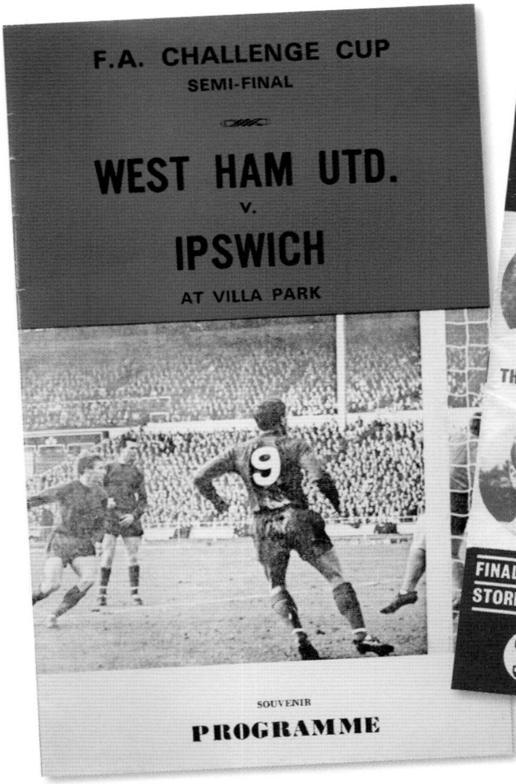

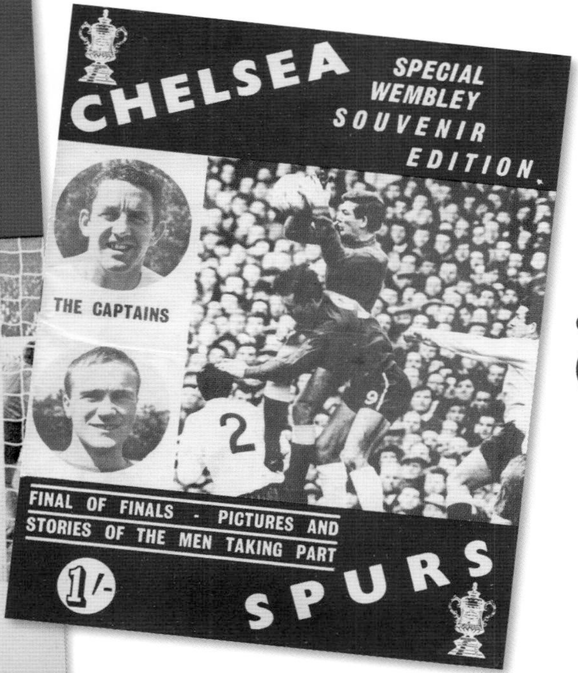

Dating back at least to the 1920s, the pirate programme was a magazine of approximately four pages, found on sale outside a ground where a big match was being played. Coincidentally, the cover might have mentioned the teams who were playing, and chucked in a key word or two such as 'FA' and 'Cup'. The pirate programme carried no advertising, no teamsheet, no half-time scoreboard A-Z – and if punters failed to enquire of the seller whether it was the 'Official Programme', well, that was their lookout.

So imagine the consternation of young Alasdair Ross, aged 13, when he was taken along by his dad for his debut Ipswich away game at Chelmsford in the Cup in 1973, and was told to run and get a prog.

Appalled by the travesty of a matchday magazine retrieved by Alasdair from an unscrupulous seller, Dad chucked the offending item on the floor and strode off to get a proper one himself.

But young Alasdair picked up the Town-Chelmsford pirate as a souvenir, and it's now worth ten times more than Dad's real deal!

Liverpool

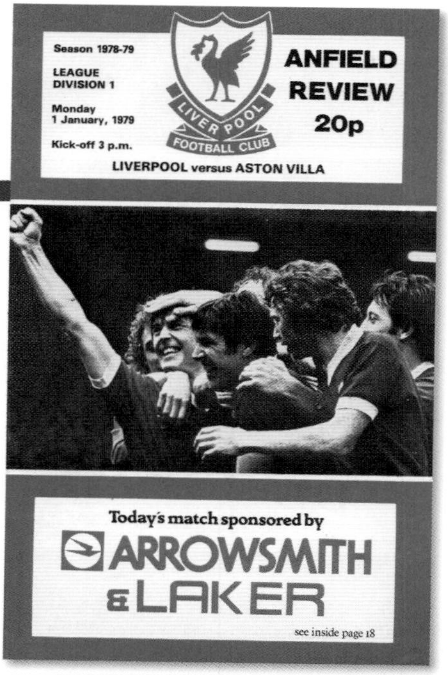

1978/79 – Unbeatable: King Kenny and a gaggle of accomplices.

1969/70 – The Kop: the most famous terrace in British football, so packed the programme could find an emergency use for a sneaky 'hot-leg' toilet break.

1976/77 – Weirdly 10 years out of date in design terms… but check the list of silverware.

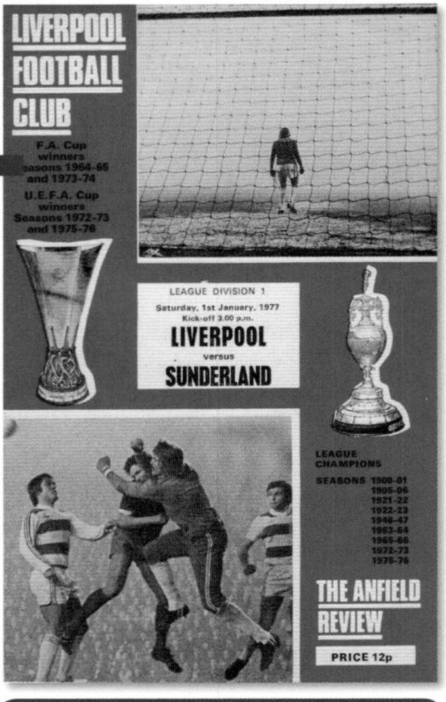

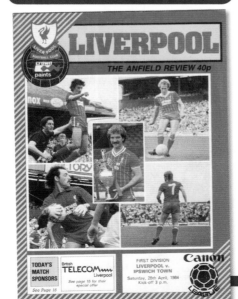

1983/84 – Low prog production values in the golden Crown Paints era. Rush, Souey and Grob all elegantly 'tached, while Dalglish hides his bare upper lip in shame.

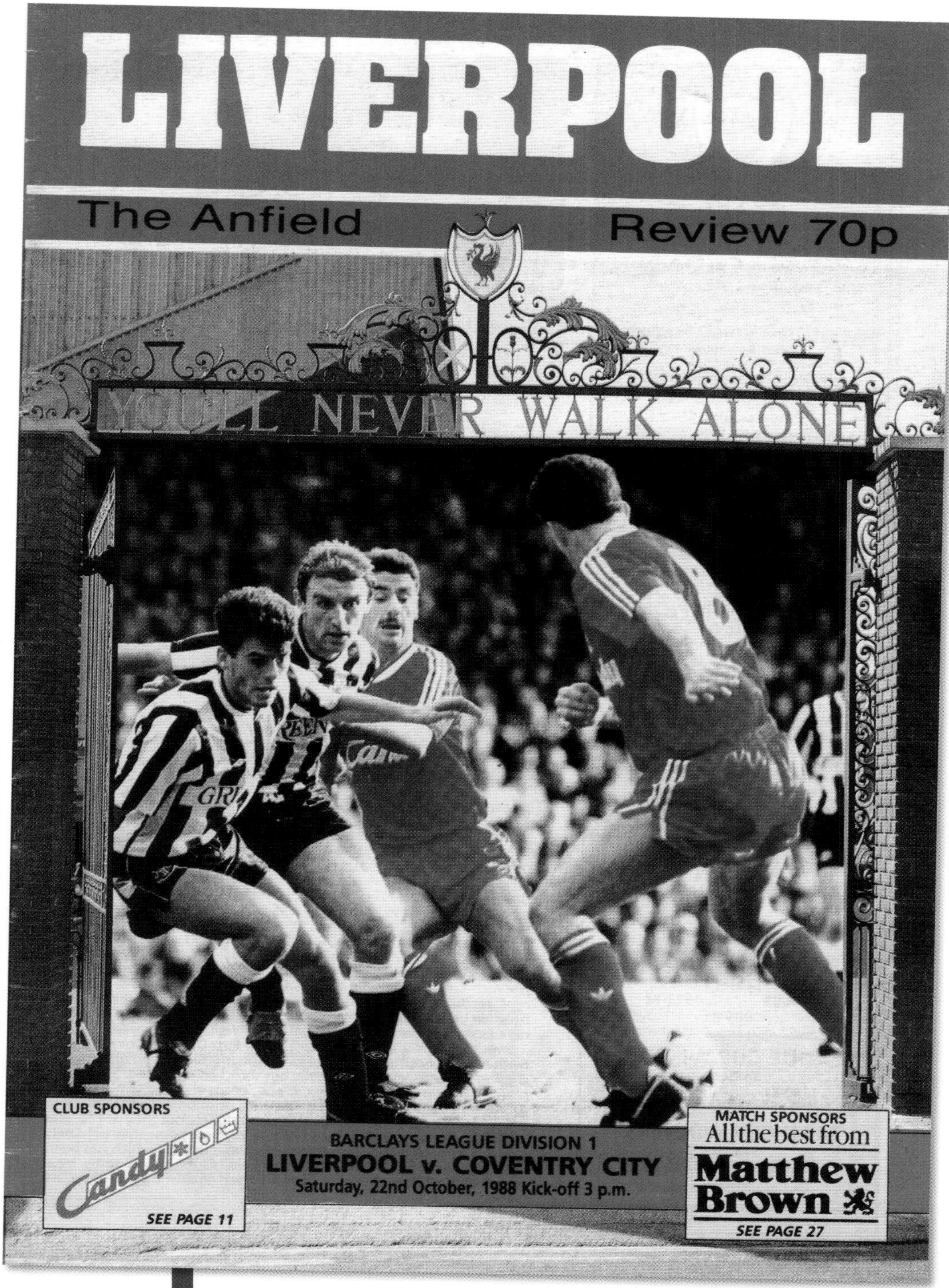

1988/89 – You don't get many more iconic photo-frames in football than the Shankly Gates at Liverpool, employed here in classic fashion to detain potent strike duo Ian Rush and John Aldridge. Later this season, the Gates would come to be indelibly associated with the tragedy at Hillsborough.

Luton Town

1975/76 – Luton were one of the earliest clubs with a branding strategy, all orange and stripes and logos. It must have been a sponsorship thing, taking on the Mister Men.

1977/78 – Ultra-vivid action featuring the only stand in football where the three banks of ad hoardings eclipsed the incidental letterbox hole left for fans to peer through.

1971/72 – An early experiment with bright orange and computer fonts and posterised public-information artwork. A glimpse into a bright future.

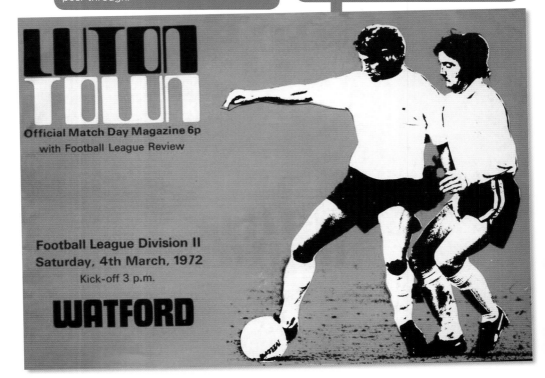

1981/82 – An infectiously joyous cover shot capturing the era of Happy Hatters, all hugs and bubble perms and ultra-tight, ultra-cool round-necked Adidas gear. The subliminal ad-hoarding comment suggests the photo editor at the time may have been a Watford fan.

1976/77 – The familiar fan perspective and field of vision make this cover, combining with the title logo to recall Saturday-night *Match of the Day*, back in the day.

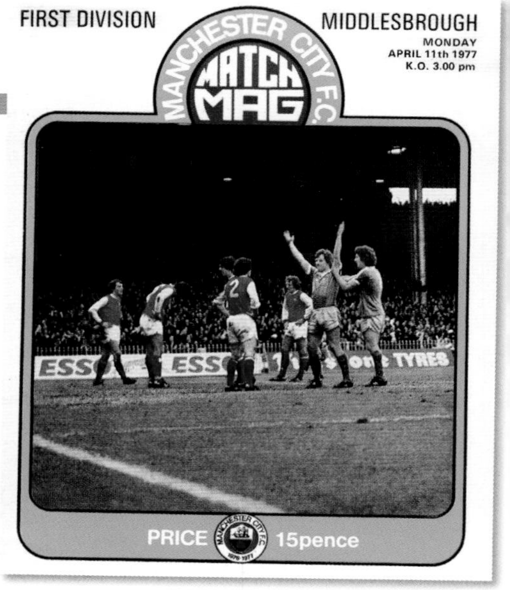

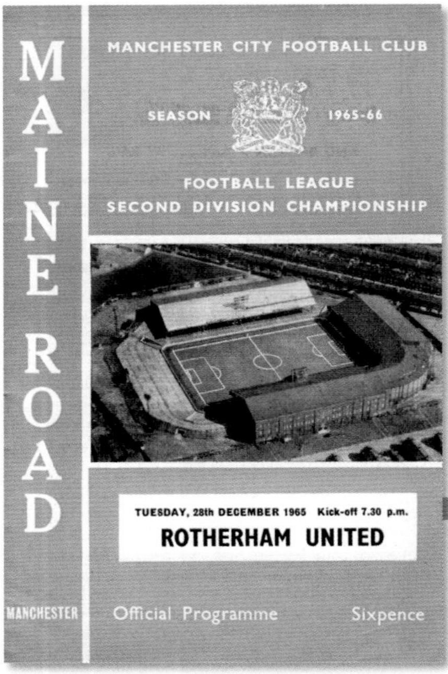

1965/66 – A rare example of the stadium name grabbing the limelight. It must have made perfect sense at the time, even in downward lettering.

1987/88 – You'll believe a man from Greenock can fly. Neil McNab and a backdrop of proper Maine Road terraces.

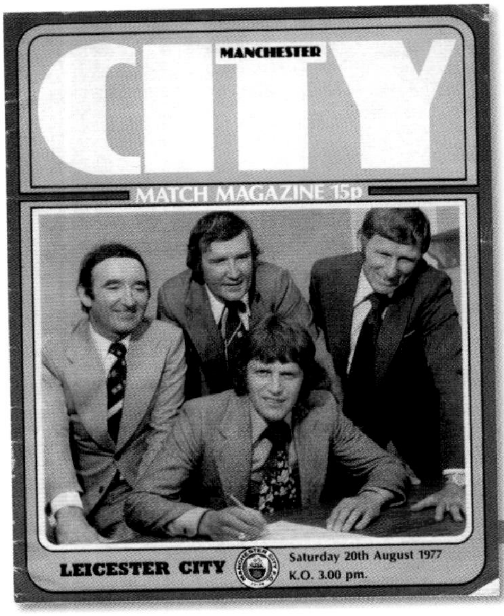

1977/78 – Never mind the Buzzcocks and noisy punk – here's Manc's more staid pop heroes Herman's Hermits signing their seventh and last multi-LP deal with EMI.

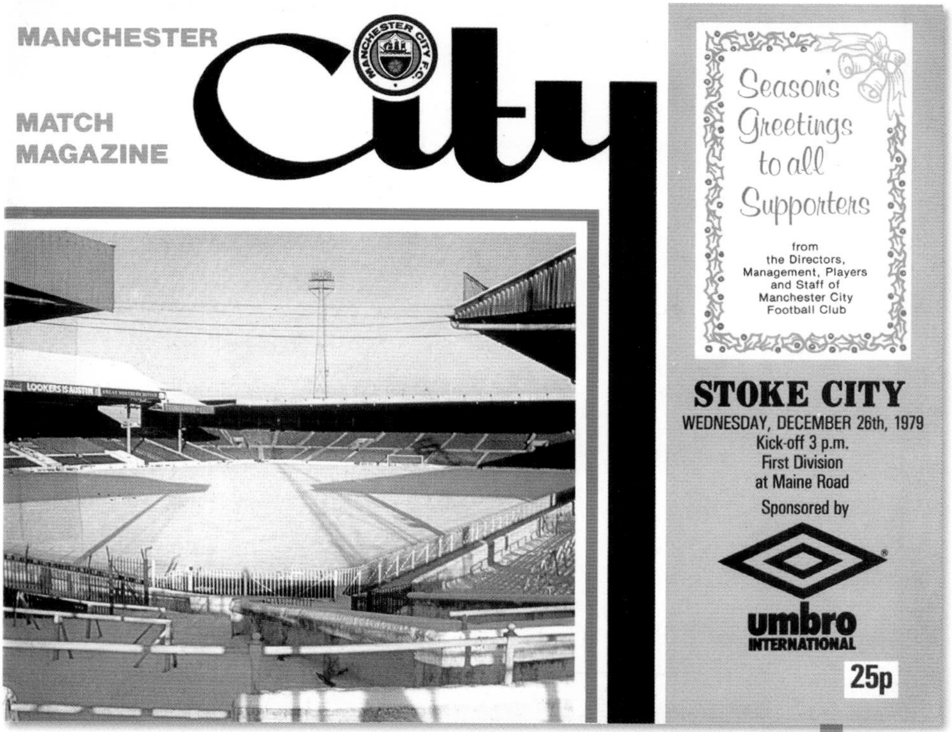

1979/80 - Kevin Cummins' debut cover shot for the City prog beautifully captures Maine Road in winter.

1982/83 - City were so pleased with their new 'schoolboy doodle'-style logo, they used it twice, persevering doggedly with the awkward landscape format.

Manchester United

1976/77 – Tommy Doc presides over nearly-Alex-Stepney, a fictional composite of Coppell, Pearson and Macari, and a down-market fan. Note the sky-blue clouds.

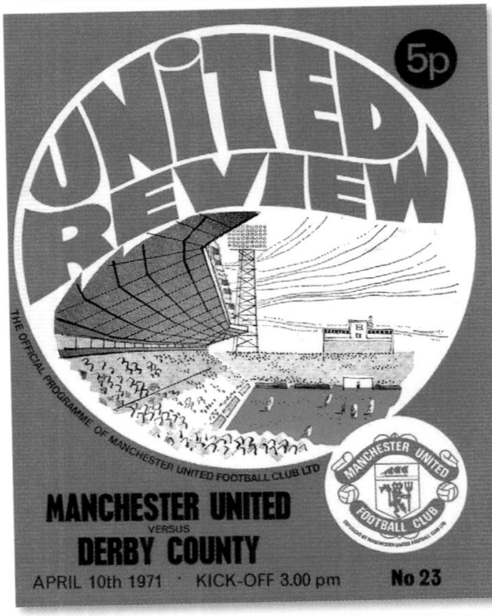

1970/71 – This is wonderful, an ideal balance of dreamlike fantasy and real-life promise, a prog completely of its time in the age of prog rock. We're talking Top 5.

1980/81 – At long last, Kevin Moran makes the cover of *Goal!* You can't go wrong with big circles.

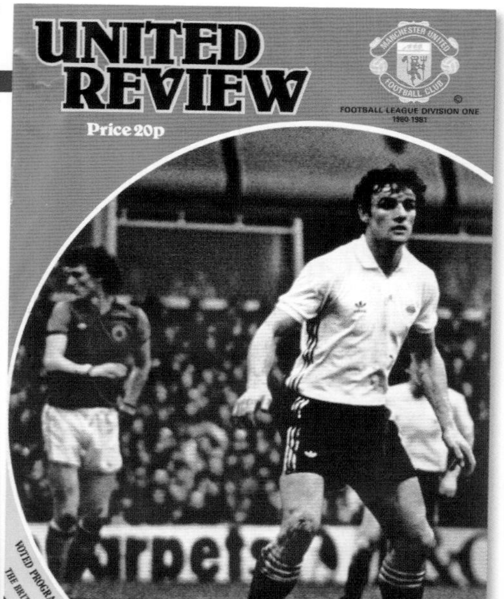

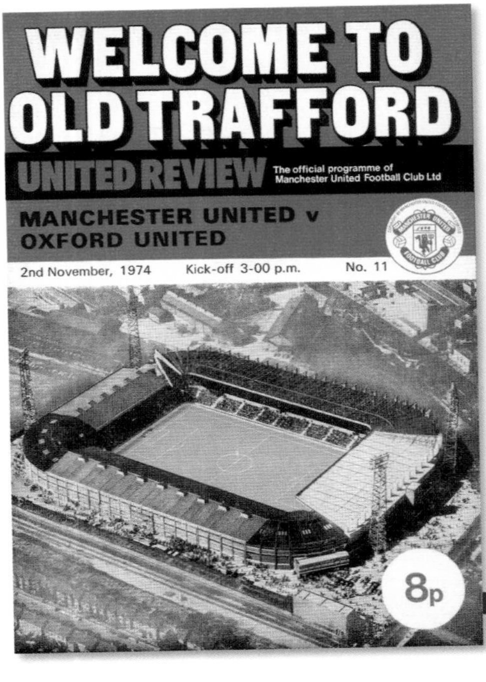

1974/75 – The grass is greener when you're suffering cutbacks down in Division Two.

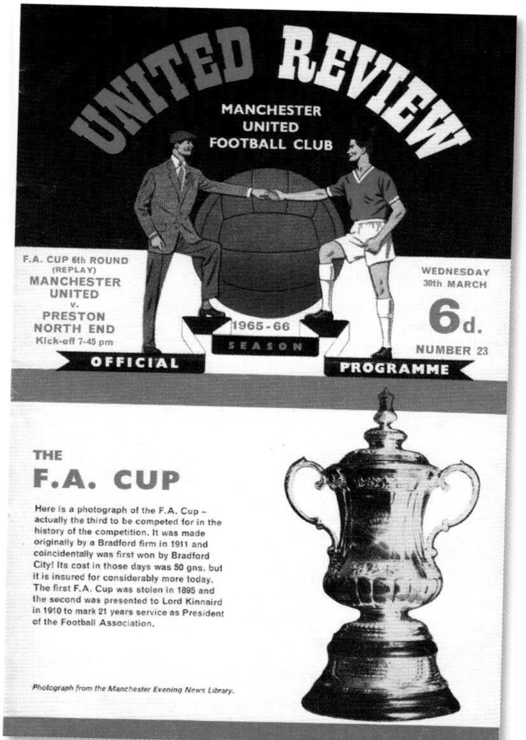
UNITED REVIEW
MANCHESTER UNITED FOOTBALL CLUB
F.A. CUP 6th ROUND (REPLAY)
MANCHESTER UNITED v. PRESTON NORTH END
Kick-off 7-45 pm
WEDNESDAY 30th MARCH
6d.
NUMBER 23
1965-66 SEASON
OFFICIAL PROGRAMME
THE F.A. CUP
Here is a photograph of the F.A. Cup – actually the third to be competed for in the history of the competition. It was made originally by a Bradford firm in 1911 and coincidentally was first won by Bradford City! Its cost in those days was 50 gns. but it is insured for considerably more today. The first F.A. Cup was stolen in 1895 and the second was presented to Lord Kinnaird in 1910 to mark 21 years service as President of the Football Association.
Photograph from the Manchester Evening News Library.

MANCHESTER UNITED FOOTBALL CLUB • OFFICIAL PROGRAMME
UNITED REVIEW
No. 23
1966-67 SEASON
6D.
M.U.F.C. v ASTON VILLA
SATURDAY, APRIL 29th
KICK-OFF 3-0 p.m.
MANCHESTER UNITED v SOUTHAMPTON, April 18th, 1967.
Although our goalless draw at Sunderland last Saturday produced a valuable point it was our 3-0 win over Southampton the previous Tuesday night that produced the pictures. Here we see one of the best goals of the season as Bobby Charlton's great shot beats Southampton's diving goalkeeper Martin. Bobby can be seen just beneath the goalkeeper. Photo courtesy the Daily Mail

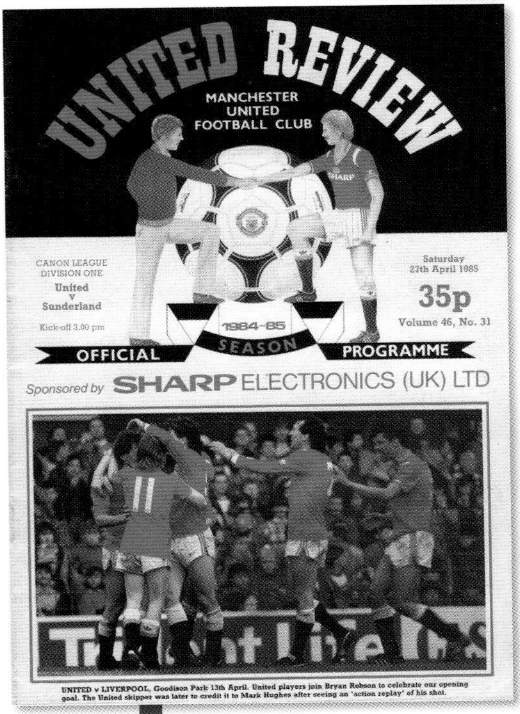
UNITED REVIEW
MANCHESTER UNITED FOOTBALL CLUB
CANON LEAGUE DIVISION ONE
United v Sunderland
Kick-off 3.00 pm
Saturday 27th April 1985
35p
Volume 46, No. 31
1984-85 SEASON
OFFICIAL PROGRAMME
Sponsored by SHARP ELECTRONICS (UK) LTD
UNITED v LIVERPOOL, Goodison Park 13th April. United players join Bryan Robson to celebrate our opening goal. The United skipper was later to credit it to Mark Hughes after seeing an 'action replay' of his shot.

UNITED REVIEW
MANCHESTER UNITED FOOTBALL CLUB
BARCLAYS LEAGUE DIVISION ONE
United v Norwich City
Kick-off 3.00 pm
Saturday 17th October 1987
50p
Volume 49, No.7
1987-88 SEASON
OFFICIAL PROGRAMME
Sponsored by SHARP ELECTRONICS (UK) LTD
SHEFFIELD WEDNESDAY v UNITED, 10th October. Bryan Robson redeems his early own goal in the best possible way — a goal in our favour to level the score.

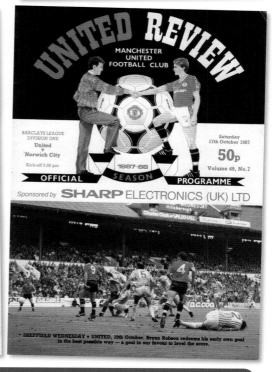

1984/85 – The evolution of *United Review*'s player-everyfan relationship. In the 60s, we moved from rosette, flat cap and gently squeezed fingers to slick mod houndstooth style. And so to the 80s, Farah slacks and Armani, and the ultimate Christmas jumper style statement.

Middlesbrough

1970/71 – Hats off to Boro for unleashing this simple, effective autographed ball idea. Strange to say it was never reused or nicked elsewhere.

1981/82 – The advantages of having a four-letter nickname, with 'Os'. Disadvantages include downward lettering and a million 'Middlesborough' spelling mistakes.

1964/65 – It's hard to say what the 1930s signwriting signified in the 60s, but the inconsistent colouring-in drove OCD prog collectors insane.

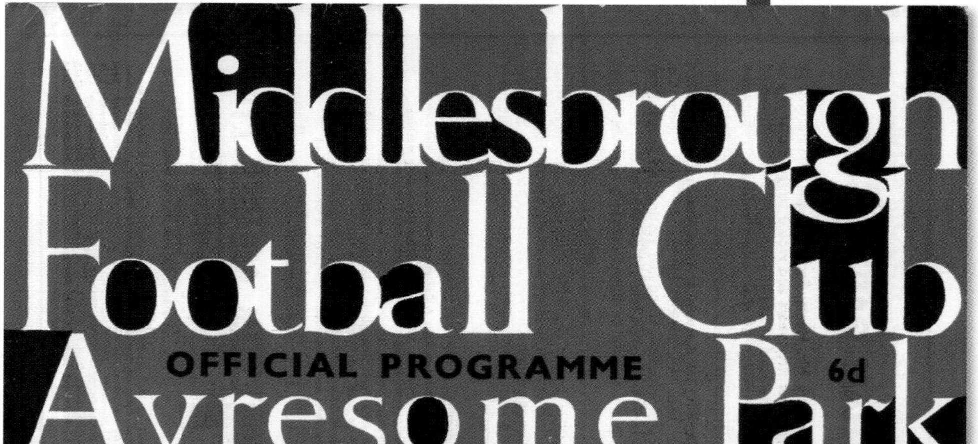

1987/88 – We like this for many reasons. It mimics the contemporary shirt's stripy panel, for starters. Post financial meltdown, the new club badge symbolises a bold and brave new beginning. Floodlit ground shots are super rare on prog covers – as is snow in August. Boro beat their local rivals 2-0. And, eventually, this turned into a promotion season.

Millwall

1966/67 – A lion playing netball. And a solid little programme from that odd historical window when Millwall wore blue-and-white stripes.

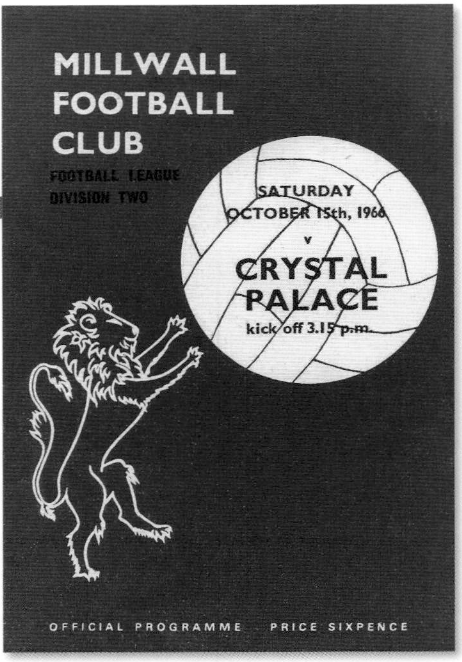

1974/75 – Most of the cover shots this season featured onfield action. This LWT studio shot is unusual, marking the last of seven seasons in all-white at The Den.

1971/72 – *Action*: that's a cool (and fitting) name for a Millwall prog. Note the lack of oppo info, so all the colour covers could be printed at the start of the season.

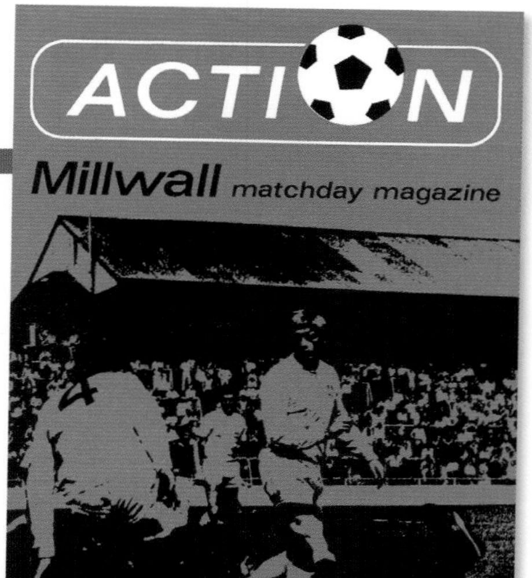

1980/81 – How cool that this Lions badge was originally half-inched from *Lion* comic. Google: 'Millwall FC badge millwall-history-org.uk' for the whole detective story.

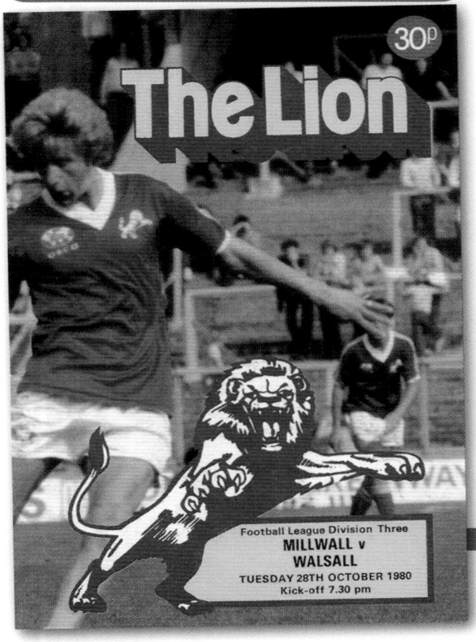

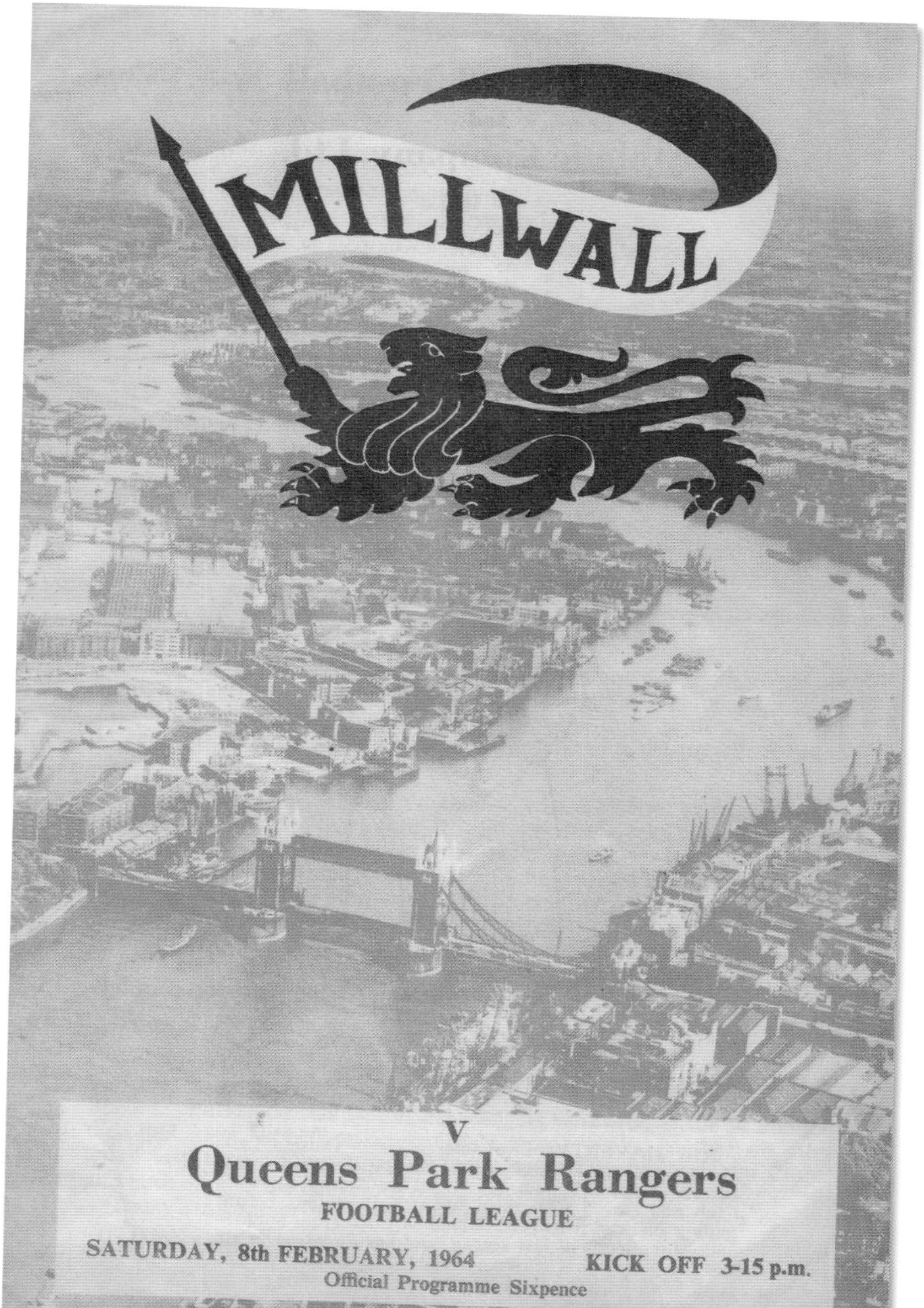

1963/64 – Everything a programme should be – a window into another place and time, complete with hints of atmosphere and zeitgeist. London looking east from Tower Bridge toward the industrial Millwall heartlands of Rotherhithe and the Isle of Dogs. Back in the days of a working river, docks, wharves and warehouses were just that – no sign of yuppie flats or Canary Wharf.

Newcastle United

1974/75 – The 'N' fashioned from a folded scarf was a little bit of design genius, a fan-friendly statement as bold as Likely Lad Bob wearing a United shirt in bed.

1971/72 – The familiar headless footballer given a dynamic, head-turning spin on a bed of lairy puce.

1972/73 – Look who's got a smart new stand, then. Brilliantly integrated into The Black 'n' White stripes, it somehow made reality pall in comparison.

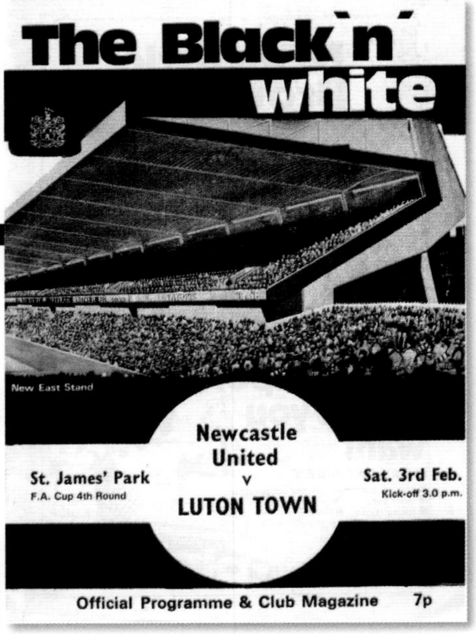

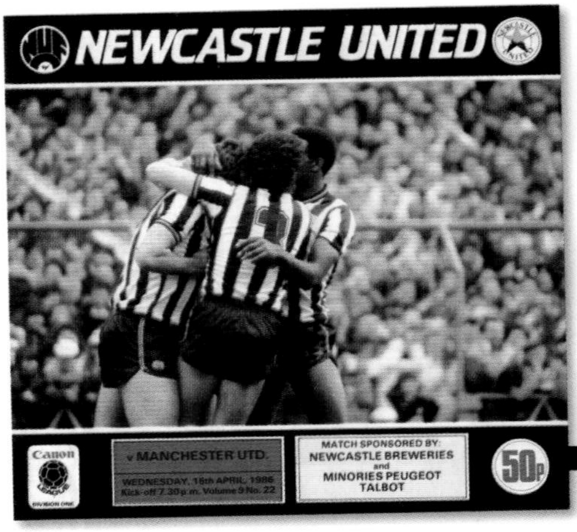

1985/86 – A bit late for a prog to go square, but perfect timing for the crash-helmet mullet perm – as modelled here by John Bailey.

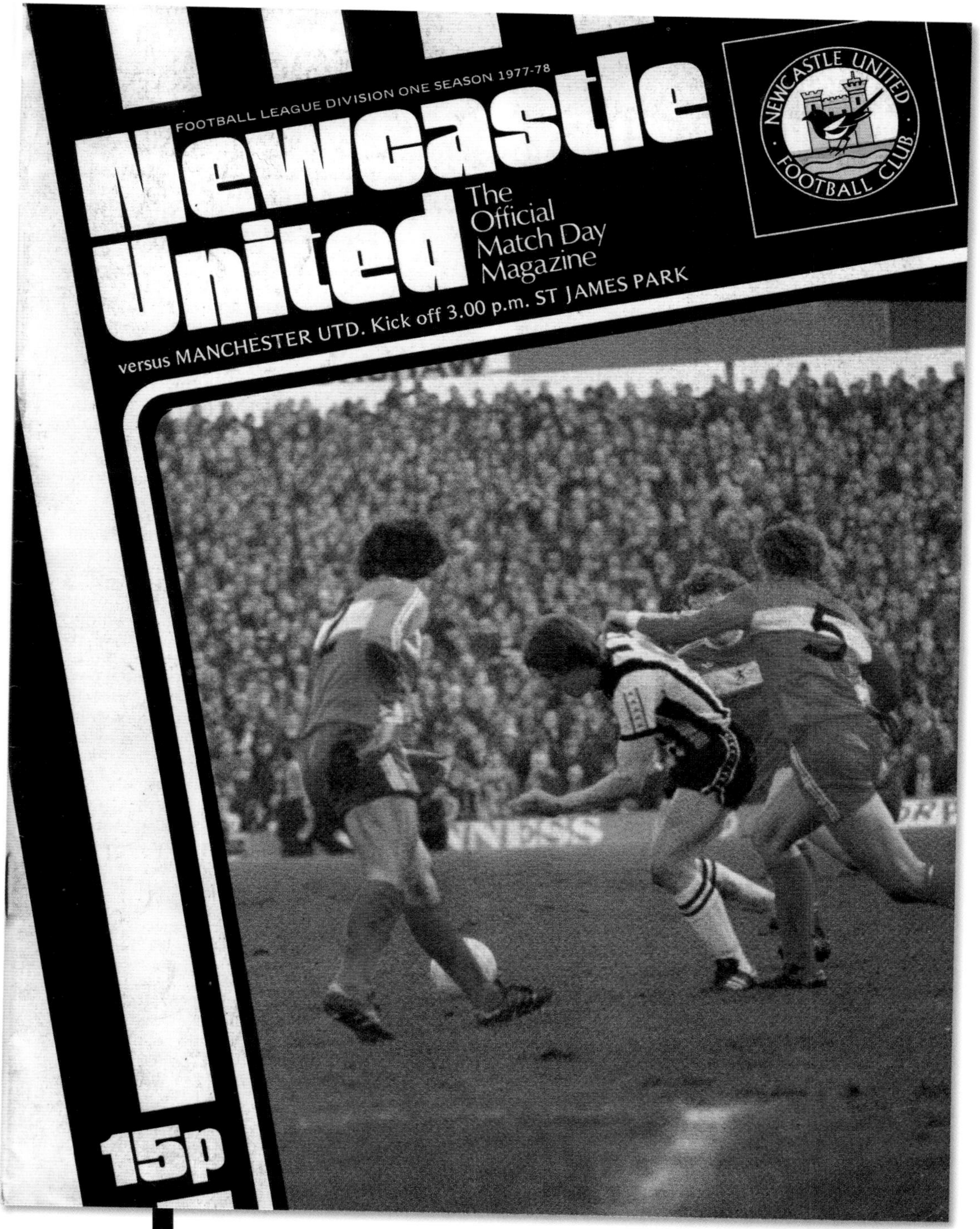

1977/78 – The offset stripy look has long been a favourite in this parish, bringing to a head a top-drawer selection of 70s highlights. A triumph of design comparable to a bumble-bee, the off-cock trick shouldn't fly for a hundred different reasons, but it does. Featuring a different action pic every issue, Middlesbrough's red ironically provides the perfect final balancing touch.

At Home With

First introduced in the mid-60s, from now on no programme could be considered complete without an 'At Home With'/ 'Off Duty' spread, where fans got to check out the wives of the stars together with their taste in soft furnishings. Now we could smirk at the way players looked oddly awkward in civilian dress, and judge them not only on the goalbanger scale but on the trendiness of their casual blouson jackets and their kids' Sunday best. *Shoot*! soon picked up the baton along with countless newspapers and mags that weren't football specific.

'At Home With' marked the dawn of the age of the footballer celebrity – no longer just a bloke with a slightly odd job which demanded he worked Saturday afternoons, like bus drivers and menswear counter assistants, but a figure who inspired awe, envy, jealousy, piss-taking, curiosity, dismissive sneers and worship in roughly equal proportions, mostly dependent on his haircut.

Nowadays, whole magazines are devoted to prying into the personal lives of the rich and famous, but there was once a more innocent glee involved in being downright nosy. Peeping behind Mike O'Grady's curtains to find him on the couch with his thrilled landlady Mrs Screen. Evaluating his slightly embarrassed smirk. Judging her on the strength of her bouffant and pearl necklace.

And crikey. Ricky Villa, Spurs 'Player at Leisure' this week, has got a primitive chess computer and it looks like he's taking a beating at the hands of his preggers wife, Cristina. "We started playing only about four months ago, and now we really enjoy it," says Ricky.

Hmm… so now we know. It's only human nature, innit?

How lucky we are that football is only really 60 per cent about what happens on the field of play.

Player off Duty 10- Graham Cro
These swinging kids are the 15-months-old identical twin daughters of Graham and Val Cross. We are assu
charge of Lisa, while Mum is keeping Andrea amused. The setting is a park near their Groby home

MERSEY MAN
Kevin Sheedy, pictured with his family at Formby Nature Reserve

16
MANCHESTER CITY MA
THE BLUES OFF-DU

Mark Bowen

Away from The Lane

JOHN FENNELLY.

OFF THE PITCH

and Lorraine Putney, it is
a case of childhood

e known each other since
the Neave Comprehensive
arold Hill. Trevor says: "I
when I stayed on an extra
ol."

vor was signed by Ipswich,
ed down to Suffolk as well.
were living together at
aine commuted to London
r three years where she
nerchant bank.

Now they have settled at Ca
Mary and on May 8 this year th
their first baby — a girl — Aimee

Away from Portman Road, Tre
chirpy cockney, enjoys playing
snooker and tennis and is a dab h
all three.

He plays off an 11 handicap at golf,
one of the lower handicap players at the
club.

Lorraine follows Trevor's career
closely and before having Aimee popped
up at most away matches.

Jeff Wealands who is featured on our centre pages match-by-match is pictured here with his wife and seven week old son Shaun.

At home with . . .

Raddy Avramovic

Raddy Avramovic has come to terms with the fact that he will never be a top golfer — and gone back to his law books.

The popular goalkeeper took 15 of the statutory 25 examinations during his time at University and is continuing to study, intending to complete the course when he returns to Yugoslavia.

He explained: "I still spend a lot of time studying — in my spare time. Steve Carter persuaded me to buy a set of golf clubs but I'm not good at it.

"I find the ball difficult to hit . . . it is too small."

Raddy is pictured in his Calverton home with his wife Bratislava and five-year-old son Ivan.

John Robson pictured at home with his wife, Jane, and their two boys, Paul (5) and Gary (3).

This won't be the happiest of Christmases for Pertti Jantunen, Bristol City's Finnish mid-field player.

For the first time he will be spending the Yuletide season apart from his wife and four year old daughter, Kia. They have returned home for the holiday period.

**"I wish I could go with them", said Pertti. "Chri... is something real-
...d, with plenty of
...etting just right.
... many friends in
...ht it best that,
...tay here because
...fe and little girl**

**... 14 months play-
...re signing for Ci-
...no English when
...untry. He is cop-
... now with the
...h is still very
... amount he has
...any difficulties,"
... helps us, but my
...ally speak any
...ghter is only just
...p a word or two
...oo young to be at**

**...riends here from
...re mostly Finnish
...d to Englishmen,
...w any complete
...meland".
...urned to Finland
...n last summer,
...hances of sight
...hen the weather
...off in the car and
... about England,
...ing".
...rtti played ice
...inter and soccer
... his wife is not**

**...any outside in-
... Bristol is quiet,
...ne in our apart-**

★

Mike O'Grady relaxes at his Wolverhampton lodgings with landlady Mrs. Screen. Mike originally planned to stay two weeks with Mrs. Screen, but has now been with her for two years!

★

ROBINS NEST

Norwich City

1976/77 – Period cocktail bar font doesn't deflect from the horror of being chased around Carrow Road by an Orient nutter.

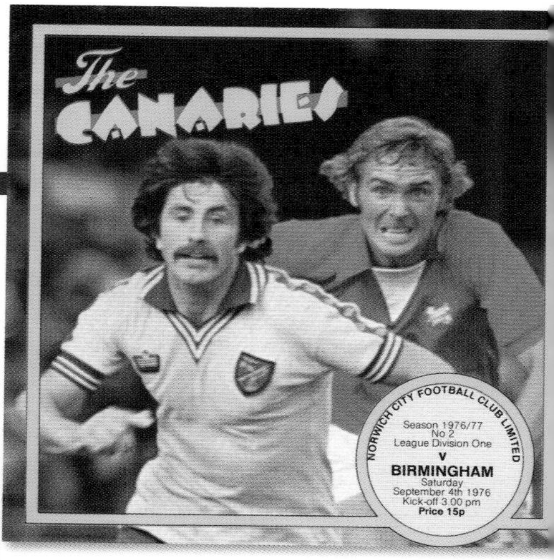

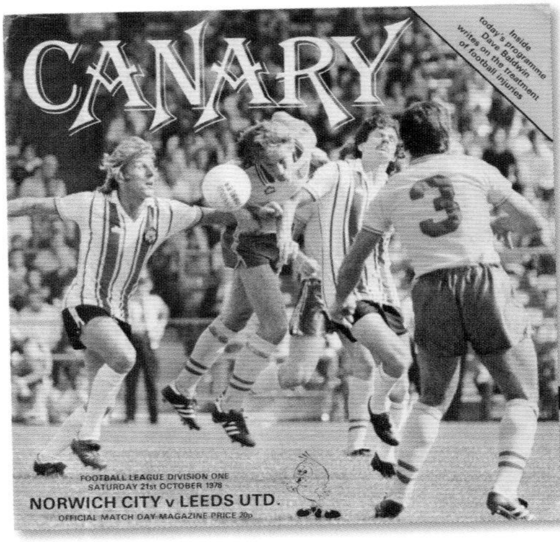

1978/79 – Soccer in the 70s Norfolk sun, a programme cover straight out of an idyllic Admiral kit advert. Tweet is a subtle touch: clearly no relation to Tweety-Pie.

1970/71 – Unimpeachable design job dating back to the dawn of the 70s – as evidenced by Graham Paddon's hair creeping collarward..

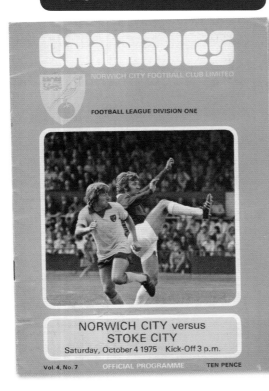

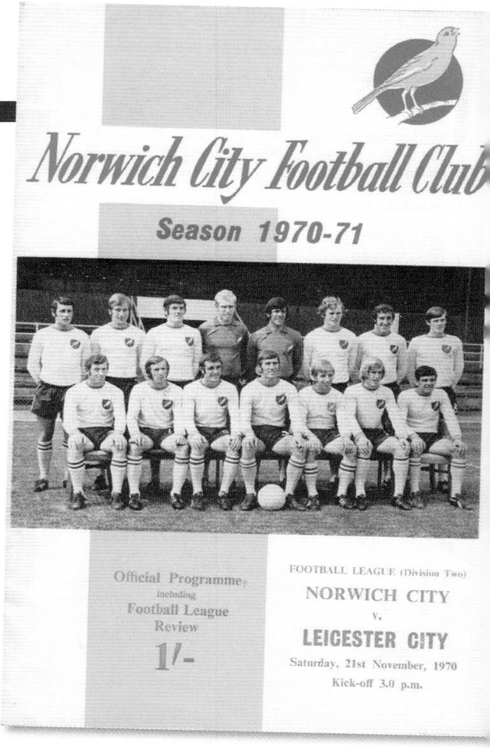

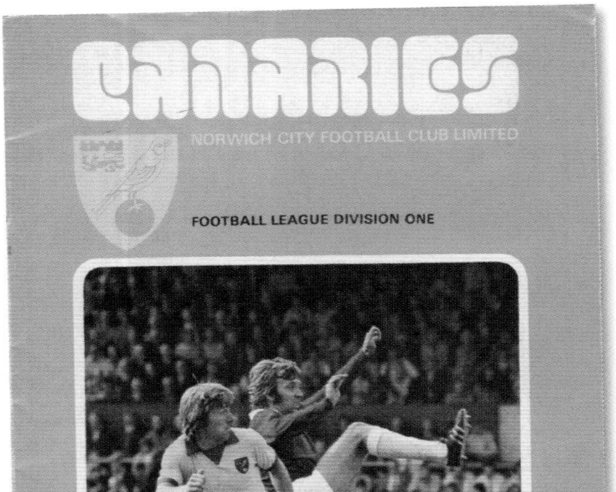

1975/76 – The club badge may have been updated back in '72, but it took this unreadably groovy techno font to definitely vault Norwich into the 1970s.

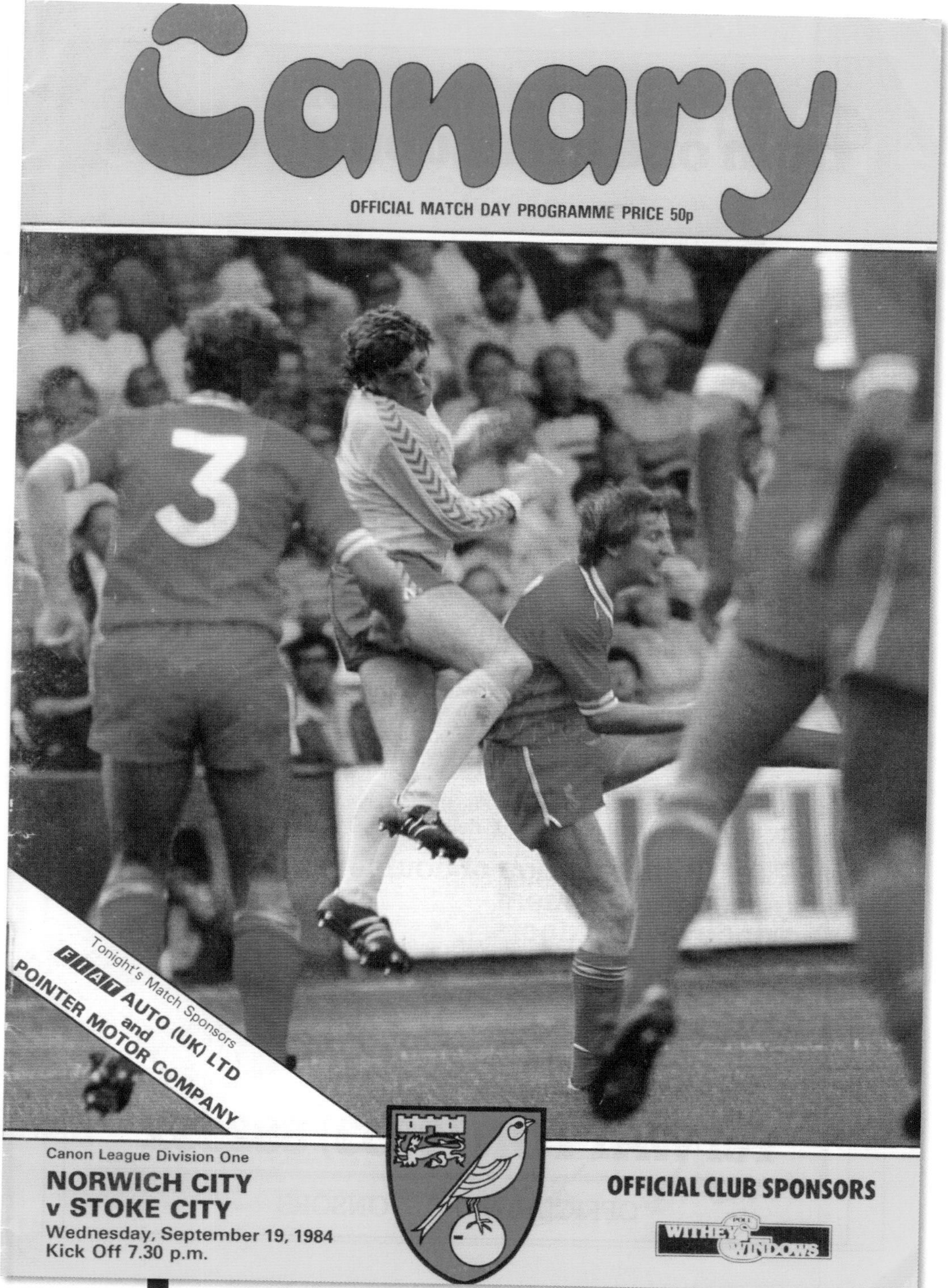

1984/85 – Quite possibly the lairiest programme cover in the history of English football, a garish shock of bright yellow, bright green and bright red – given a final tweak of perfection by Steve Bruce's sense-strimming Hummel kit up against a solid wall of Umbro Reds. Smashing holiday brochure font. Nice touch, too, flipping to *Canary*, after previously toying with the plural and the definite article.

Nottingham Forest

1967/68 – Most clubs would only feature the Division One trophy if they'd recently lifted it. Forest's use was pre-emptive by a decade.

1972/73 – Truly terrific cover which positively shouts 'Forest'. Only at third glance do you question the club's immense pride in an entrance off a 60s industrial estate.

1986/87 – A sidelong look at prog design, featuring Neil Webb and three tricky trees thrown in for balance.

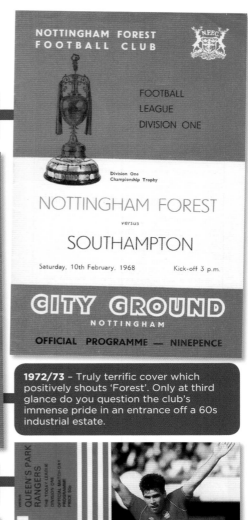

1978/79 – Cloughie wins the First Division and League Cup straight after promotion, and entrusts cops with the cups. Forest 2-0 Liverpool en route to Euro glory.

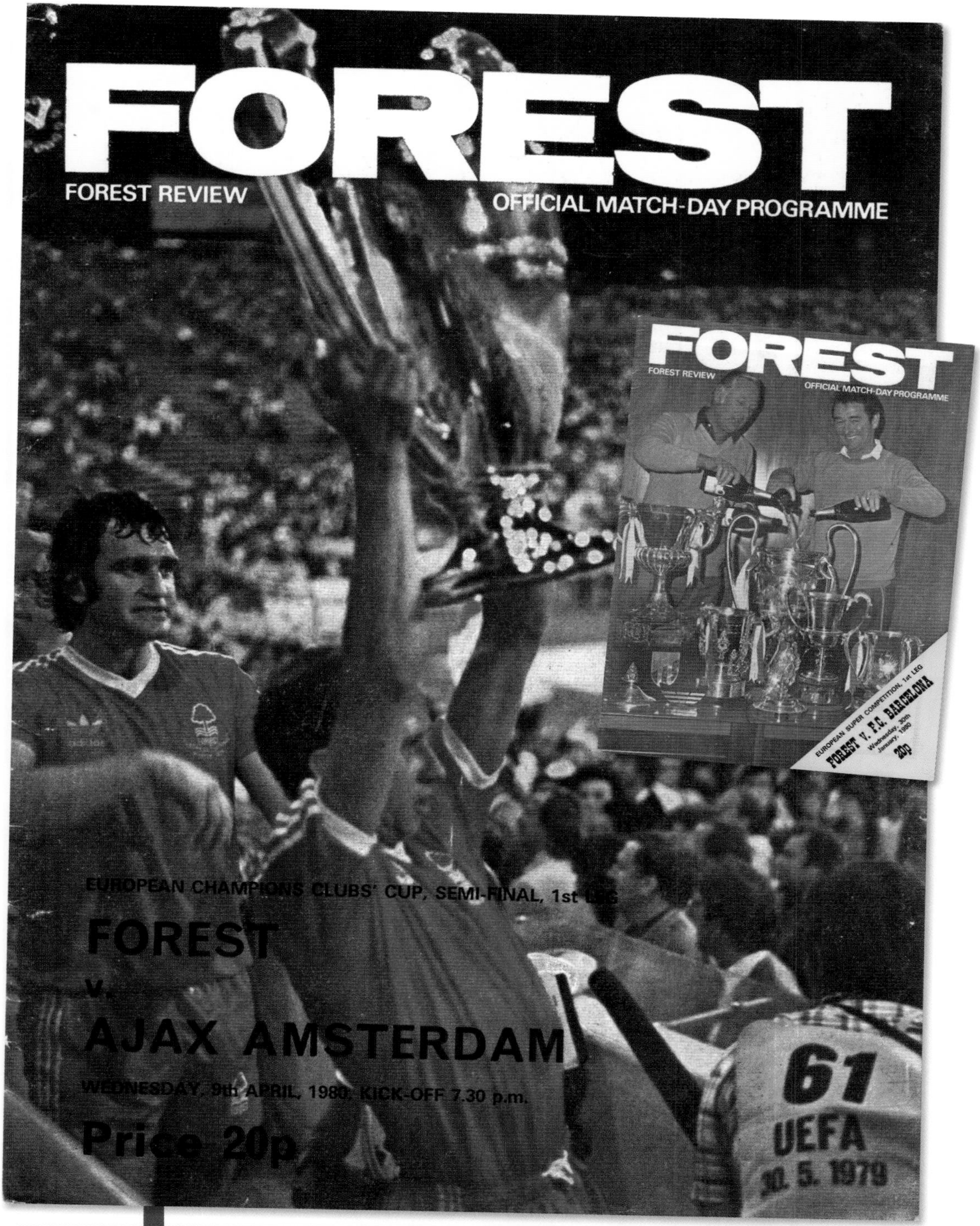

1979/80 – Flicking through piles of Forest progs from the glory era, it's striking how low-end the print job was, all blurry and patchy. But maybe ours is a prime case of Great British attention to the wrong detail. They beat Ajax (pron: 'Ajax') 2-0 here in the semi of the European Champion Clubs Cup. Never mind the quality, admire the silverware.

Notts County

1983/84 – Hold on, it's the futuristic font from our favourite Villa prog, reused here nearly a decade on. They were right, see?

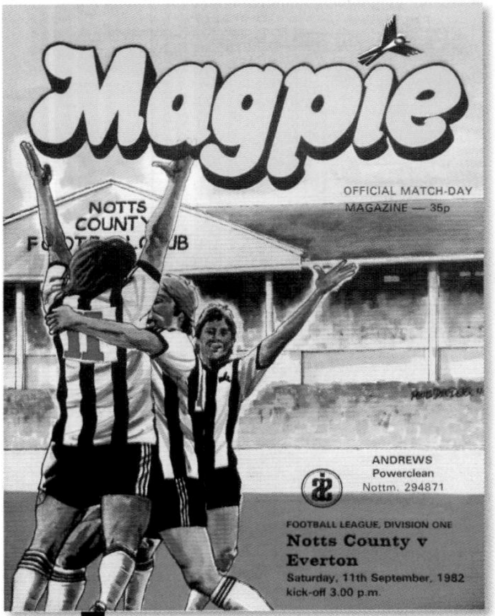

1982/83 – Who better to capture the carnival amosphere of the Magpies in the First Division than a circus poster illustrator? Roll up, roll up!

1983/84 – Exciting *Scorcher*-style action is the promise, combined with the grounded gable boast of being the oldest League club in world football. But who did they play?

Oldham Athletic

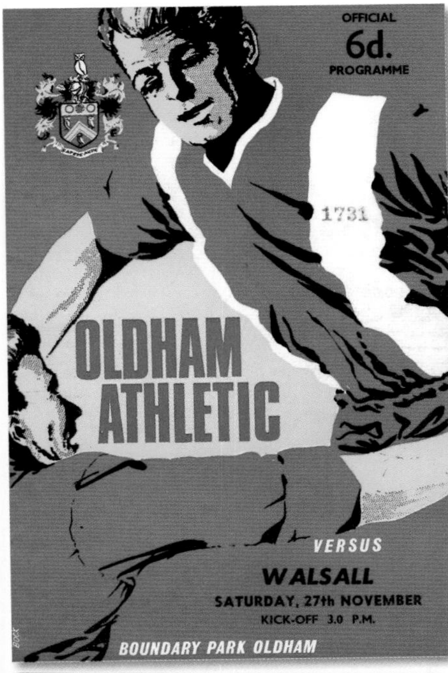

1965/66 – The irresistible essence of a game of football. Come and watch the Blue-and-Whites of Oldham grappling, or perhaps dancing with the, er, Blues?

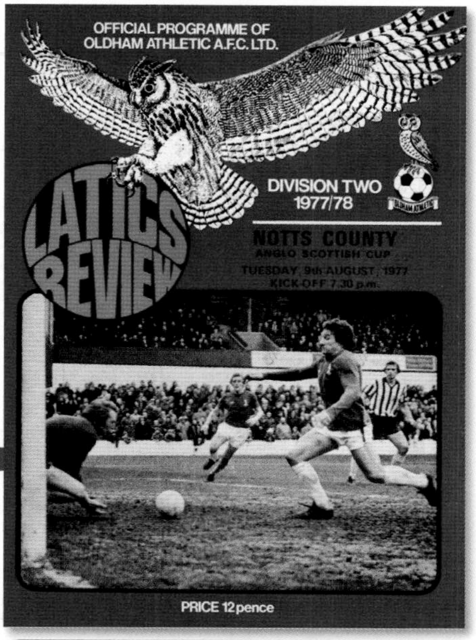

1977/78 – An alarmingly large owl attacks a hippy football under the disapproving swivel-headed glare of the more modest original.

1962/63 – Oh, for simpler times. The sheer joy of football encapsulated in a smiling player, pink capital letters and the original town crest.

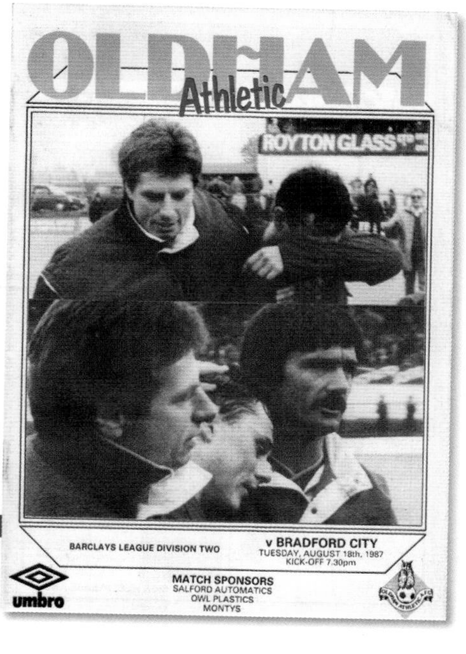

1987/88 – A fresh start for a new campaign – and not one but two pics of Tommy Wright blubbing after last season's play-off failure. Canny use of colour, mind.

1988/89 – Oh yes, okay then. Leyton Orient. From the pink fanzine nadir of the late 80s.

1979/80 – The unique, classic Admiral 'braces' kit echoed subtly in a tidy showcase of 70s design.

1975/76 – Fleetingly trendy, impractical landscape orient(geddit?)ation allows for ginormous krautrock tagging.

1964/65 – The U's third League campaign, having switched names from Headington United in 1960. Stiil no 'Oxford' mentioned on the Dreaming Spires cover.

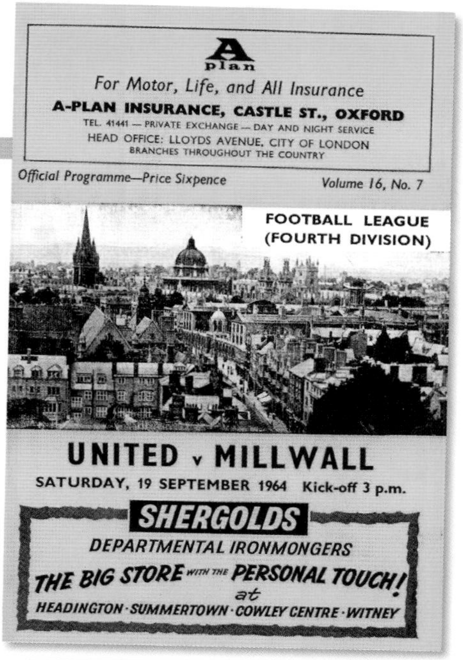

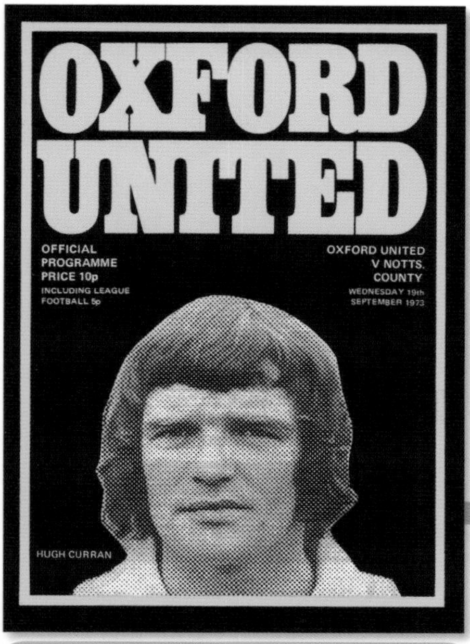

1973/74 – Less doubt who's at home here, but the overall effect is accidentally funereal.

1985/86 – Just a couple of weeks after Oxford's Wembley Milk Cup victory over Reading. My new minicomputer is a Wang (ironically HQ'd in Cambridge).

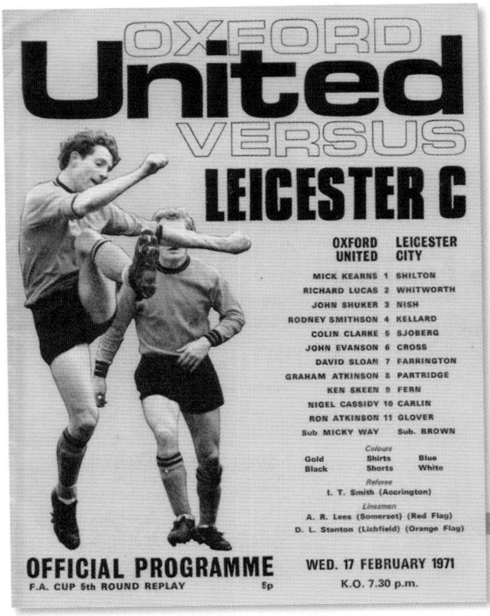

1970/71 – Cutout covers were rare at this time, and as a nipper I remember being struck by the edgy look. The big 'VERSUS'. The shockingly cazh 'Leicester C'.

Peterborough United

1980/81 – ‘Photograph courtesy of *Peterborough Standard*’; but don’t think the prog designer is going to change his front page to accommodate it. Posh bloke 3/10.

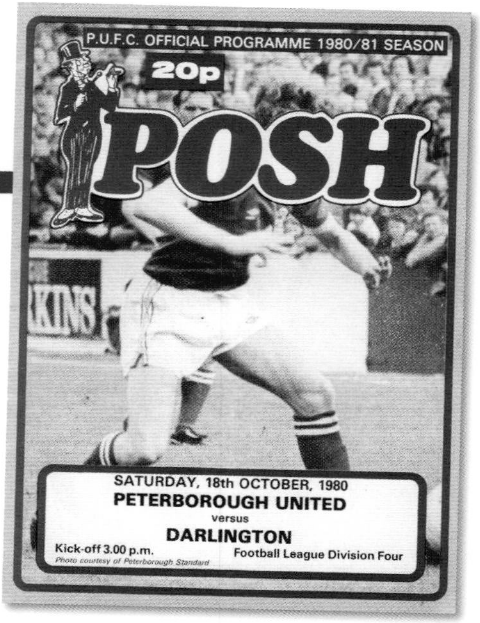

1981/82 – It’s only November 28th and the Posh have already got their decorations up, in tandem with an unconvincing clipart-style posh bloke (2/10).

1968/69 – We like architectural drawings, especially ones with fictitious little trees and roof ads. This match featured the League debut of Scun’s Kevin Keegan.

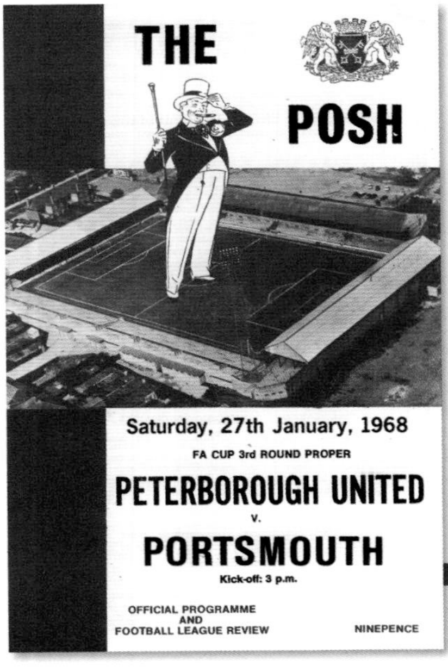

1967/68 – Hard to see why they didn’t just hang on to this giant Posh bloke cavorting like a circus ringmaster in the centre-circle at London Road (9.5/10).

Plymouth Argyle

1968/69 – To outsiders, Plymouth were always all about the kit, this magnificent green hooped number with black trim and ship badge the most iconic of the lot.

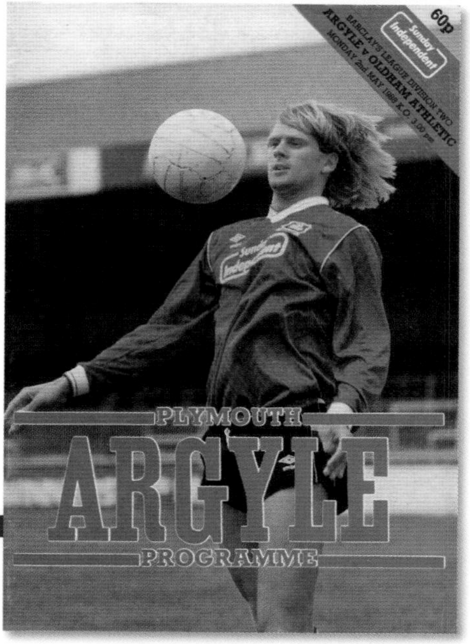

1987/88 – Just to underline the bright green oddness of being a Pilgrim, here's the greeniest green programme in League history.

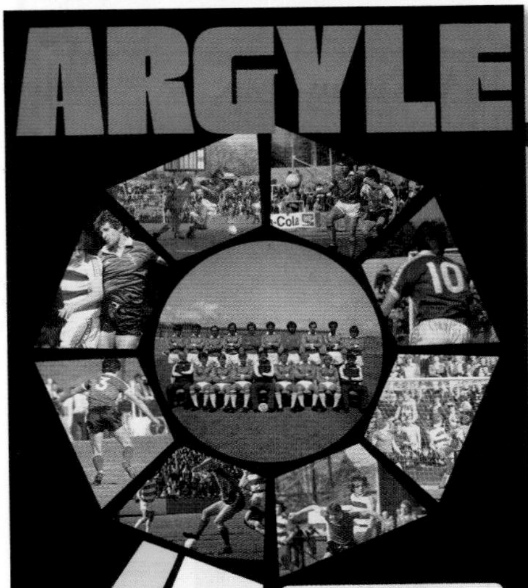

1981/82 – Argyle were one of the many lower-league clubs to benefit from a smart Duplex Litho prog upgrade...

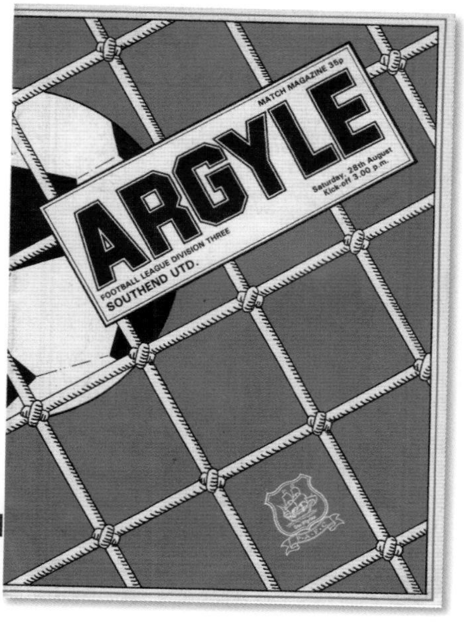

1982/83 – Which, we're sorry to say, was short-lived. Back to a rather shoddy effort next season, albeit with some authentic maritime knots in the net.

Portsmouth

1965/66 – This distinctive naval cover was first used in 1952, and the day-tripping delights of HMS *Victory* had serious staying power.

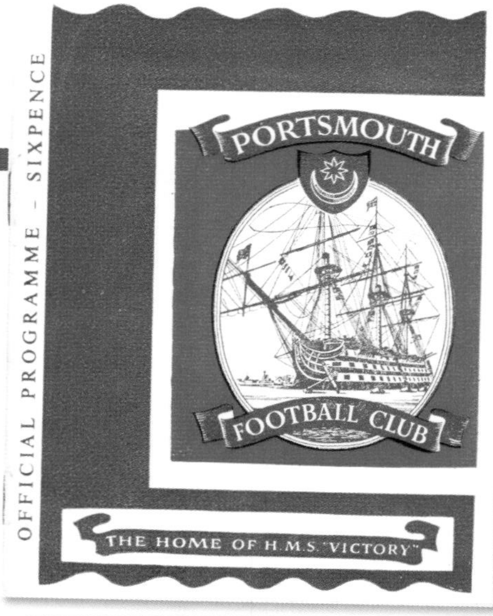

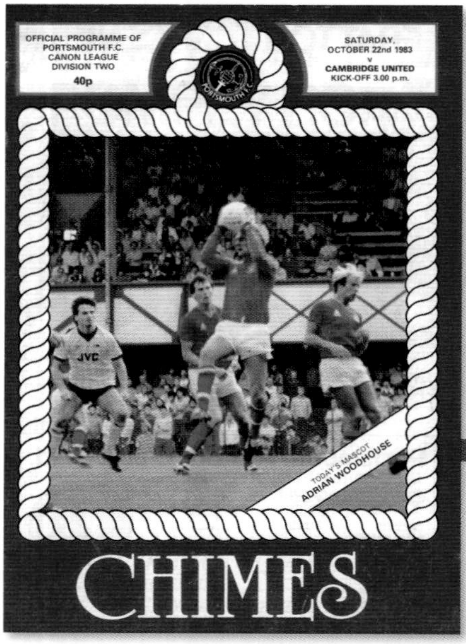

1983/84 – As if to outdo Plymouth on the previous page, Pompey weigh in (and quite possibly anchor) with a hefty length of nautical rigging. Great name, *Chimes*.

1988/89 – The South Coast's big 'Mouth derby finds Pompey in apposite Admiral kit. Iffy downward writing further soiled by Market Carrier Bag font for the 'The'.

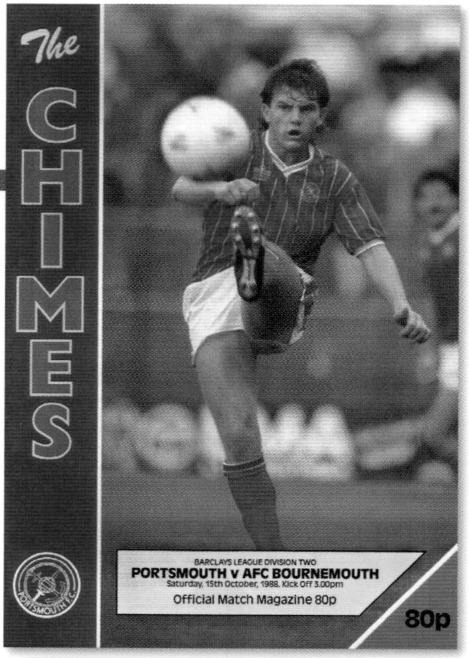

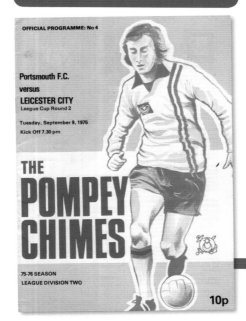

1975/76 – The shock of the cool white kit just had to be reflected in the programme, modelled by a necessarily anonymous player who is very nearly Peter Marinello.

1967/68 – Ker-pow! The age of *Victory* is tossed overboard as Lokomotiv Pompey dive into Soviet-style modernism with some abandon. The Byzantine emperor's crescent on the badge; the heroic players engaged in figurative class struggle: squint and you could almost be in Azerbaijan.

Testimonials

When was the last time you went along to pay your respects to a great old servant of your club, putting up with the prospect of a meaningless friendly against big local rivals – it's never quite the same, on their days off – in order to chip in to the loyal clubman's retirement nest egg as he looked forward to living in temporarily reduced circumstances and having to get a proper job? Eh?

There's no such thing as a testimonial match any more. Lining the pockets of a multi-millionaire with the proceeds of a kickaround against a team with the suffix 'XI' doesn't count. The vital elements of long service, need, mutual gratitude and respect are all absent.

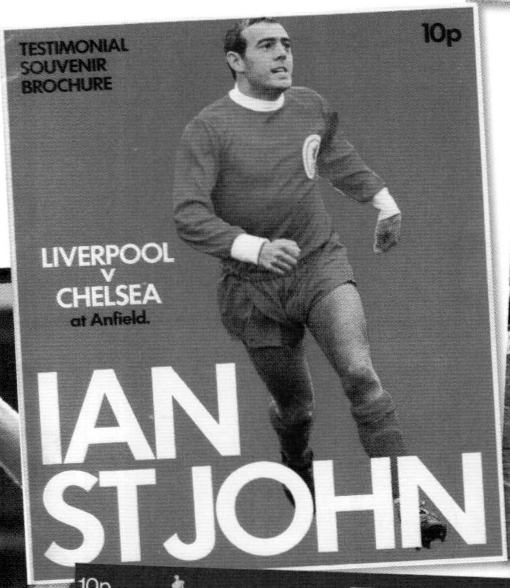

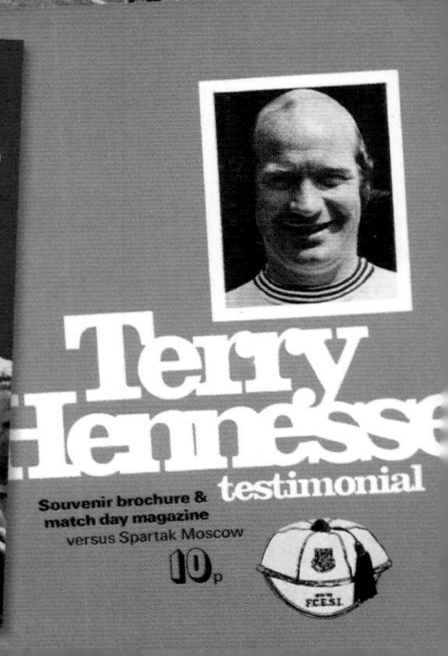

Eddie Gray
EDDIE GRAY
LEEDS UNITED
v
SUPER LEEDS
Wednesday 28th March 1979
Souvenir Brochure 30p

Sammy
MANCHESTER UNITED
FOOTBALL CLUB
TESTIMONIAL MATCH
23 NOVEMBER 1981

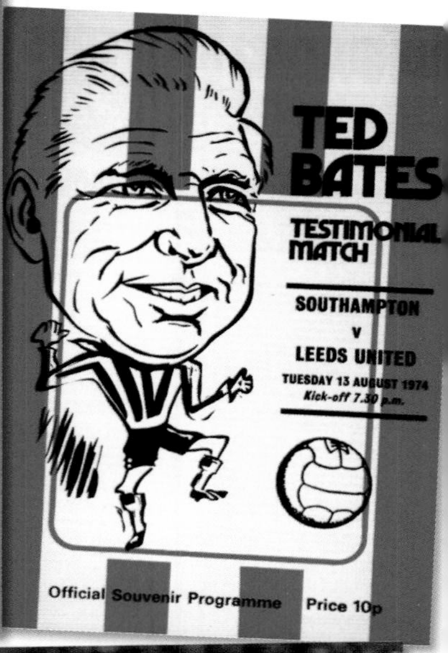

TED BATES
TESTIMONIAL MATCH
SOUTHAMPTON
v
LEEDS UNITED
TUESDAY 13 AUGUST 1974
Kick-off 7.30 p.m.
Official Souvenir Programme
Price 10p

PAT JENNINGS
STIMONIAL MATCH
At Tottenham Hotspur Ground
TUESDAY, 23rd NOVEMBER, 1976
Kick-off 7.30 p.m.
OTTENHAM HOTSP
v ARSENAL
ficial Souvenir Programm

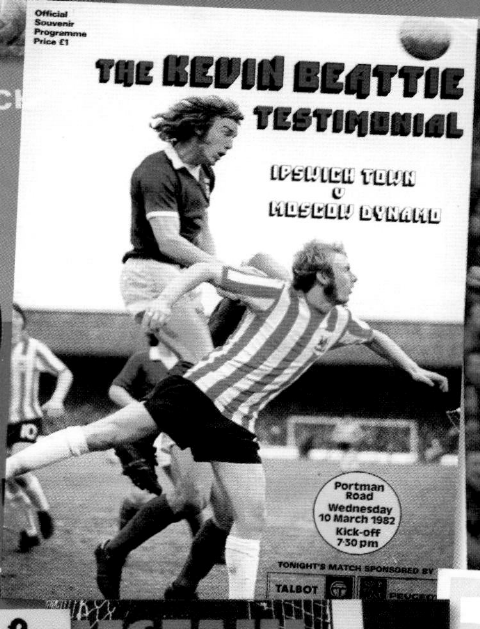

Official Souvenir Programme Price £1
THE KEVIN BEATTIE TESTIMONIAL
IPSWICH TOWN
v
MOSCOW DYNAMO
Portman Road
Wednesday 10 March 1982
Kick-off 7·30 pm
TONIGHT'S MATCH SPONSORED BY
TALBOT

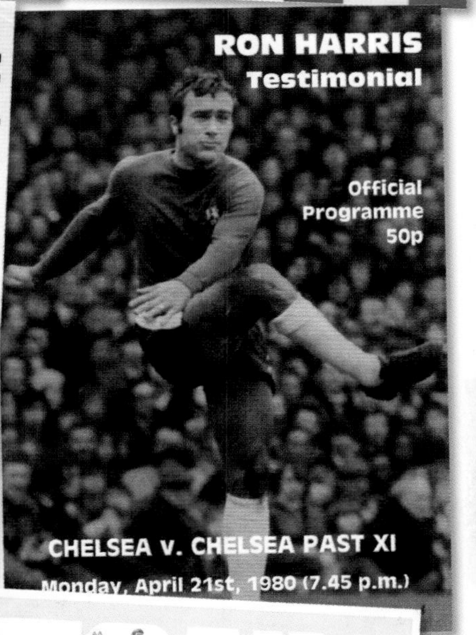

RON HARRIS
Testimonial
Official Programme
50p
CHELSEA V. CHELSEA PAST XI
Monday, April 21st, 1980 (7.45 p.m.)

£1 Programme
including full colour poster
TESTIMONIAL
HEARTS v EVERTON

McFAUL
McALPINE
A Testimonial for WILLIE McFAUL
NEWCASTLE UNITED v MANCHESTER CITY
20p

TONY BOOK
TESTIMONIAL
MATCH
NOVEMBER 27th 1974
MANCHESTER
CITY XI
VERS
ALL STARS XI
Kick-off 7·30p.m.
MAINE ROAD
PRICE 15p

Queens Park Rangers

1977/78 – Stan Bowles accepts the Player of the Season award from Scottish comedian Kevin Bridges in his tuff Superhoops knitwear and enamel regalia.

1984/85 – Fashion victim: John Byrne's micro-shorts have disappeared almost completely up his, er, shirt.

1981/82 – A third variation on the long-running 'QPR' look. The Hoops only really ever had two templates.

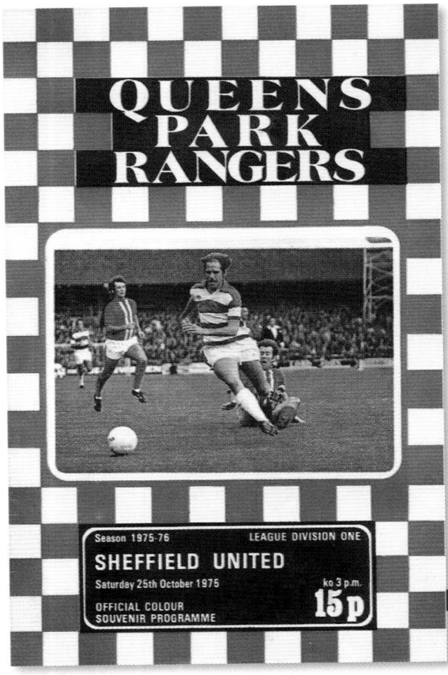

1973-77 – The nasty black panels and colour pic should have ruined it, but the chessboard look was strong enough to survive the affront.

1967-73 – This is optimism: the mod heartlands of Shepherd's Bush reflected in a multicoloured op-art splash of colour at Loftus Road. Rod would have approved.

Reading

1978/79 – There's an agreeably psychedelic 70s kids' TV show feel about this thoughtful row of elms symbolising doomed Elm Park.

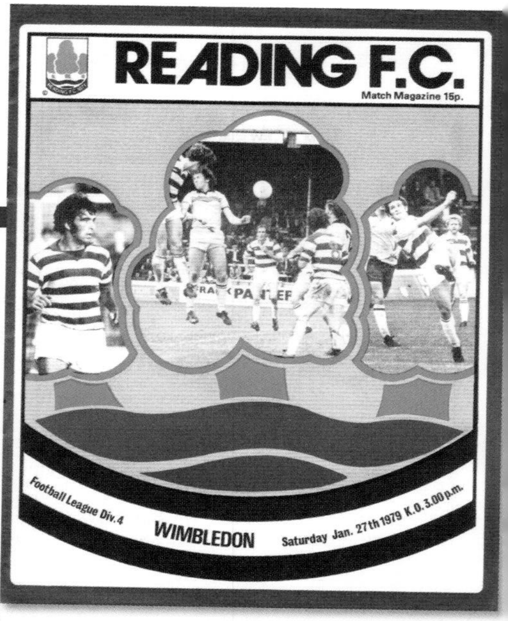

1981/82 – The clean, clear Duplex Litho look captures £150,000-rated Royals star Kerry Dixon in his pomp.

1969/70 – We love the vintage Penguin/Pelican Book look, as recently brought back to life on the hilarious Scarfolk Council website.

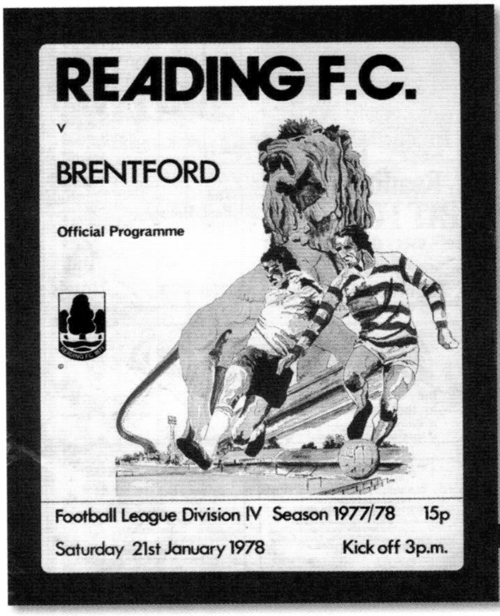

1977/78 – Could the 31-foot Forbury Lion be football's only cover star erected in a public park to commemorate a battle in Afghanistan in 1880? We believe so.

1975/76 – The fan-unfriendly format coupled with the film poster look. It makes us yearn to see *The Pink Windmill,* starring Ian McShane and Jenny Agutter.

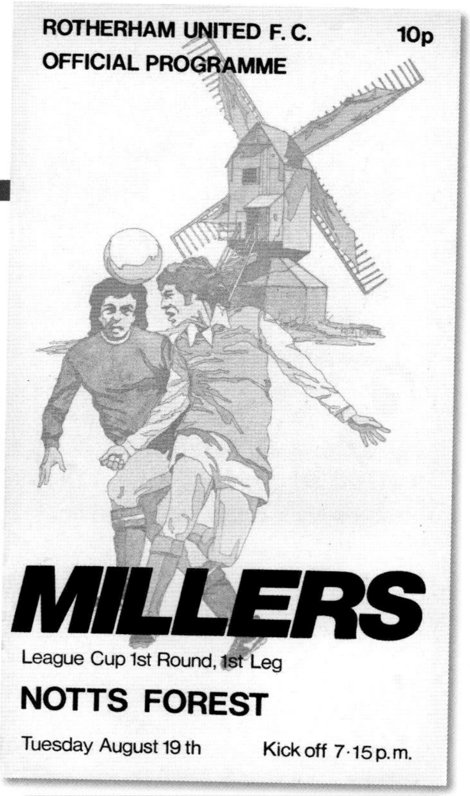

1966/67 – The hipster lavender and cerise look must have gone down a storm in Yorkshire in the Spring of Love.

1978/79 – This baby smashes straight into our Top 5 prog names, ignoring in cavalier style the old adage: 'Don't make promises you can't keep'.

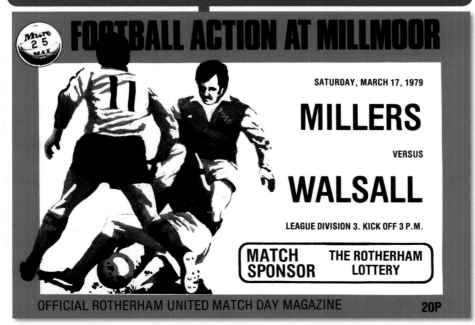

1973/74 – Magnificent, literally groovy font, instantly recalling Mexico 70 and the dawn of Adidas. Bring it back.

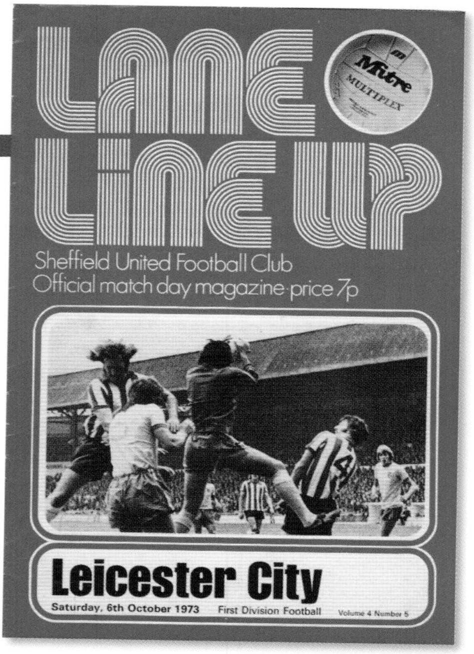

1987/88 – Fabulous lettering coloured in off a Letraset ruler. And a generous aerial shot of Bramall Lane taking in a fair chunk of Sheffield's industrial heritage.

1976/77 – Time to go through the... pentagonal window. Back to an era of a smart new Admiral kit with a new badge, and the great Alan Woodward.

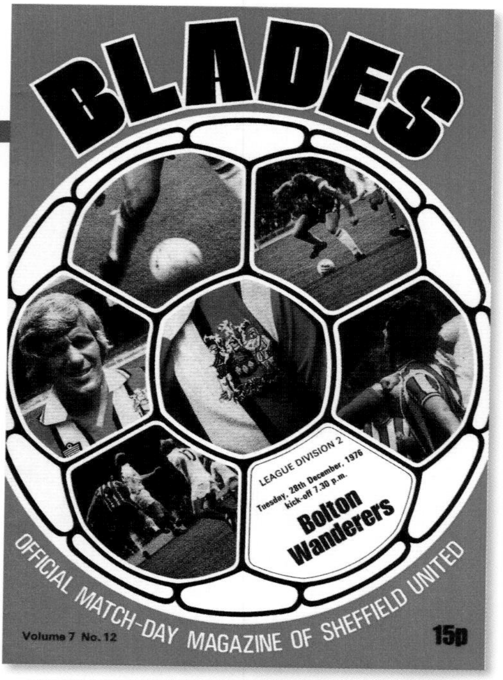

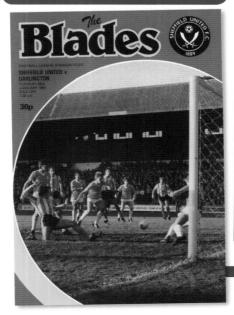

1981/82 – *Goal!* power. You can't beat a big circle on a red background.

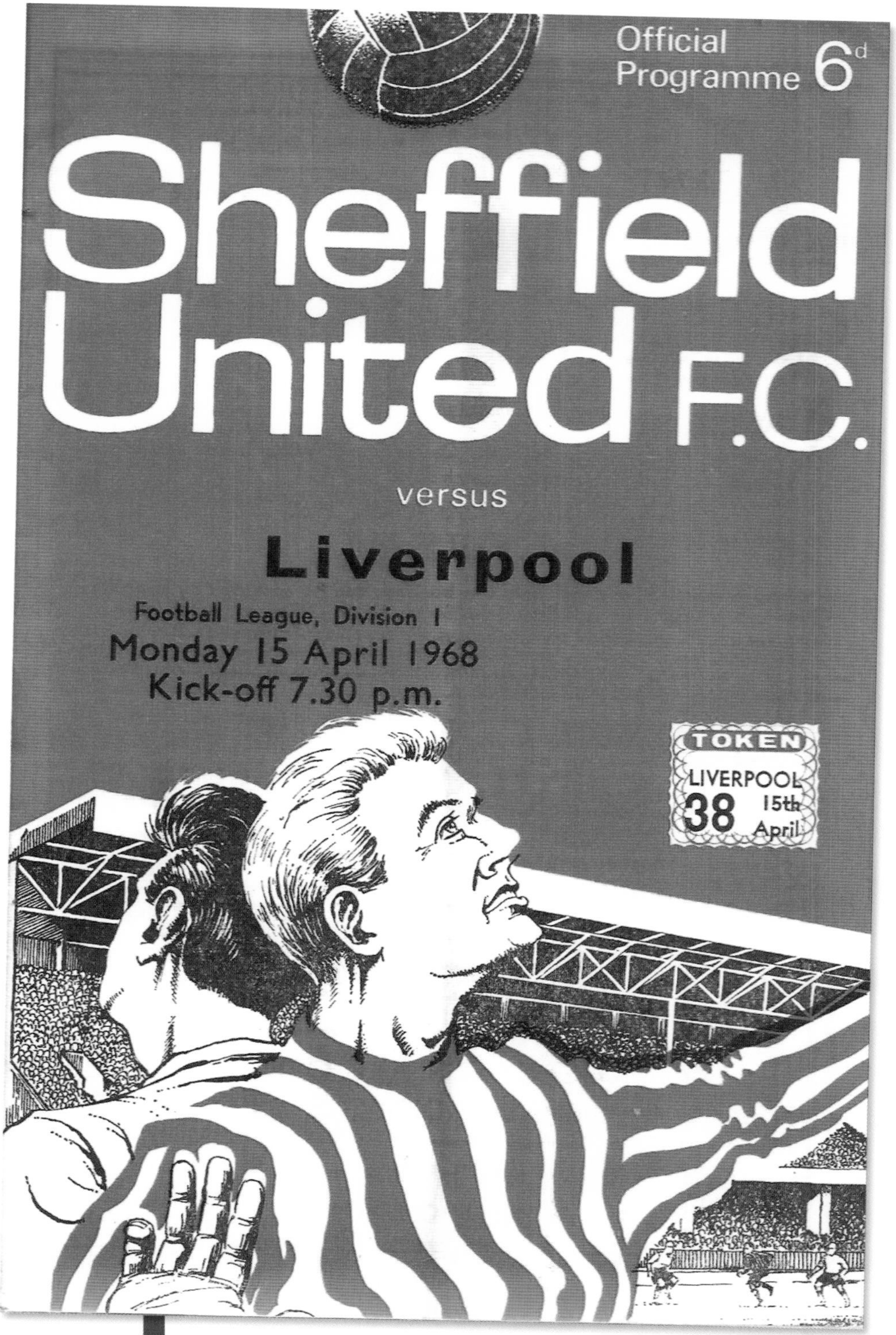

1967/68 – A passing cloud catches the eye of the Blades centre-forward, who reflects on the long-forgotten whereabouts of the ball as his jersey begins to go all soft and wavy. He tries to cling to reality, but soon dissolves into the grass on the open cricket-pitch side of Bramall Lane.

Sheffield Wednesday

1984/85 – It was bitter up on t'moor, playing in horrible sleet before a crowd huddled at the back of the terraces. The 'Spy Who Came in from the Cold' font is curiously apt.

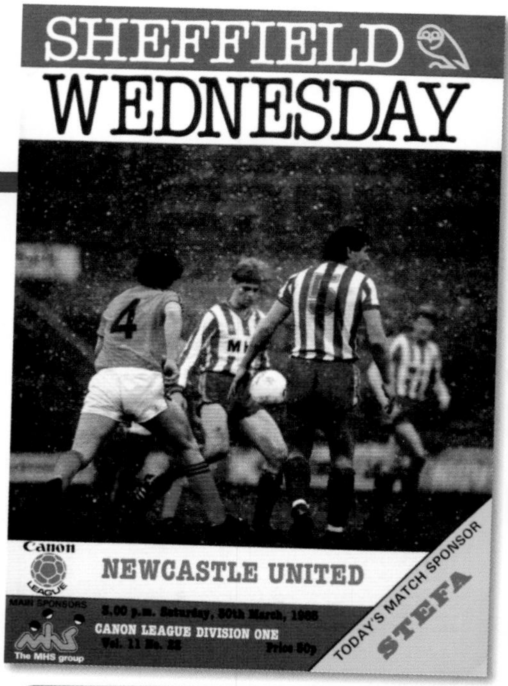

1965/66 – An odd cover designed to proudly show off the mechanics of the new cantilever stand. No club did epic as well as Sheff Wed.

1974/75 – Did we say, we like programmes with 'The' in the title? Especially used BIG, and with an infectious conga line wending its way through the outline of the stadium.

1970/71 – What a title. As if in response to the Blades' unfocused aerial shot on the previous spread, Wednesday weigh in with a BBC *Panorama*-style logo making Hillsborough the centre of the universe. At the time, it looked very *Joe 90* to these eight-year-old eyes.

1983/84 – A section of crowd that's obviously staged – spot the tea-lady, the physio, the receptionist – attacked by giant shrew shock.

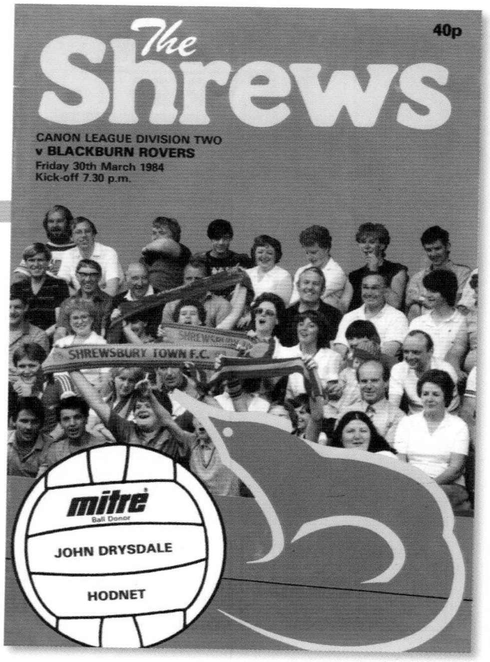

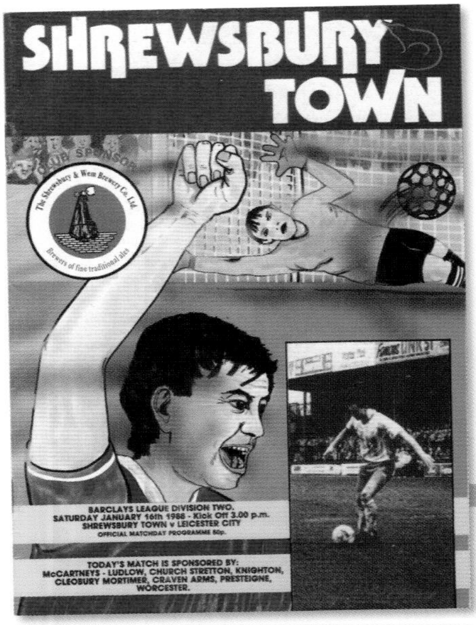

1987/88 – This is so bad it's weird. What's with the hazy brown trail further soiling the terrible graphic? And that ball? And that face? And that afterthought inset?

1982/83 – Interesting, if inexplicable, use of three tumbling oblongs here. That training kickaround looked a corker, though – starring a heroic Nigel Pearson.

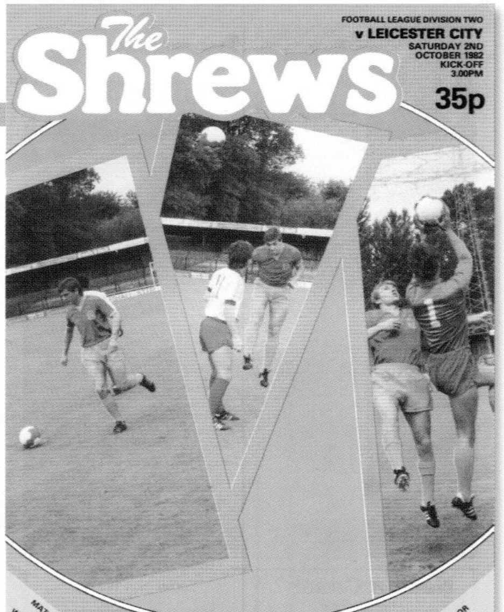

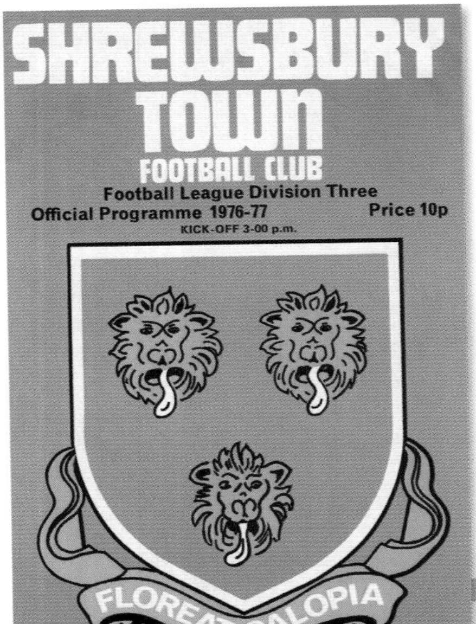

1976/77 – Even Shrewsbury's town arms is a bit of an oddity. Lions rampant with big lolling tongues.

Half-Time Scoreboard

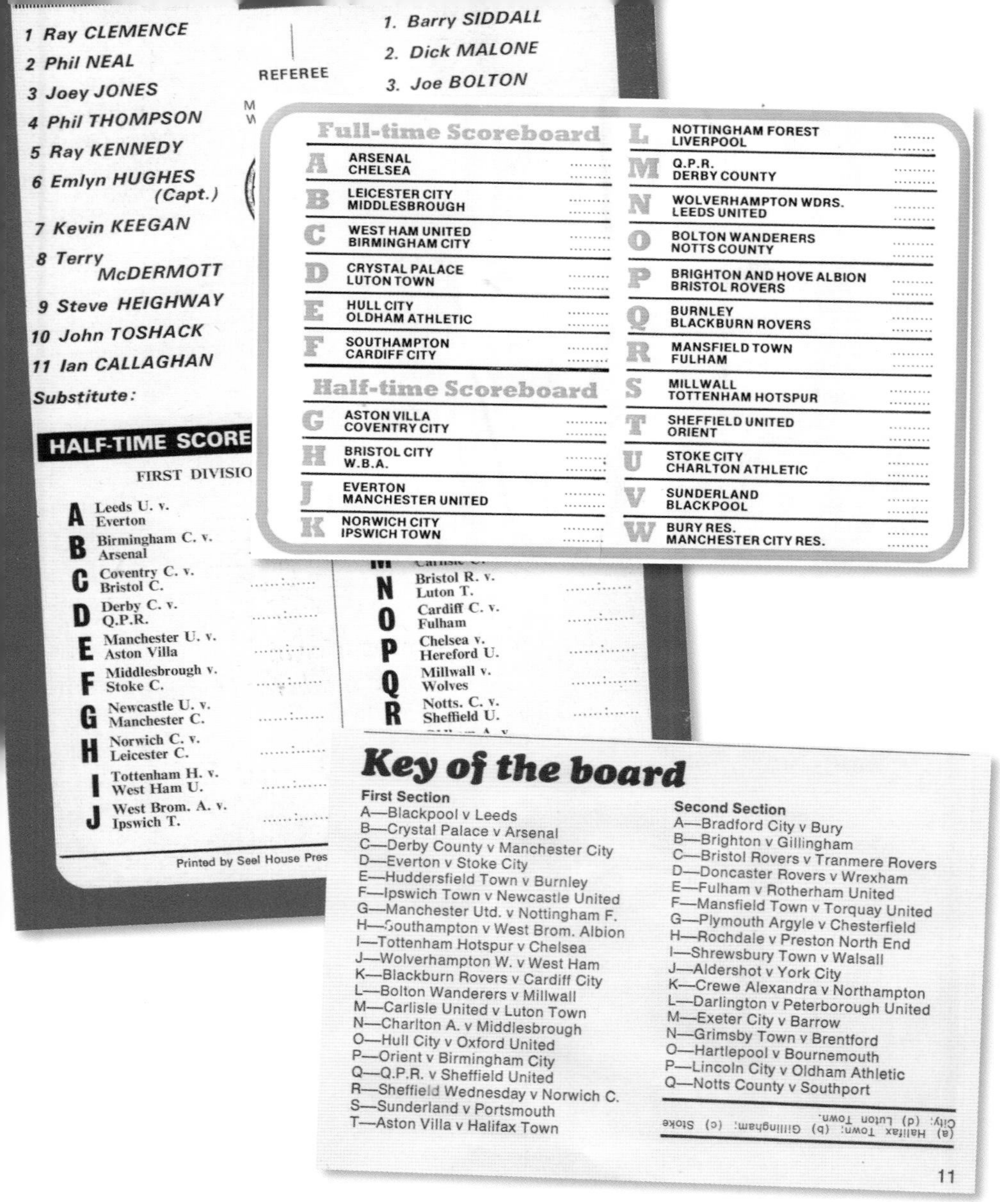

1 Ray CLEMENCE
2 Phil NEAL
3 Joey JONES
4 Phil THOMPSON
5 Ray KENNEDY
6 Emlyn HUGHES (Capt.)
7 Kevin KEEGAN
8 Terry McDERMOTT
9 Steve HEIGHWAY
10 John TOSHACK
11 Ian CALLAGHAN
Substitute:

REFEREE

1. Barry SIDDALL
2. Dick MALONE
3. Joe BOLTON

HALF-TIME SCORE

FIRST DIVISIO

A Leeds U. v. Everton
B Birmingham C. v. Arsenal
C Coventry C. v. Bristol C.
D Derby C. v. Q.P.R.
E Manchester U. v. Aston Villa
F Middlesbrough v. Stoke C.
G Newcastle U. v. Manchester C.
H Norwich C. v. Leicester C.
I Tottenham H. v. West Ham U.
J West Brom. A. v. Ipswich T.

N Bristol R. v. Luton T.
O Cardiff C. v. Fulham
P Chelsea v. Hereford U.
Q Millwall v. Wolves
R Notts. C. v. Sheffield U.

Printed by Seel House Pres

Full-time Scoreboard

A ARSENAL / CHELSEA
B LEICESTER CITY / MIDDLESBROUGH
C WEST HAM UNITED / BIRMINGHAM CITY
D CRYSTAL PALACE / LUTON TOWN
E HULL CITY / OLDHAM ATHLETIC
F SOUTHAMPTON / CARDIFF CITY

Half-time Scoreboard

G ASTON VILLA / COVENTRY CITY
H BRISTOL CITY / W.B.A.
J EVERTON / MANCHESTER UNITED
K NORWICH CITY / IPSWICH TOWN
L NOTTINGHAM FOREST / LIVERPOOL
M Q.P.R. / DERBY COUNTY
N WOLVERHAMPTON WDRS. / LEEDS UNITED
O BOLTON WANDERERS / NOTTS COUNTY
P BRIGHTON AND HOVE ALBION / BRISTOL ROVERS
Q BURNLEY / BLACKBURN ROVERS
R MANSFIELD TOWN / FULHAM
S MILLWALL / TOTTENHAM HOTSPUR
T SHEFFIELD UNITED / ORIENT
U STOKE CITY / CHARLTON ATHLETIC
V SUNDERLAND / BLACKPOOL
W BURY RES. / MANCHESTER CITY RES.

Key of the board

First Section
A—Blackpool v Leeds
B—Crystal Palace v Arsenal
C—Derby County v Manchester City
D—Everton v Stoke City
E—Huddersfield Town v Burnley
F—Ipswich Town v Newcastle United
G—Manchester Utd. v Nottingham F.
H—Southampton v West Brom. Albion
I—Tottenham Hotspur v Chelsea
J—Wolverhampton W. v West Ham
K—Blackburn Rovers v Cardiff City
L—Bolton Wanderers v Millwall
M—Carlisle United v Luton Town
N—Charlton A. v Middlesbrough
O—Hull City v Oxford United
P—Orient v Birmingham City
Q—Q.P.R. v Sheffield United
R—Sheffield Wednesday v Norwich C.
S—Sunderland v Portsmouth
T—Aston Villa v Halifax Town

Second Section
A—Bradford City v Bury
B—Brighton v Gillingham
C—Bristol Rovers v Tranmere Rovers
D—Doncaster Rovers v Wrexham
E—Fulham v Rotherham United
F—Mansfield Town v Torquay United
G—Plymouth Argyle v Chesterfield
H—Rochdale v Preston North End
I—Shrewsbury Town v Walsall
J—Aldershot v York City
K—Crewe Alexandra v Northampton
L—Darlington v Peterborough United
M—Exeter City v Barrow
N—Grimsby Town v Brentford
O—Hartlepool v Bournemouth
P—Lincoln City v Oldham Athletic
Q—Notts County v Southport

(a) Halifax Town; (b) Gillingham; (c) Stoke City; (d) Luton Town.

11

Not long ago, while at a match, I was checking on the scores of our fellow promotion contenders on Livescore.com. It was taking a little longer to download than usual (probably about eight-tenths of a second) and I was poking the screen of my iPhone in an exasperated fashion.

And then I thought: "Whoa there! Whoa there, old son... when did we get so impatient?"

A few short years back, before we carried around the collective knowledge of the world in the palm of our hand, we had to wait until half-time to see how the other games were going. Then they'd be viewed on the electronic scoreboard, accompanied by boos or cheers, as appropriate.

Travelling even further back through the mists of time to the late Sixties (which now appears technologically equidistant between the Saxons and Samsung) most grounds employed a simple but effective code which allowed supporters to see the scores around other grounds. It involved a chap with a wooden box full of metal plates with numbers on them, arranging them next to a row of letters, usually situated on the front wall of a stand. In the days when a programme cost a shilling, everybody bought one, and you turned to the appropriate page to crack the code.

And, somehow, we got by.

Southampton

1968/69 – The early-season hopefulness of the official team photo, all smart new kit, the smell of fresh red paint and new-mown grass in The Dell air.

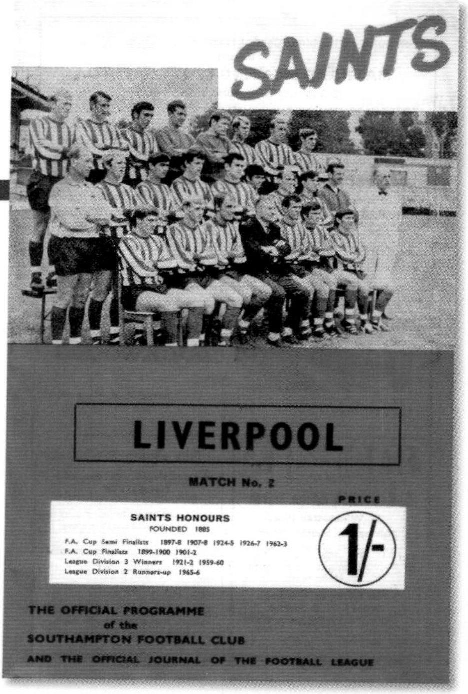

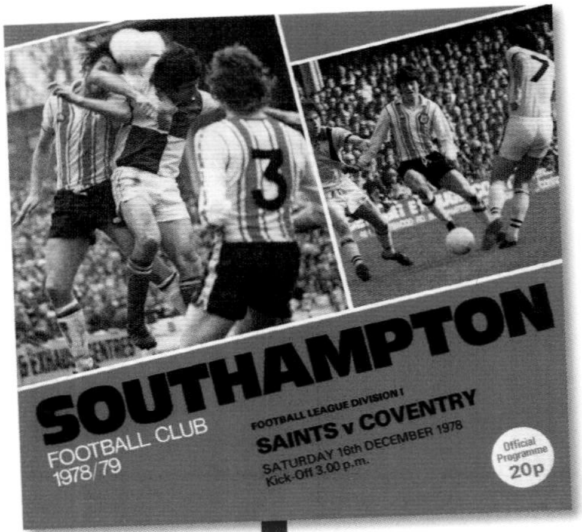

1978/79 – The rush to square format turned up the odd gem. Cover shots from the previous promotion season when both Saints and Spurs remade the grade.

1982/83 – Can we be the only programme collectors who reckon the Isle of Wight doesn't feature on nearly enough covers? What a splendid cabaret font.

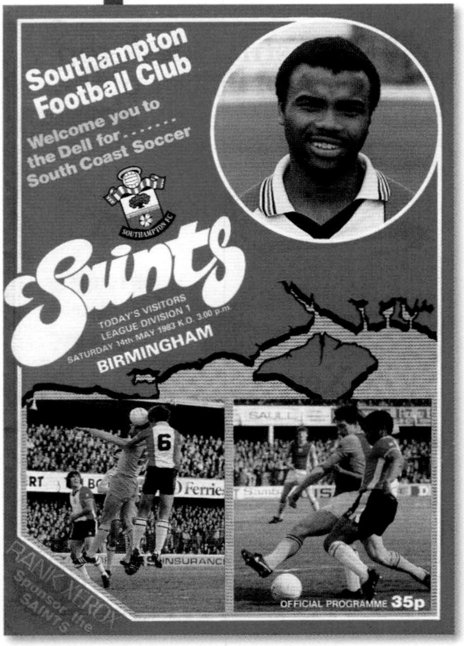

1973/74 – Southampton accidentally invent the fanzine.

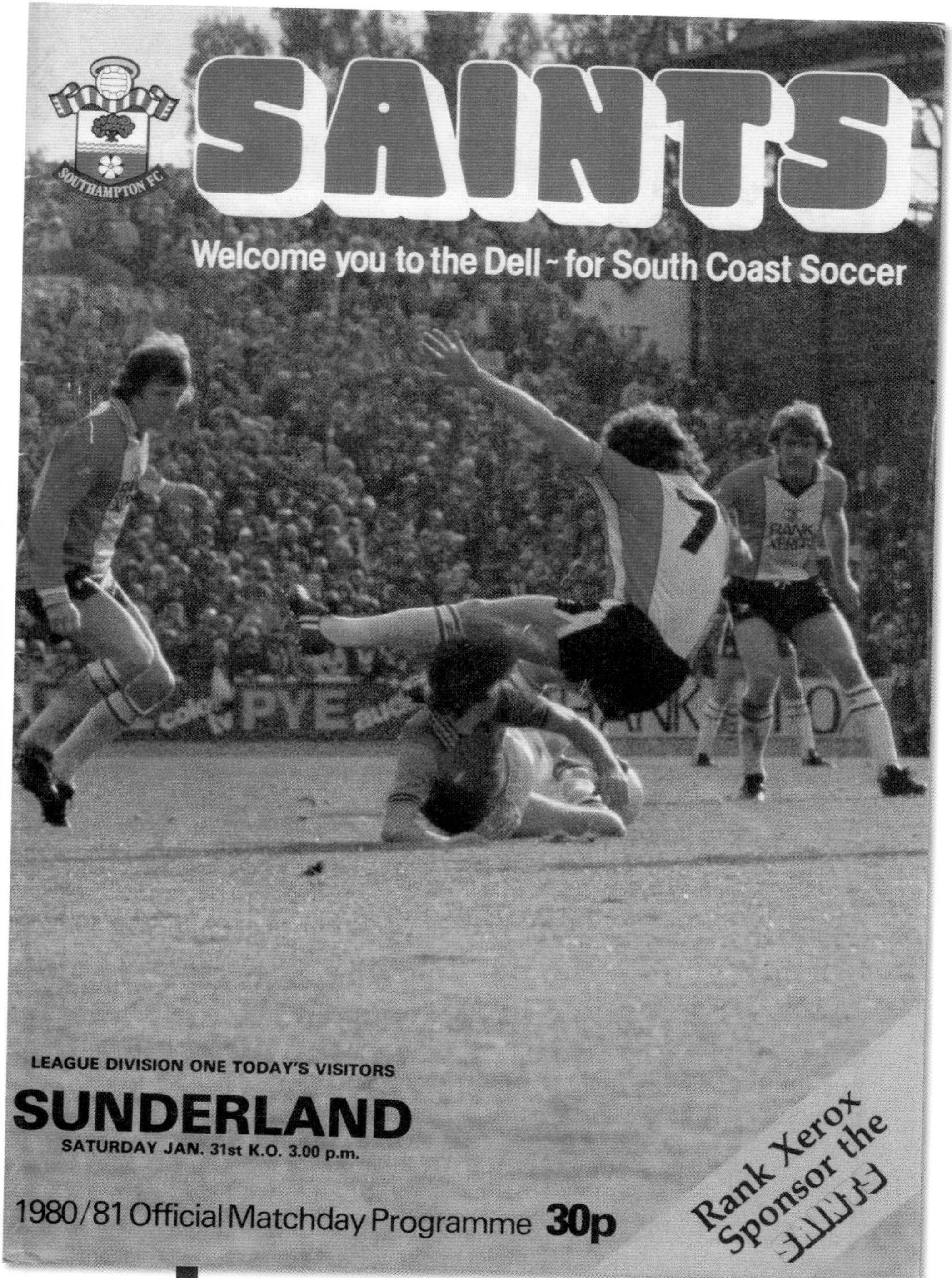

1980/81 – We love the way you can see right into this cover shot, into the crowd past Keegan, Channon and Holmes in their fantastic Patrick kit, and beyond to the trees outside The Dell. It's a sunny Saturday afternoon scene with a warm South Coast welcome that almost makes us want to be Southampton fans, back in the day.

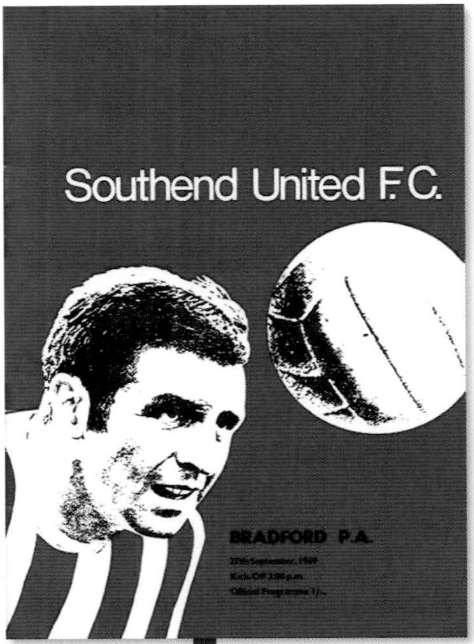

1969/70 – What a shame that the editor's daughter's pencil study of a Shrimper was replaced with a real one a few matches into the season. The hair was quite good.

1974/75 – Twin attractions here: the seaside-theatre sex-farce 'Run For Your Wife' font coupled with a Coffer-badge boot logo (and tiny football).

1990/91 – The dangers of spray mount in a confined office. A stand has been removed and Roots Hall relocated into a watersports idyll by the pier. And is that a clown?

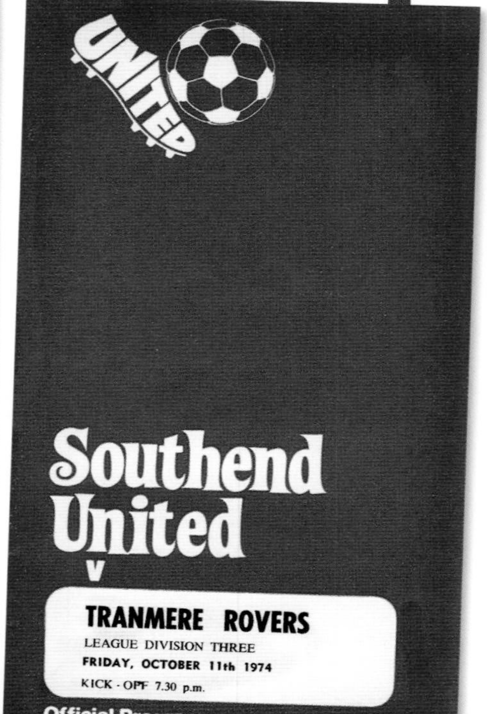

Stockport County

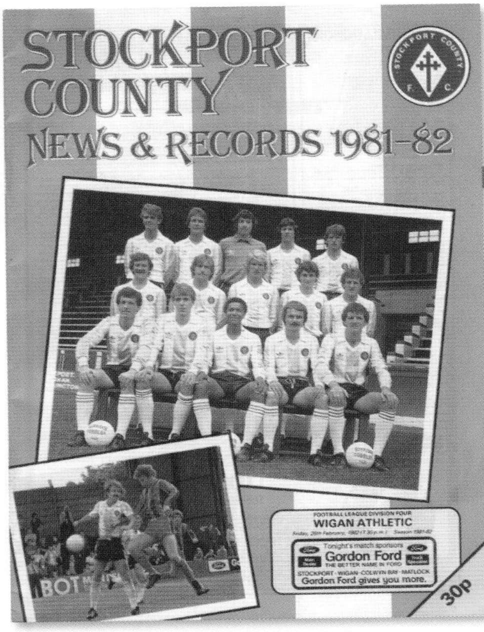

1981/82 - 'News & Record' is what publishers Duplex Litho meant to say - while the Stockport team itself was meant to be mistaken for World Cup holders Argentina.

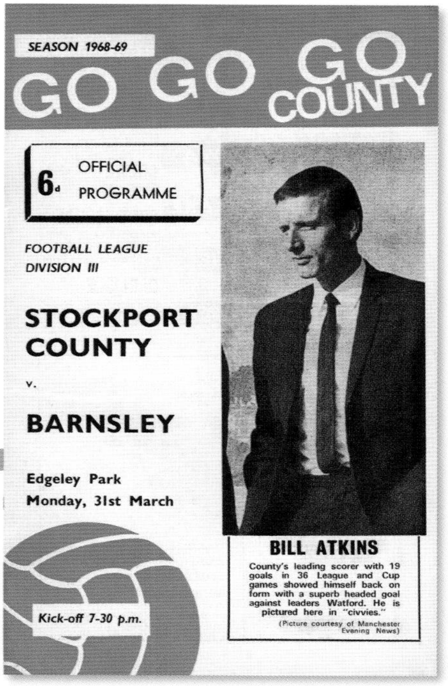

1968/69 - Surely one of the finest prog titles ever? However, by March, it might have been hoped that an action shot of the club's top scorer could be procured.

1983/84 - Love the with-it digital watch font. The infant Mick Quinn. The way the '100' centenary logo is so hard to spot, making you wonder... why the antique pics?

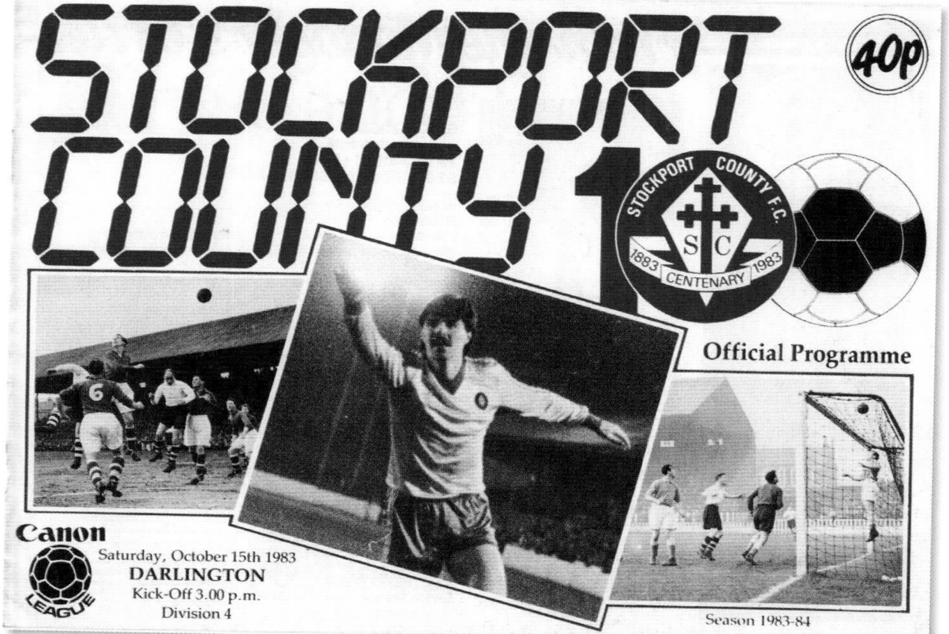

Stoke City

1967/68 – We wish we'd got a quid for every time this ace pop-art image has been reproduced in a fanzine/magazine/blog/book. Ker-ching: we couldn't resist.

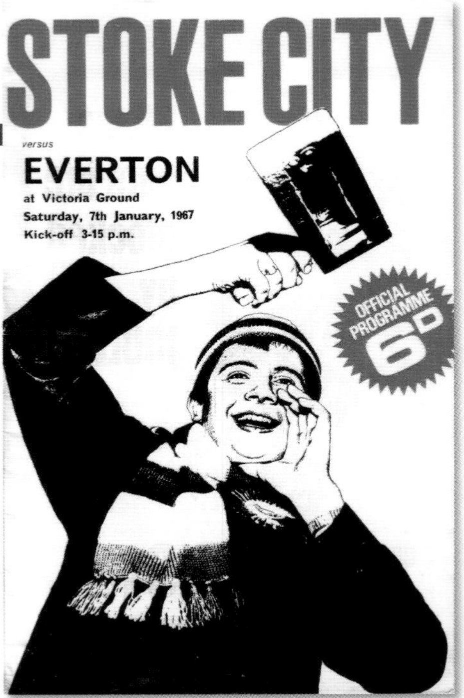

1969/70 – Never mind Stockport, what we meant to say was *The Ceramic City Clipper* is easily the best prog name ever. With Banksy cutout art and Pele, too.

1976/77 – The endless possibilities of the composite cover, with colour pics revolving fortnightly. Dodds and dog. Superman Shilts. The failed header. 'Til next time.

1973/74 – Wow: magnificent. It's got everything. Having hit upon the perfect Stokie prog cover, why did they ever change?

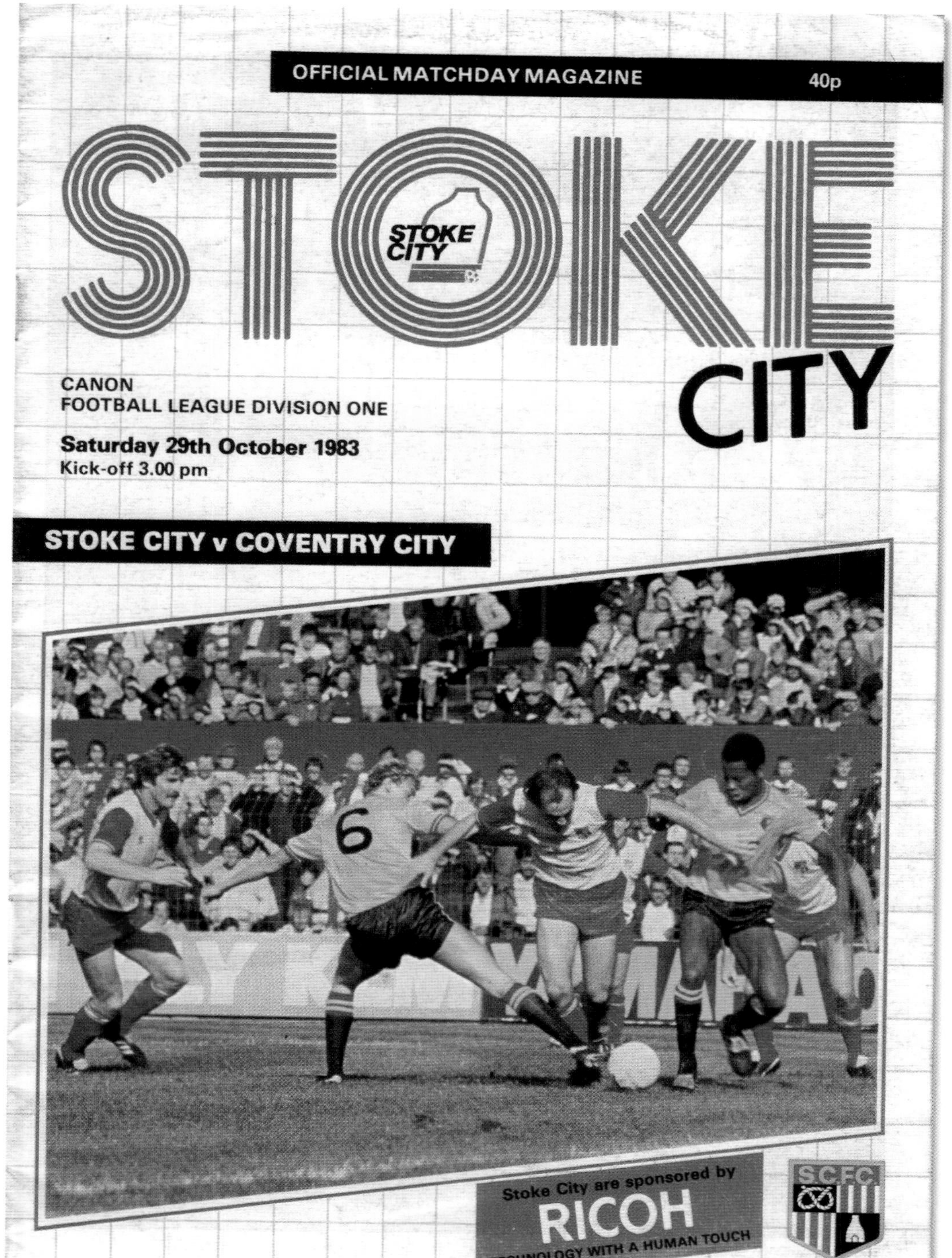

1983/84 – Archetypal 80s crap, based on the 'graph paper' look beloved of the contemporary *Smash Hits* mag. Early branding confusion is rife, with two club logos and a Mexico 70 font that is no longer quite cutting edge. To top it all, the Potters' 80s kit hits an all-time low, with Umbro micro stripes that made it look pink. Must do better on so many fronts.

Cup Finals

Give this book to your mum and let her have a flick through looking for bronzed Vaseliney legs and interior decorating hints from the inevitable 'At Home With' spread… and then ask her which programmes she thinks are the most valuable.

Well, it's obvious, innit? The FA Cup final is the English game's showcase, the biggest game of the year – it's footy glamour central, with *Cup Final It's a Knockout* on all morning and a helicopter escort for the team coaches back in the days before satnav.

Even today you can find eBay sellers and blokes with car-boot stashes of childhood treasures who mistakenly assume their 1976 FA Cup final prog must be worth a tenner of anybody's money. It's 40 years old, after all. Practically an antique. And Southampton beat Man U. You must remember, it was a proper turnip for the books, a classic. In Hampshire, there are streets and babies named after Bobby Stokes. There's city, even.

Coh, I remember going up to Mr Sherrard's corner shop on the morning of the match and he had a big pile of the programmes on sale with the papers. All the kids used to go and buy one every year – and the same thing must have happened in tens of thousands of newsagents all over the country.

It's got to be worth twenty quid of anybody's money. Tell you what, meet you halfway and call it fifteen.

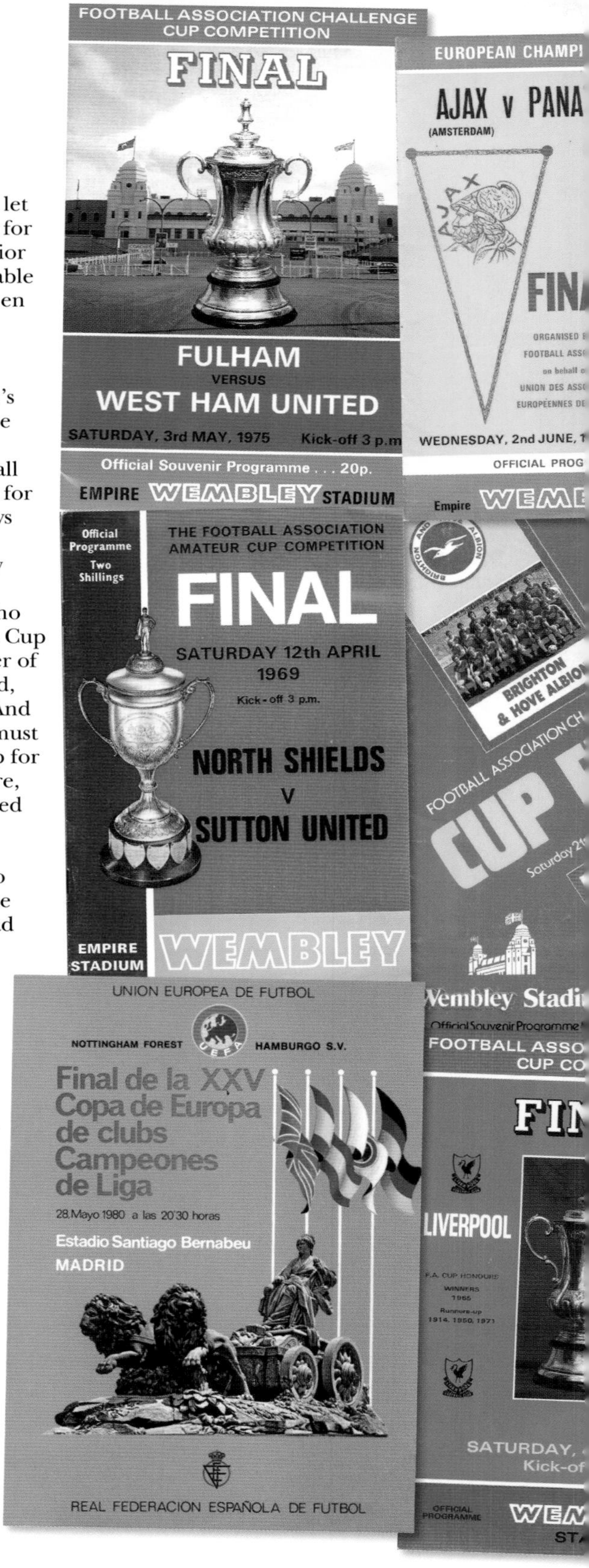

The Football League
CUP FINAL
Aston Villa
v
Everton
Saturday 12th March 1977
Kick-off 3pm
WEMBLEY STADIUM
Official Souvenir Programme 25p
WOLVES 71-72
U.E.F.A. CUP FINAL 1st LEG
Molineux Wednesday May 3rd, 1972 kick-off 7.30 p.m.
WOLVES v TOTTENHAM
Official Souvenir Programme . . . 10p.
Scottish
CUP FINAL
CELTIC v RANGERS
Hampden Park · Saturday 8th May 1971 · Kick-Off 3pm
OFFICIAL PROGRAMME 10p
EUROPEAN CHAMPION CLUBS' CUP-FINAL TIE
CLUB BRUGGE KV
LIVERPOOL F.C.
Wembley Stadium
NORWICH CITY
THE FOOTBALL LEAGUE
CUP FINAL
SATURDAY 3rd MARCH 1973
KICK OFF 3.30 pm
TOTTENHAM HOTSPUR
Official Programme Ten Pence
Incorporating Cup Final Issue of "League Football"
WEMBLEY
Official Programme One Shilling
THE FOOTBALL ASSOCIATION CHALLENGE CUP COMPETITION
FINAL
SATURDAY MAY 20th 1967
Kick-off 3 pm
CHELSEA
v
TOTTENHAM HOTSPUR
EMPIRE STADIUM
WEMBLEY
EUROPEAN CUP WINNERS' CUP
FINAL TIE
TSV MÜNCHEN 1860
v
WEST HAM UNITED
MAY 19th 1965
WEMBLEY
Kick-off 7.30 p.m.
OFFICIAL PROGRAMME
ONE SHILLING
Football Association Challenge Cup Competition
CUP FINAL
Arsenal v Manchester United
Saturday 12th May 1979 Kick off 3pm
Wembley
Official Souvenir Programme 50p
OFFICIAL PROGRAMME
Scottish
CUP FINAL
RANGERS (HOLDERS) v. DUNDEE
KICK-OFF 3 P.M.
HAMPDEN PARK, APRIL 25, 1964

Sunderland

1965/66 – Peer into the muddy crystal football and you can very nearly make out the future: a new programme cover design next season.

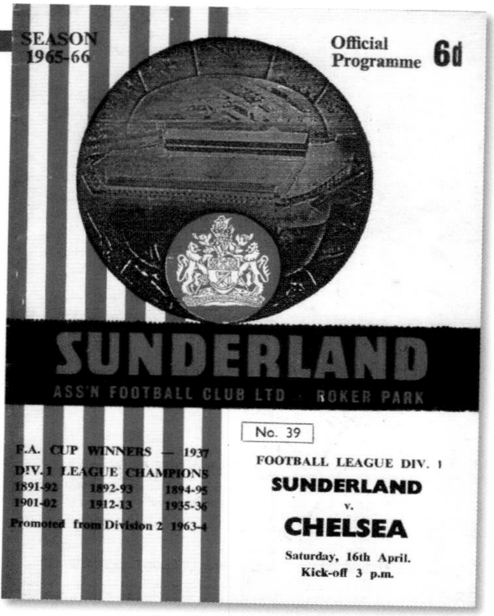

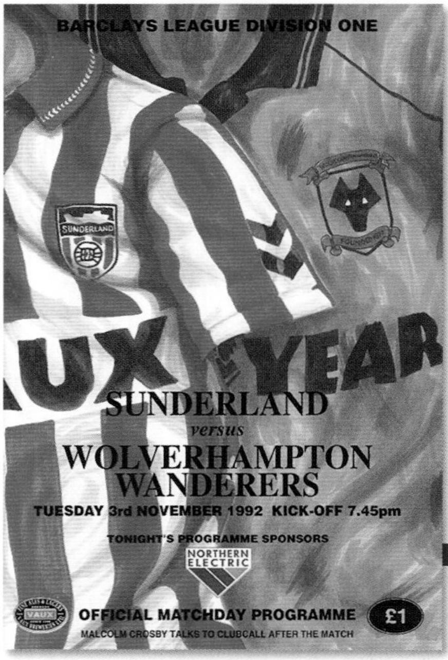

1992/93 – Now here's a real rarity. A programme from the 90s, no less – and one whose production actually involved a skill.

1983/84 – It's the boxes at the bottom that let down this Roker cover. No design, no Guinness logo or toucan. Just raw text courtesy of the John Bull Printing Outfit No. 7.

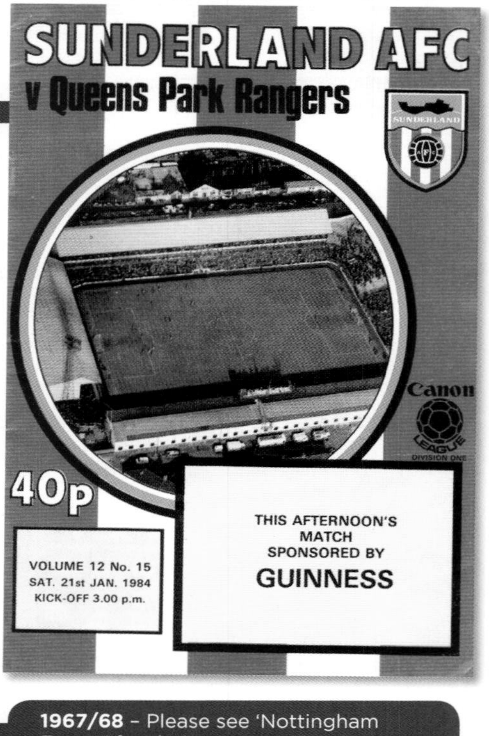

1967/68 – Please see 'Nottingham Forest' for derisory comment.

1976/77 – Absolutely awe-inspiring. A frontline fan's eye view of Roker action, and an intimation of the intimidating Roar.

1977/78 – See 'Newcastle United' for high praise. The same Sunderland printer was responsible for both progs, and must have hoped no one would ever find out!

Swansea City

1961/62 – Clever eye motif, complete with eyebrow underlining the club name and centre-circle for an iris. When red was Swansea's automatic third colour.

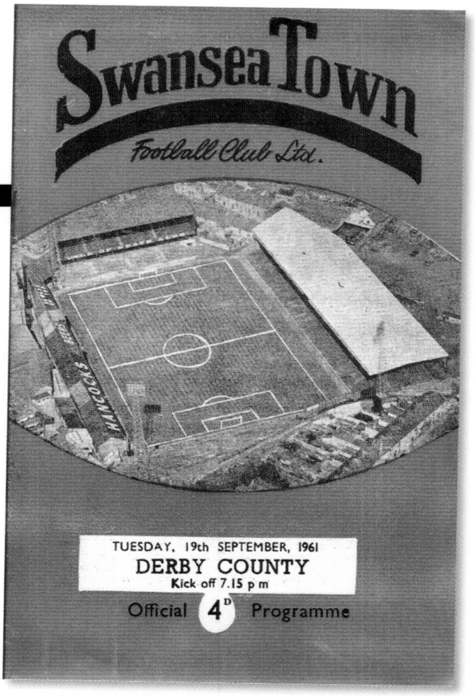

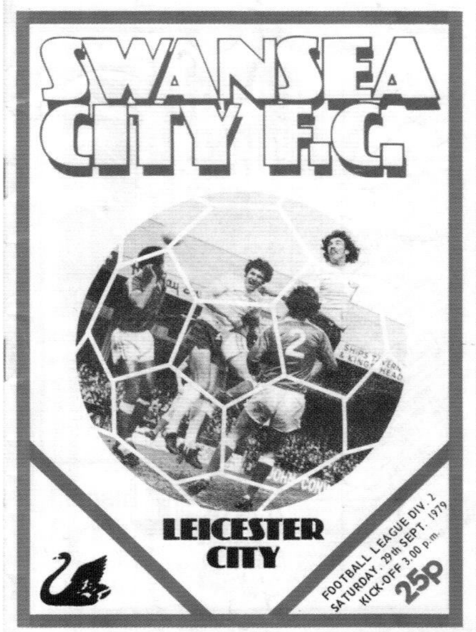

1979/80 – Art Deco Swans on the rise, en route from Division Four to One.

1984/85 – The lowest of the low. A whole cover devoted to a horrible corporate ad. It's curtains.

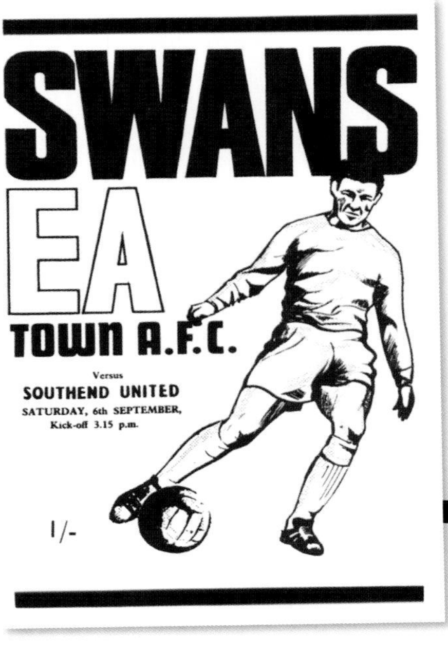

1969/70 – Deconstruction Time Again: truly terrific stuff, handily explaining the derivation of the club's nickname for fans who had never previously cottoned on.

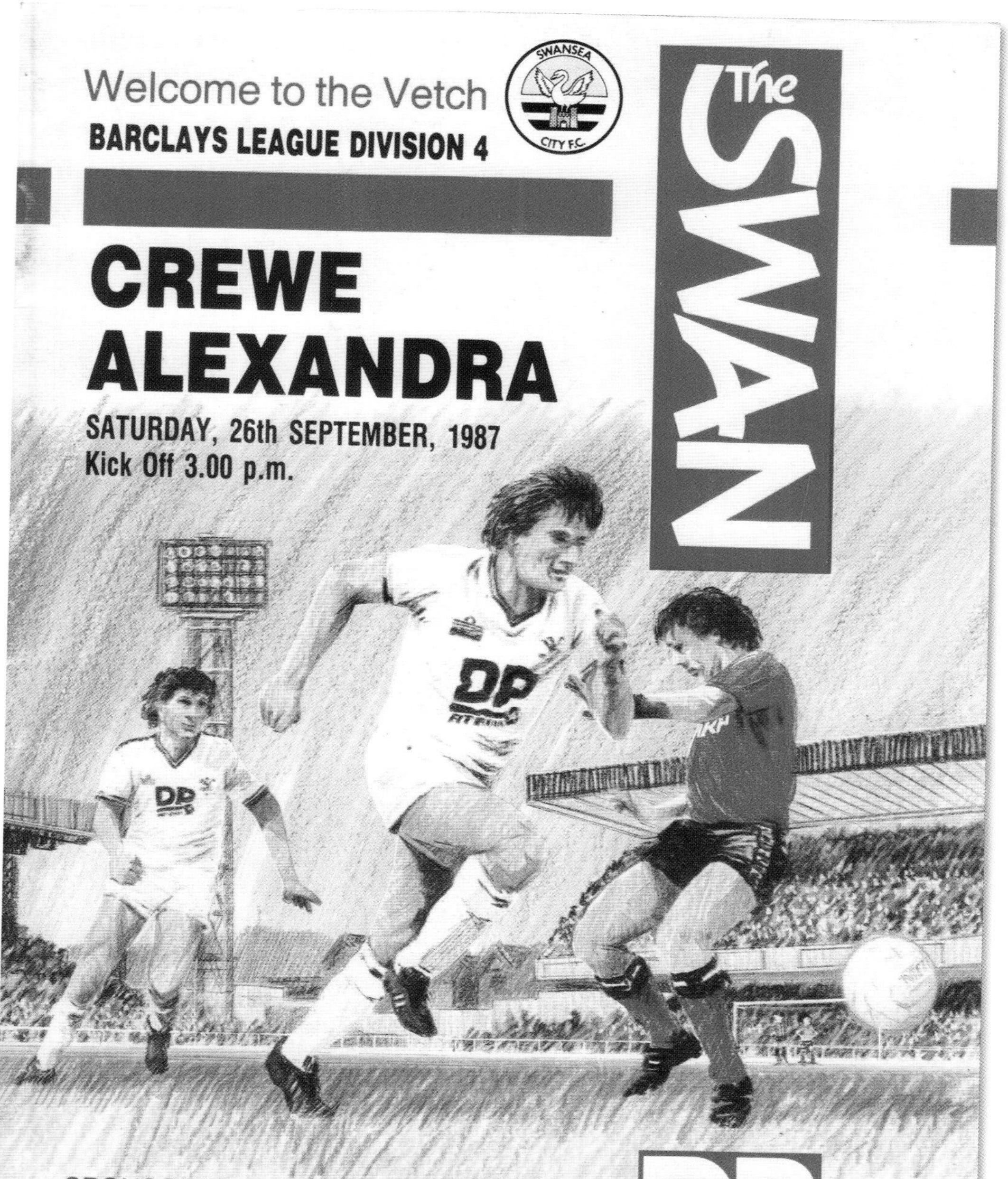

1987/88 – The abstract brilliance of the 60s and the failures of '95 are somehow synthesised in this ultimate SCFC product: a football programme created in the style of a calendar for The Swan takeaway. It's China v South Korea on the cover and egg foo-yung on the menu. We love the delicate explanation of what 'DP' stands for, and the way the crayoned sky peters out.

Swindon Town

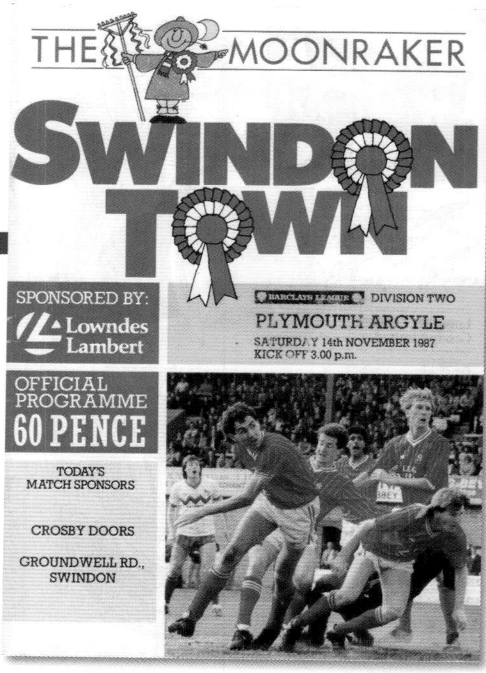

1987/88 – We like cartoon mascots, especially off-message ones nowt to do with Robins or Railwaymen. How great, to name your prog after local Wiltshire smugglers.

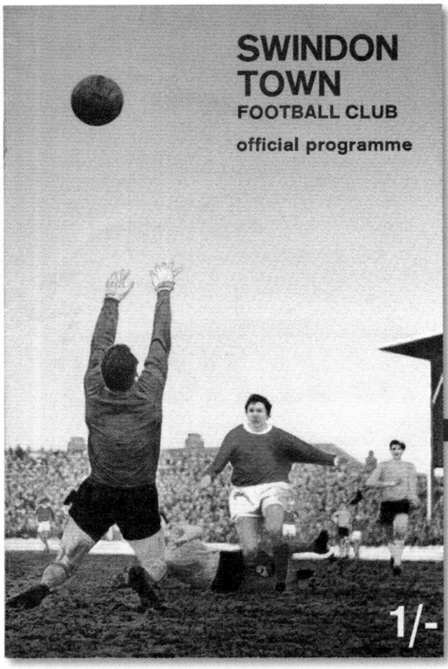

1969/70 – An almost-brilliant eyecatching cover, ruined only by the recolouring job which makes the Swindon forward appear four stone overweight.

1978/79 – You might think it's a decade late for the headless action look, but it's quite in keeping with the dynamic arrowed logo – one of the mod revival's coolest.

1968/69 – No pics and nothing to say? Put your faith in a robin from a Giles cartoon out of the *Daily Express*.

Torquay United

1974/75 – The Gulls try winging the Midlands-copyright psychedelic look, but end up creating a fearful swamp monster.

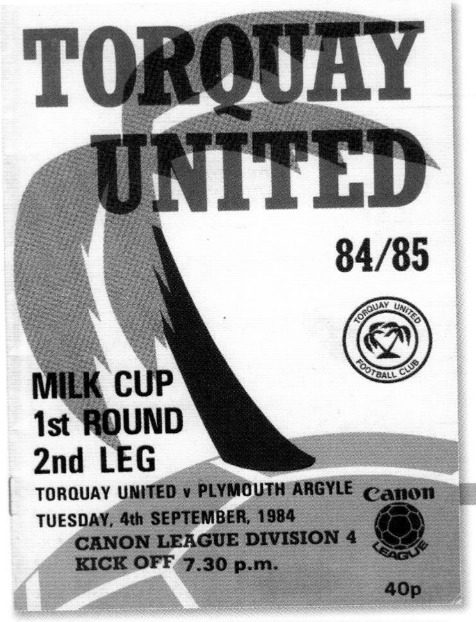

1984/85 – Milking it: visit the tropical desert island of Torquay on the English Riviera.

1967/68 – Who needs footer when you've got Oddicombe Beach? Unbelievably, it was a step up from the micro-pleasures of the seafront Abbey Gardens, last season.

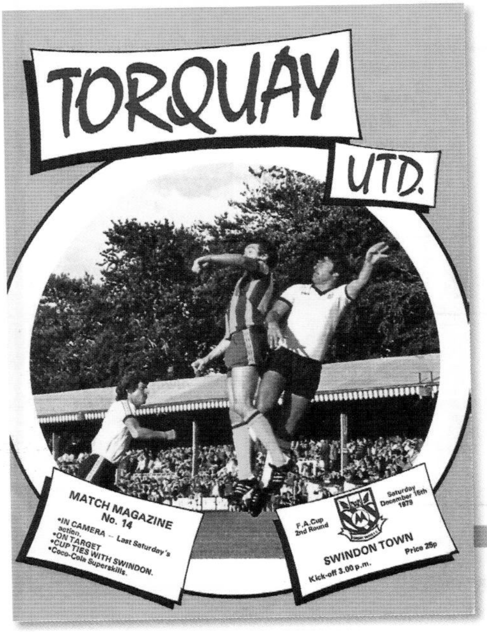

1979/80 – If Basil Fawlty had gone to a match round the corner from his palace of 2-star pleasures, this would have been the programme he bought.

Tottenham Hotspur

1975/76 – Spurs remained resolutely behind the times throughout the 60s and 70s, refusing to bow to the temptations of free love, fast talk or design fads.

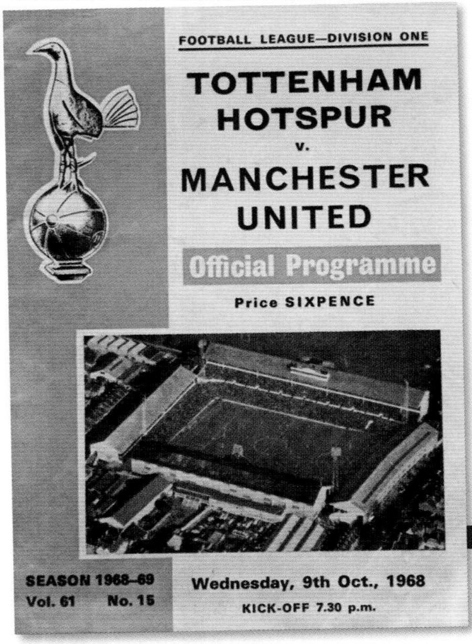

1968/69 – Like many schoolboys of the time, the club stood steadfastly by their hand-drawn cock.

1982/83 – We like cartoon mascots, but this tooled-up Foghorn Leghorn makes us realise Spurs may have been right all along.

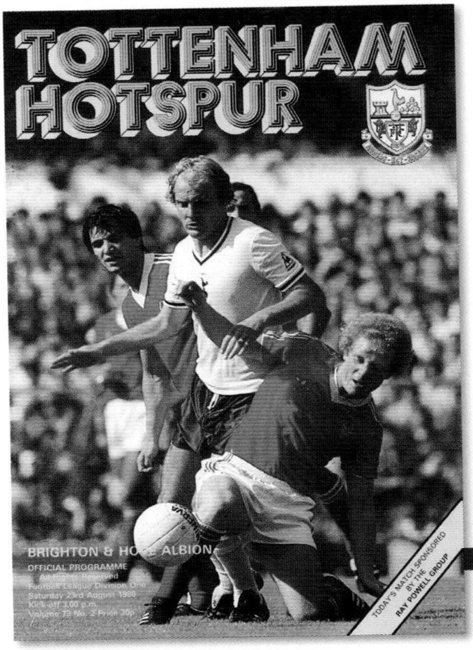

1980/81 – It's a Fact: Coventry City, yes; Leeds, yes; even Bradford City. But no one can remember Terry Yorath ever playing for Spurs.

1984/85 – Even by the mid-80s, the club logo and flag fluttering from Spurs' mast look distinctly vintage. But the neat echo of the players' self-coloured shorts helps to make this a memorable issue from the difficult crossover period into modernity. At a glance, Mark Falco's arm and neck get all mixed up with Garth Crooks's shirt (and tongue), to hilarious effect.

Sex Sells

Coventry City could probably lay claim to introducing scantily clad 'lovelies' to the football programme world in the early 70s, when *The Sky Blue* transformed itself into a lifestyle magazine. The Sky Blue Girl of the Match added a certain something to the back page, which us nine-year-olds couldn't quite put our fingers on…

By the 1980s, plenty more clubs had realised that Dad may be more likely to shell out his 40p if there was a bubble perm and tight shorts on the cover – no, not Kevin Keegan – and suddenly everyone was at it. You can almost count the goosebumps at Middlesbrough as three Northern ladies jump for the sheer joy of being at Ayresome Park, while a lass from Derby tries to convince us that sitting on the pitch in your pants is the most natural thing in the world.

Meanwhile, at St Andrews, The Blues' marketing department went for the jugular, milk-ing their appeal in a campaign that thrust their shirt sponsors to the fore, which took a lotta bottle in an era when inexcusable sexism was sometimes still confused with the okay sort. Her milkshake brings all the boys to the yard.

But the short short shorts at West Brom and even the hamstring stretches involving gym-porn outfits at Loftus Road are all fairly innocent compared to the goings-on at Aberdeen. A lady wearing an unprecedented (even in our own heads) football kit with stockings and

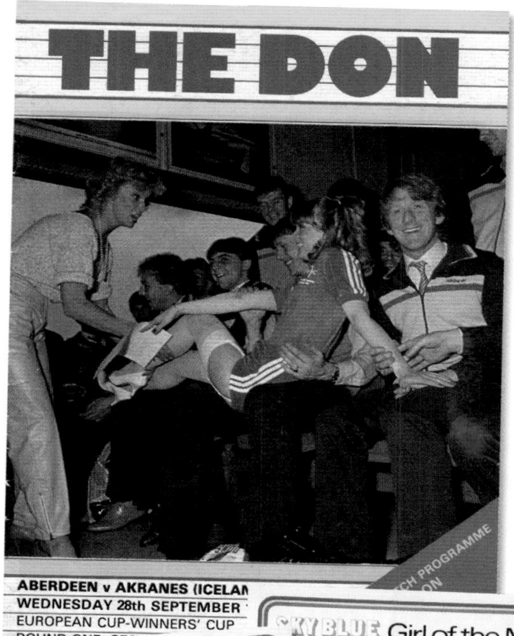

suspenders combo has been draped over the Dons. A young Gordon Strachan, wearing the expression of a man who has just remembered that his wife reads the programme, guards his groin.

Troublesome business, this sex. But it sells.

Tranmere Rovers

1968/69 – One of the strangest uses of full colour, with heavy accent on the badge. Forest/ Sunderland-style pride in the modern is extended to a foyer staircase.

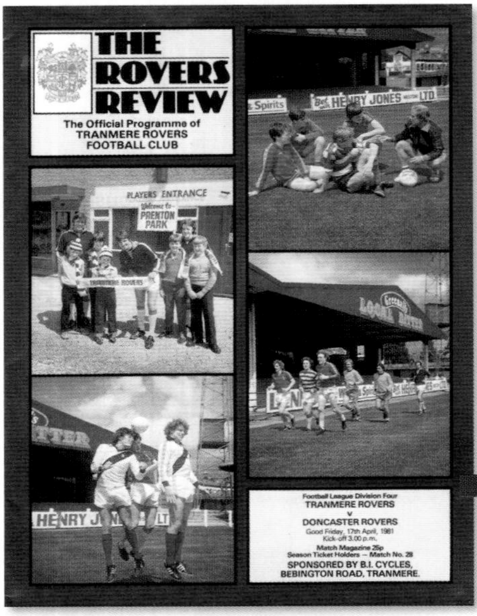

1980/81 – There's a real 'Penny Lane' vibe here, on a glorious sunny day out in Birkenhead.

1969/70 – What a difference a season makes. Rovers plunge headlong into the future.

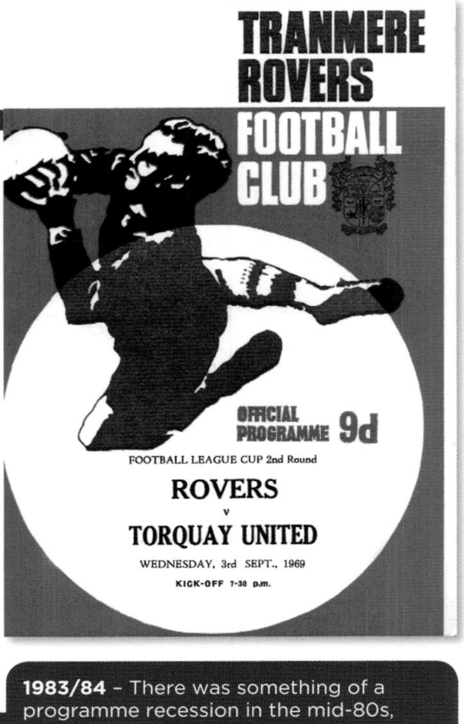

1983/84 – There was something of a programme recession in the mid-80s, in case you weren't already aware. Miserably poor fare.

Walsall

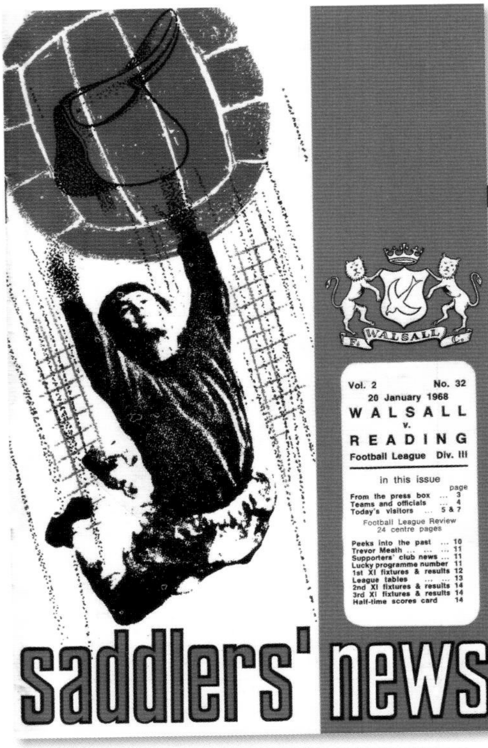

1967/68 – Feel the pride in the Saddlers' superimposition of their local industrial speciality on the flying leather football. Children make them in Taiwan now.

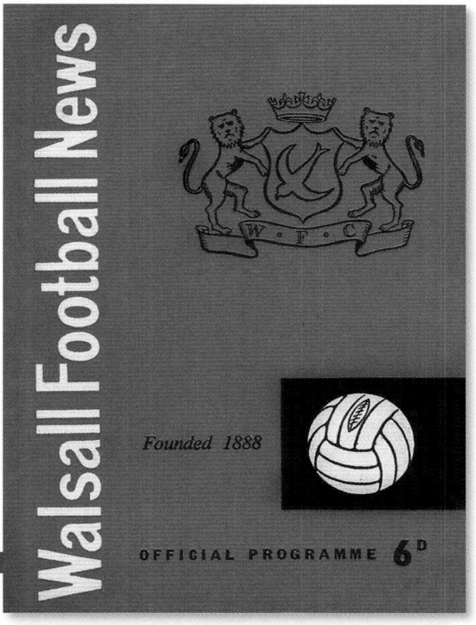

1965/66 – *Walsall Football News* is an idiosyncratic name for a programme, but this is a thoughtful job on the mini handbook model.

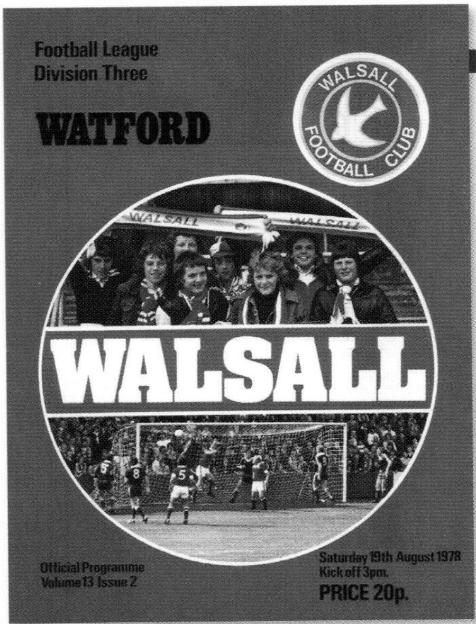

1978/79 – A sigh-inducing array of catalogue bomber jackets, Woolworths denim, trackies, knotted scarves and even a Fonzie-style baseball jacket from the Bull Ring.

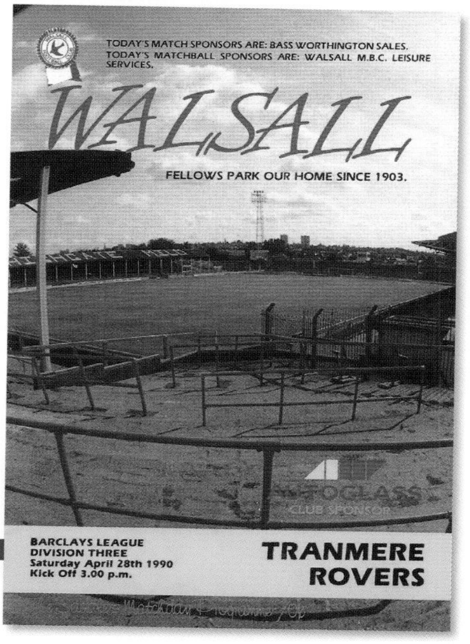

1968/69 – It's still humbling, stunning, the death of a football ground. All those shared memories left without a home. RIP the wonderful mild-only Highgate Brewery, too

1971/72 – Harry, the ultimate cartoon mascot, was soon to inhabit pride of place on Watford's adventurous asymmetrical twin-vertical-sash Umbro shirt. Kiss the Hornet.

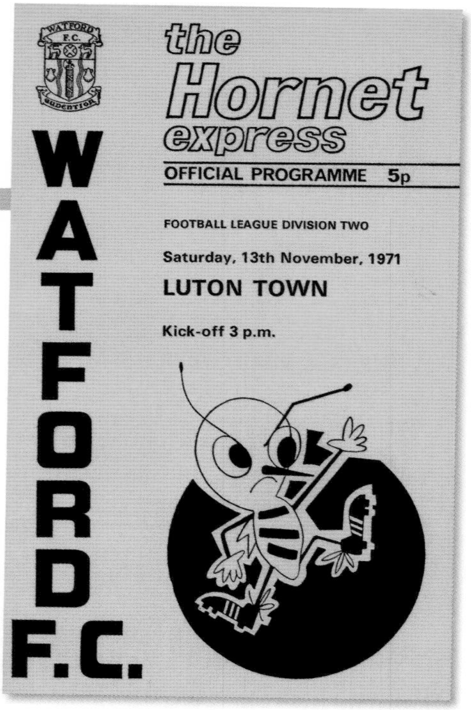

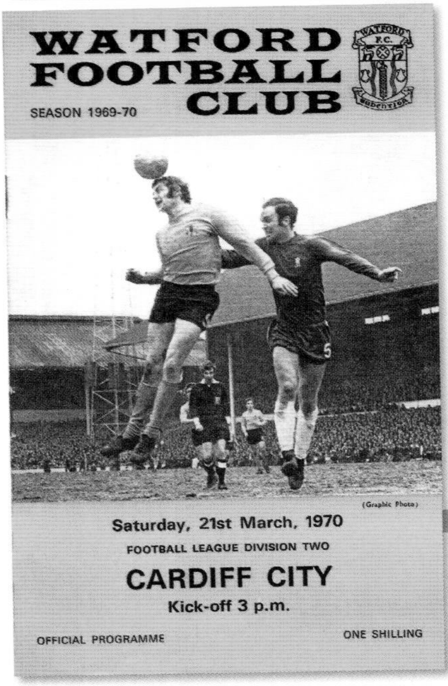

1969/70 – The season before the *Hornet Express* rebrand, the Hornets beat Stoke and Liverpool to reach the FA Cup semis, losing out to Chelsea at White Hart Lane.

1978/79 – Hornets on the rise from the Fourth to the First, stopping off here to leapfrog Chester and Plymouth in a Third Division promotion year.

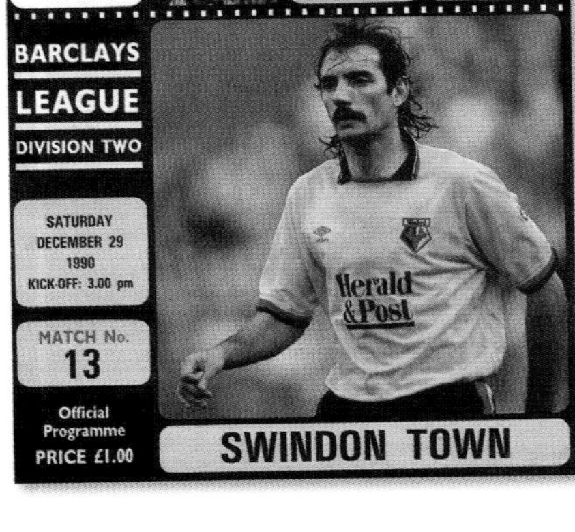

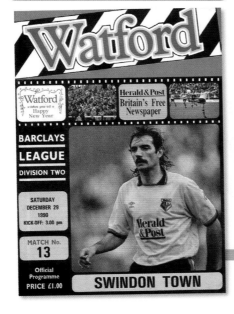

1990/91 – Yes, we're fond of the 'filmstrip' look, but Watford overegg the pudding here, throwing in a clapperboard as well.

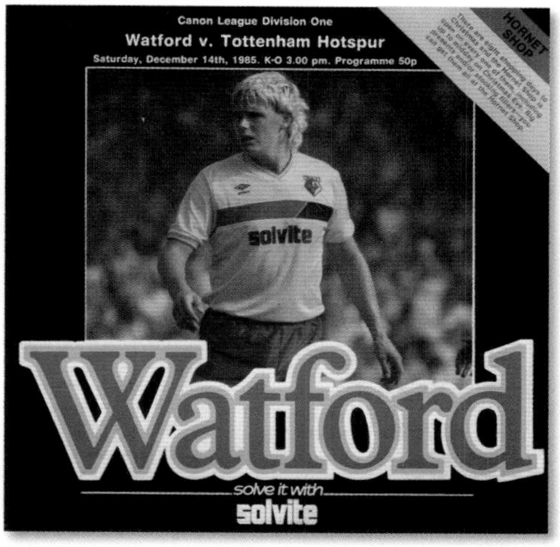

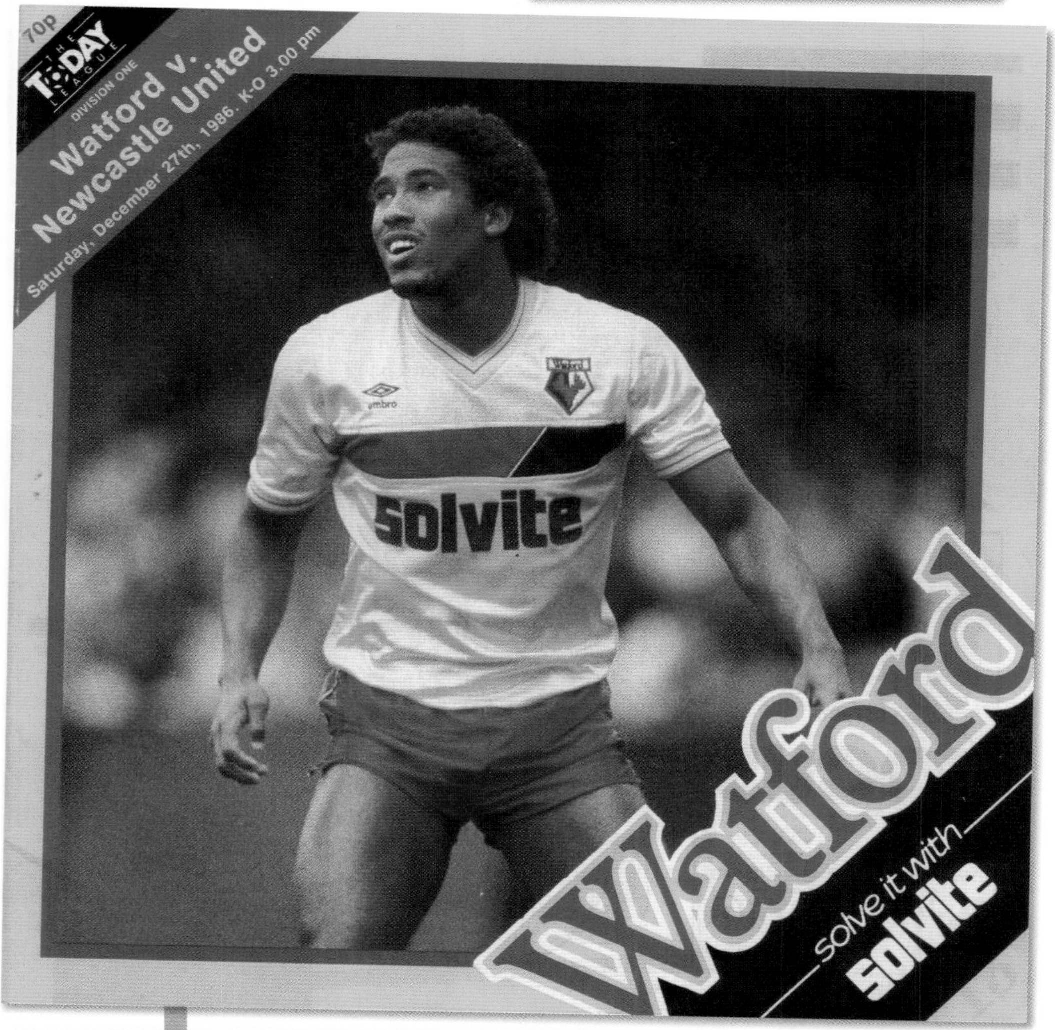

1983-87 – Watford were one of the first clubs to get a feel for modern branding and use it to their advantage. The unique red-and-yellow colourway, logo and showbiz celebrity chairman were all over Vicarage Road.

West Bromwich Albion

1983/84 – The cartoon crowd is an agreeably bizarre touch here, framing Ken McNaught. We like how Albion's corrugated roof features again, as it did opposite.

1975/76 – There's a home-kit version of this artful wonder, too; but the contrasting colours and Scrabble-style synchronicity make this a Baggies classic.

1967/68 – Elegant, bold and balanced. Were the Baggies' programmes the best of the lot?

1978/79 – What a trio: Bryan Robson, Len Cantello and Tony Brown. 'God' gets to play support.

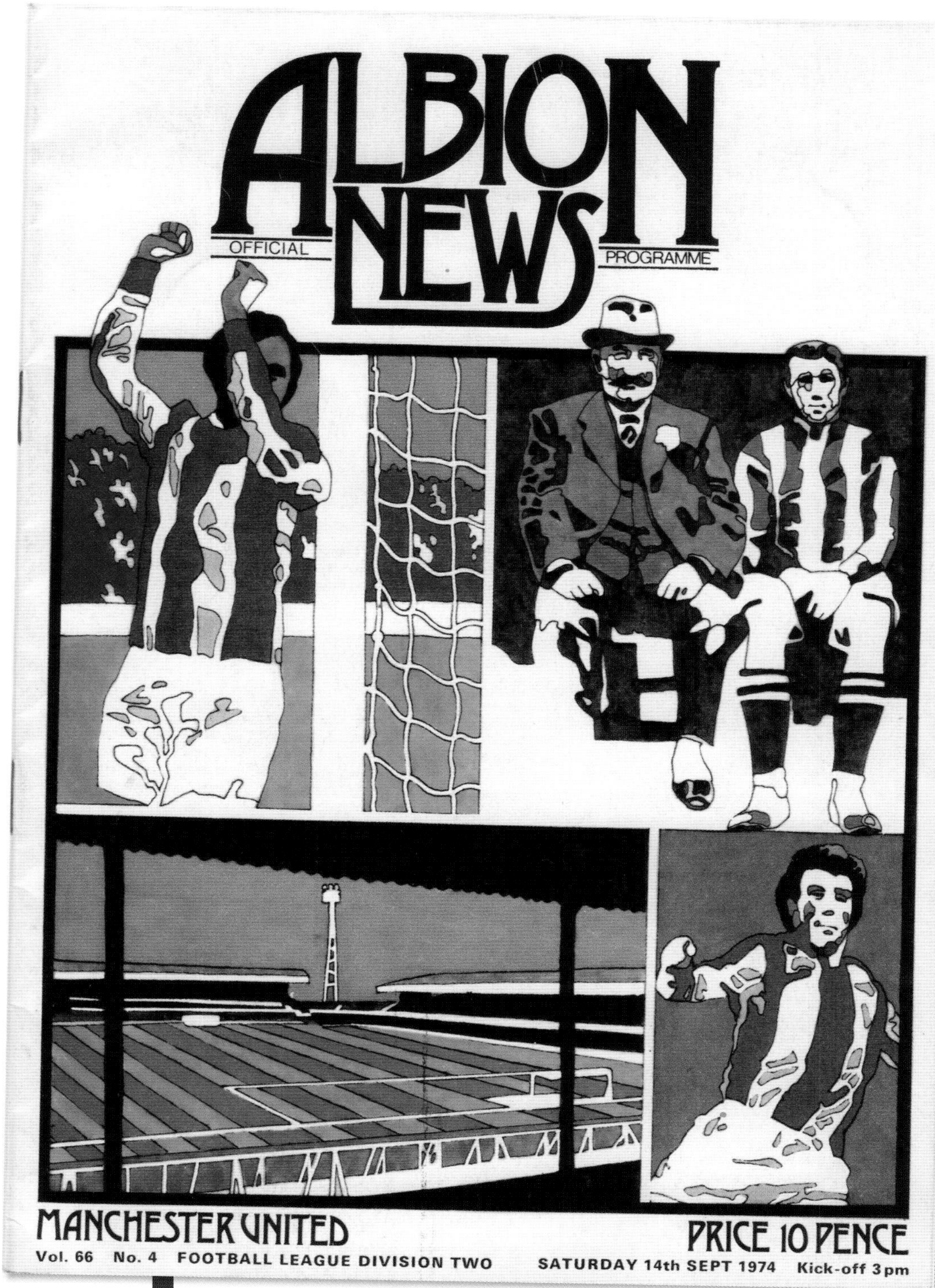

1974/75 – It's a pointless and impossible task, weighing up the incomparable attributes of thousands of football programmes produced over 35 years. But this is our fave. Edwardiana meets the 70s seamlessly in a colourful splash of cutting-edge nostalgia that's right up there with *Sergeant Pepper* and *Butch Cassidy & The Sundance Kid*.

1983/84 – Brooking no argument: the first year after the fall of the traditional *Hammer*.

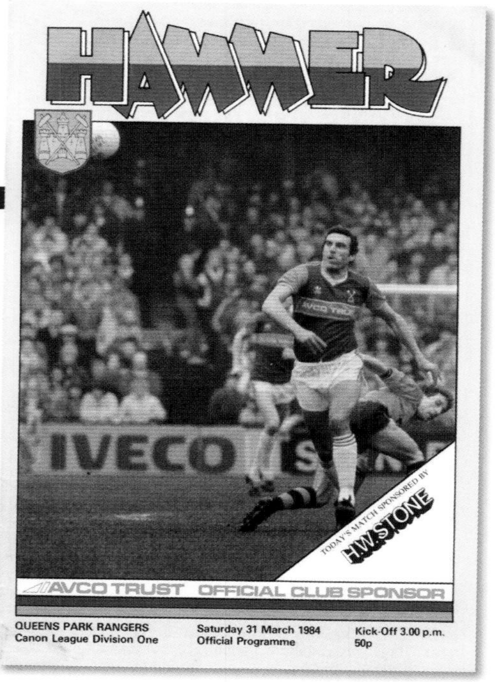

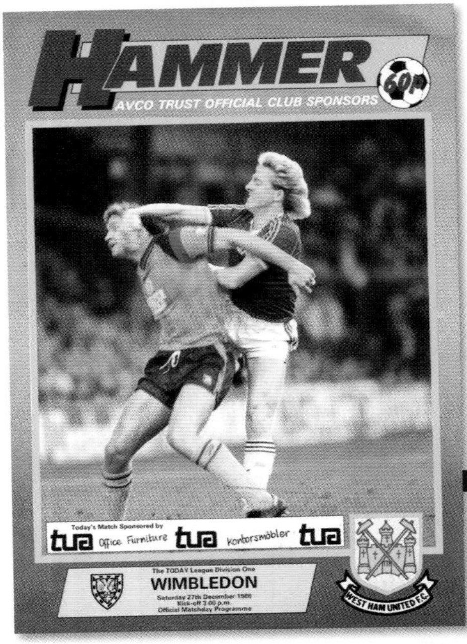

1986/87 – Frank McAvennie thumps Saint Kevin Bond in the chops. A straight retrospective red, these days.

1988/89 – Strange how pink was considered a legitimate sub for claret before branding got an Iron grip. A thoughtful *Hammer*.

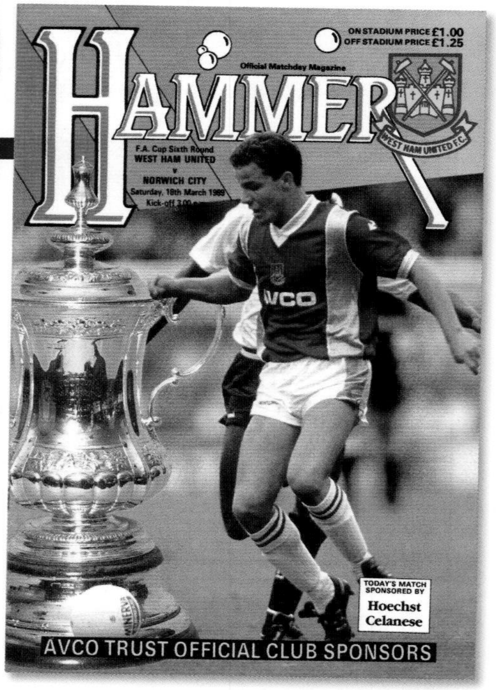

1961/62 – Pre-Hammer-History, when dinosaurs and spivs ruled the East End, and Ron Greenwood was the new boss.

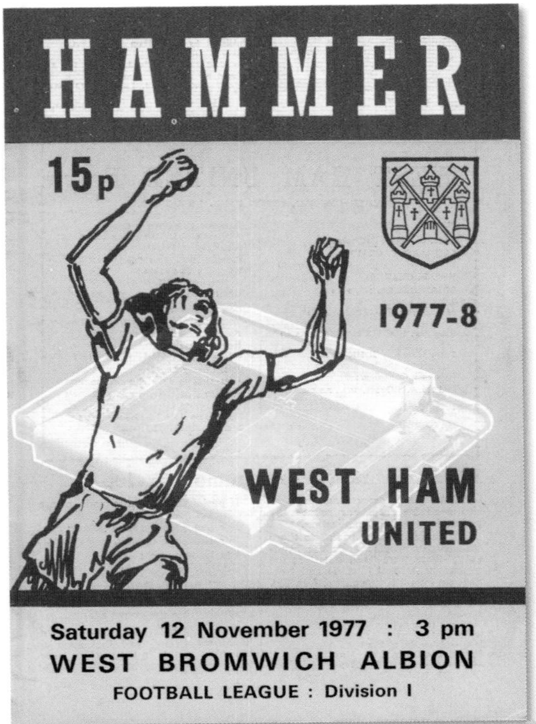

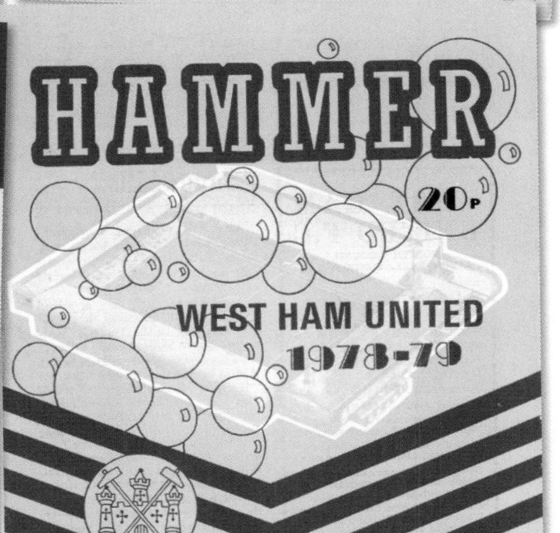

1969-83 – A perfectly iconographic set of *Hammer* programmes was produced with form and function, fans' pockets and posterity in mind. Alan Taylor in heroic Cup semi-final mode. Crossed iron-worker's hammers. An echo of the fabulous Admiral chevron kit. And bubbles.

Wolverhampton Wanderers

1967/68 – Wolves' world is going round in circles. It never appeared on the shirt, but this was actually the official club badge for a short period.

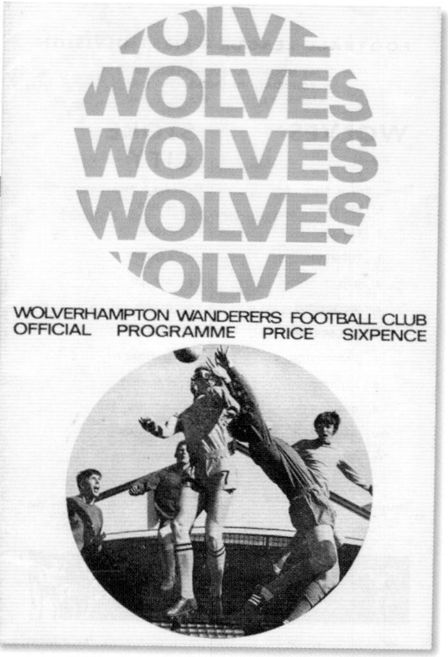

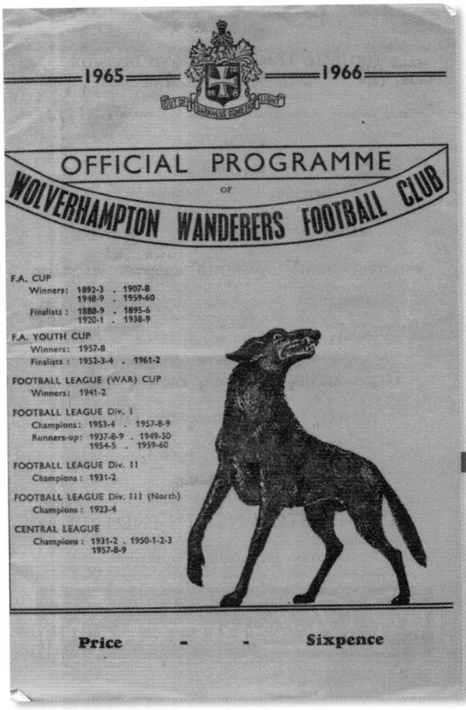

1965/66 – Pure danger: Wolves' wolf was of Shakespearian rather than Disney descent.

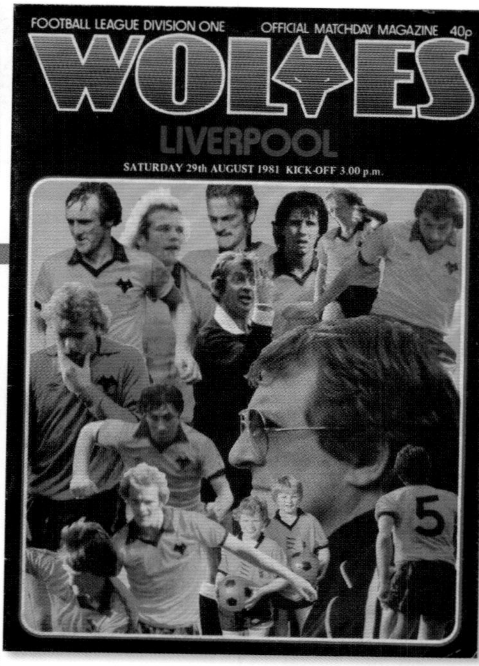

1981/82 – A cool handmade collage that recalls phonebox-cramming competitions – all cheekily built around the cracking image of the ref flicking the Vs.

1983/84 – Read from right to left, this graphic symbolises the rollercoaster plunge Wolves were about to take from Division One to Four in short order.

1970/71 – Brilliant WW graphic, post Volkswagen. A cartoon roughness about the background swatch which would have raised eyebrows at the time. Scooby-Doo salted in as a guest star. And memories of a 1-0 victory over Chelsea at Molineux on a grey Saturday afternoon, as God intended. All this for 5 new pence.

Wrexham

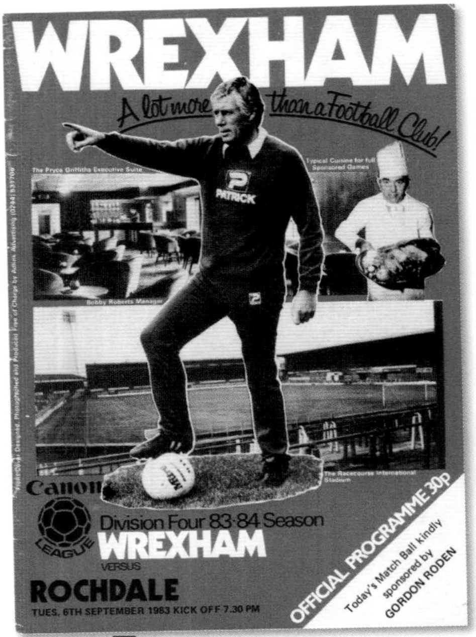

1983/84 – 'A lot more than a football club': there's an International Stadium, a swanky Executive Suite and Typical Cuisine for full Sponsored Games.

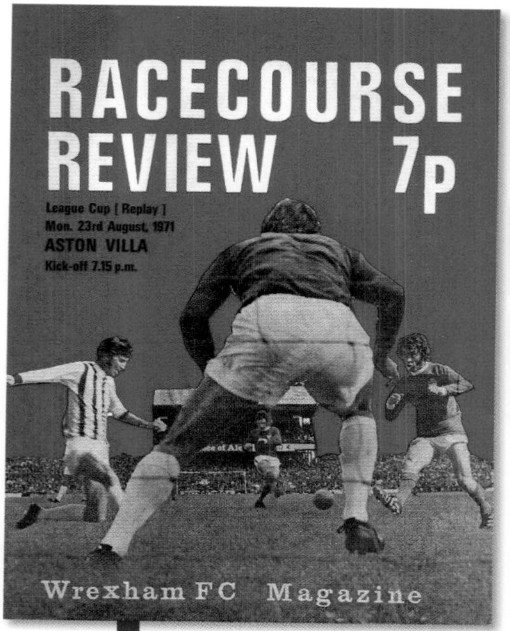

1971/72 – A review (a magazine, too) of a goalie's big bottom obscuring a wonderfully tiny stand. All yours for a huge price: 7p.

1977/78 – Wrexham skipper Gareth Davis at Wrexham market. Animals donated by fans were sold for his testimonial fund - and raised £600!

York City

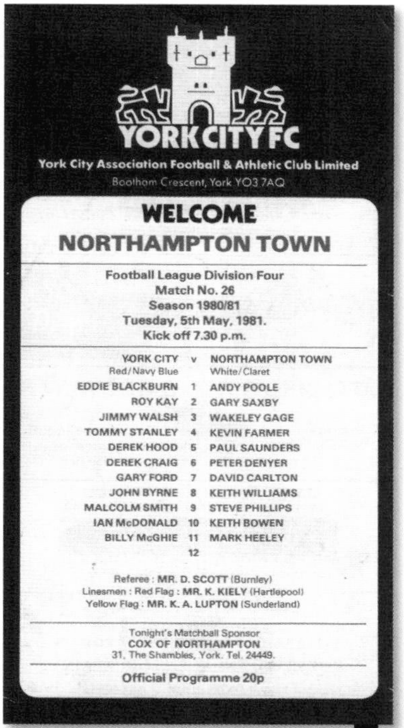

1980/81 – A format rarity in York's fold-out leaflet, which expanded from 16 sides into one large sheet, and was then blown away by the wind.

1975/76 – An aerial battle for a 'CY' badge, which wasn't really as successful as Leeds' 'Smiley' – all this in the highly original Umbro 'Y' kit era.

1964/65 – The Minstermen randomly adopt a comedy stance with their rib-tickling cartoon and comic font look. Well, it was different.

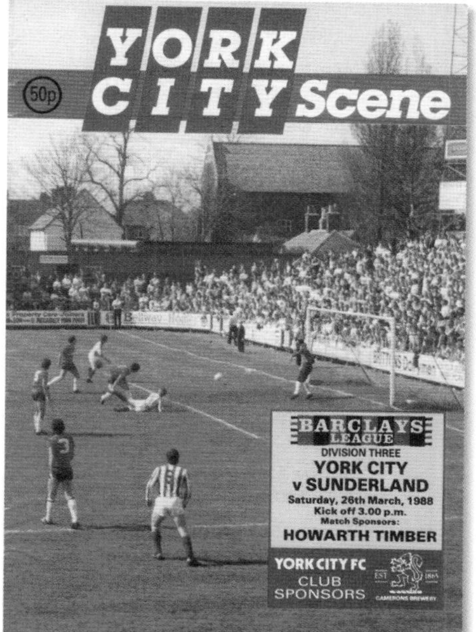

1987/88 – More low-key pleasures from the lower leagues. The trees overhanging the terraces. St Luke's Church in full view. The Yorkie ad up the floodlight pylon...

Manager's Notes

"We are now in a position where the club is finally out of debt which means that we can look around to improve the side," Stoke's Tony Waddington concentrated determinedly on the positives. "I am sure that a great many clubs will have to do what we have just done by the sale of Jimmy Greenhoff and Alan Hudson."

"I'm not one for superstitions," Pompey supremo Ian St John protested shakily, "but a victory tonight would finally cast any doubt from my mind about bogeys."

"Thank goodness January is over!" sighed Bristol City manager Alan Dicks by way of a goodbye. "The good New Year start we all hoped for did not materialise and very little has gone right for us. We were knocked out of the Cup, have failed to win in our last seven matches and had all our plans ruined by icy weather when the match at Aston Villa was postponed. We now hope our fortunes will pick up for the rest of the season."

"Graham [Taylor] and I will insist that our teams stick to their footballing principles," Luton Town boss David Pleat presumed. "We have not achieved our results by strong-arm tactics. We hope the terrace supporters will get behind the teams but not over-react."

"It is appropriate that we entertain for our first game in 1980," Stoke City's Alan Durban said confusingly, "the undisputed British side of the Seventies."

"There will, of course, have to be a great deal of improvement on our performance at Cardiff on Saturday. I would put that down as our worst of the season. It was a good point," Bristol City's Norman Hunter made a sudden, unexpectedly upbeat claim, "but a most disappointing game to watch."

"During our stay we were met by the British Ambassador and his wife," namedropped Leicester City's Jimmy Bloomfield, "and spent some time with one of the local sheikhs who looked after us very well indeed."

"Whenever I think of Brighton, I used to think about an 8-2 defeat by Bristol Rovers, and then an inglorious FA Cup exit to a non-league side. In case you happened to be on another planet at the time, they were the kind of results Peter Taylor and I got when we first went to manage Brighton after leaving Derby." But trust Cloughie to weigh self-deprecation with a cryptic googly. "They have come a long way since those days (perhaps because they have not got a good manager)."

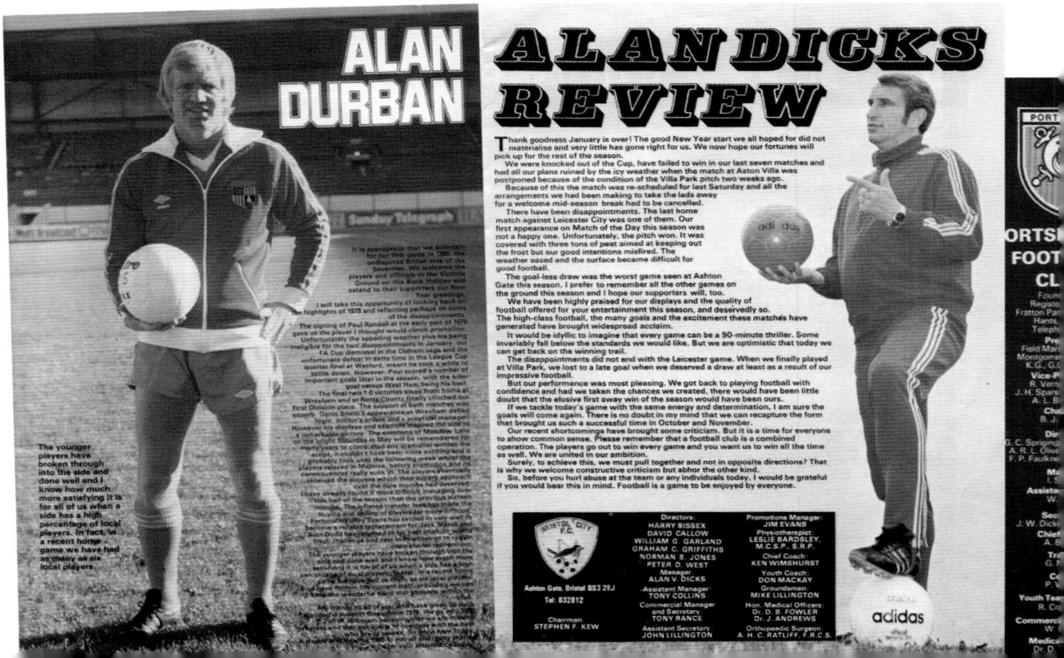
ALAN
DURBAN
The younger players have broken through into the side and done well and I know how much more satisfying it is for all of us when a side has a high percentage of local players. In fact, in a recent home game we have had as many as six local players.
ALAN DICKS
REVIEW
Thank goodness January is over! The good New Year start we all hoped for did not materialise and very little has gone right for us. We now hope our fortunes will pick up for the rest of the season.
We were knocked out of the Cup, have failed to win in our last seven matches and had all our plans ruined by the icy weather when the match at Aston Villa was postponed because of the condition of the Villa Park pitch two weeks ago.
Because of this the match was re-scheduled for last Saturday and all the arrangements we had been making to take the lads away for a welcome mid-season break had to be cancelled.
There have been disappointments. The last home match against Leicester City was one of them. Our first appearance on Match of the Day this season was not a happy one. Unfortunately, the pitch won. It was covered with three tons of peat aimed at keeping out the frost but our good intentions misfired. The weather eased and the surface became difficult for good football.
The goal-less draw was the worst game seen at Ashton Gate this season. I prefer to remember all the other games on the ground this season and I hope our supporters will, too.
We have been highly praised for our displays and the quality of football offered for your entertainment this season, and deservedly so. The high-class football, the many goals and the excitement these matches have generated have brought widespread acclaim.
It would be idyllic to imagine that every game can be a 90-minute thriller. Some invariably fall below the standards we would like. But we are optimistic that today we can get back on the winning trail.
The disappointments did not end with the Leicester game. When we finally played at Villa Park, we lost to a late goal when we deserved a draw at least as a result of our impressive football.
But our performance was most pleasing. We got back to playing football with confidence and had we taken the chances we created, there would have been little doubt that the elusive first away win of the season would have been ours.
If we tackle today's game with the same energy and determination, I am sure the goals will come again. There is no doubt in my mind that we can recapture the form that brought us such a successful time in October and November.
Our recent shortcomings have brought some criticism. But it is a time for everyone to show common sense. Please remember that a football club is a combined operation. The players go out to win every game and you want us to win all the time as well. We are united in our ambition.
Surely, to achieve this, we must pull together and not in opposite directions? That is why we welcome constructive criticism but abhor the other kind.
So, before you hurl abuse at the team or any individuals today, I would be grateful if you would bear this in mind. Football is a game to be enjoyed by everyone.
BRISTOL CITY F.C.
Ashton Gate, Bristol BS3 2EJ
Tel: 632812
Chairman: STEPHEN F. KEW
Directors: HARRY BISSEX, DAVID CALLOW, WILLIAM G. GARLAND, GRAHAM C. GRIFFITHS, NORMAN B. JONES, PETER D. WEST
Manager: ALAN V. DICKS
Assistant Manager: TONY COLLINS
Commercial Manager and Secretary: TONY RANCE
Assistant Secretary: JOHN LILLINGTON
Promotions Manager: JIM EVANS
Physiotherapist: LESLIE BARDSLEY, M.C.S.P., S.R.P.
Chief Coach: KEN WIMSHURST
Youth Coach: DON MACKAY
Groundsman: MIKE LILLINGTON
Hon. Medical Officers: Dr. D. B. FOWLER, Dr. J. ANDREWS
Orthopaedic Surgeon: A. H. C. RATLIFF, F.R.C.S.
adidas

JIM SMITH

"Now we need the win-at-home habit..."

I recall that I began my last article by saying what a pleasant change it made to be writing my comments with two successive wins behind us.

Well, now I can improve on that by pointing out that we have three successive *away* wins under our belt, a situation which I feel must help to build everyone's confidence in the right direction.

However, that is only part of the story. I have to be equally honest and agree that we must now get over the barrier—or is it merely a little hump?—of not having put our results together at home in the League.

I am sure most of you will have realised by now that it is a very tight, evenly-matched Second Division in which you are just as likely to pick up points away as you are at home.

It was for this reason that I was not *too* upset that we only drew at home to Bristol Rovers. Provided you can avoid defeats it is, in a way, immaterial where you get the majority of your victories.

However, it goes a little deeper than that. We must now set about achieving the habit of winning consistently at home not only because we ... successful season underway but ... the supporters, need to see us at ... d be able to celebrate exciting ... erformances at St. Andrew's.

... n get into that happy habit and ... vay form going then folks will ... we are on our way to something

... feature of our current situation ... bs me a little is the number of ... her clubs in whom we are sur- able to pick up a newspaper, especially a week-ends, without us being linked wit someone.

Some of the reports have an element of truth of course, because it is a fact that we are always making inquiries to establish which players are available if required.

However, we are always being quoted as interested in players when there is no truth whatsoever. This, I feel, stems from the fac that we sold a player for a million pounds an there is a general assumption that we hav cash to burn. That attitude annoys me an leads me to state emphatically that we are onl interested in buying when we feel the player i question is absolutely right for Birminghan City.

What's more anyone who does join us nov will have competition on his hands.

I would like to say how well the players i defence have done in pulling out of that ba start. Jeff Wealands, Terry Lees, Joe Ga lagher, Tony Towers and Mark Dennis hav combined well to bring more stability to th side.

We do, of course, have Pat Van Den Hauw out for some time with a back injury whic leaves us short of defensive cover. This is situation which I must consider very carefull

Finally a pat on the back for Steve Lyne Three goals in his first four League and Leagu Cup games for the Club are a reward for h hard work.

Now we have Keith Bertschin and Don Give challenging for a first-team place against ... the very competition that we must have ...

VICTORIA VIEWS

I am sure in the New Year that there are going to be a lot of good players coming on to the transfer market at bargain prices.

The ambition at this club has always been to make the team a better one. Nothing has changed in this respect and all my efforts as manager of Stoke City will be aimed in this direction.

We are now in a position where the club is finally out of debt which means that we can look around to improve the side. I am sure that a great many clubs will have to do what we have just done by the sale of Jimmy Greenhoff and Alan Hudson.

These were not Tony Waddington transfer deals but Stoke City sales. They were made purely in the financial needs of the club.

I am aware that I am under pressure because of their departures but it was just something that the club had to do.

We are obviously concerned about our position for Stoke have always been a club who have gone out and enjoyed their football and this needs a sense of security from a player's view.

But we have a lot of good players here and the younger ones in particular need the encouragement of supporters. I would ask supporters to back the players who are 100 per cent behind the club.

We shall be working hard at improving our game. There is a tremendous spirit in the club and everyone is determined to get the right results.

I want this club to be successful and I am sure this is the New Year wish of everyone connected with Stoke City.

It was unfortunate that the December postponements meant that we missed out on the chance of reaching the accepted 20 point mark before Christmas. The games are now in hand and it is up to us to make the most of them.

The return of John Mahoney gives us an extra dimension for we have missed him during his cartilage troubles.

Whatever happens the outlook at this club will always be to provide the best possible side for the Potteries.

TONY WADDINGTON

STOKE CITY F.C. CO. LTD.

ALBERT HENSHALL · THOMAS DEGG · PERCY AXON · ALEX HUMPHREYS · SANDY CLUBB · BILL WILLIAMS

Directors — Chairman: ALBERT HENSHALL, F.C.C.A., Vice-Chairman: THOMAS DE... PERCY AXON, ALEX HUMPHREYS, SANDY CLUBB, M.B., Ch.B., M.R.C.O.G.

Manager: TONY WADDINGTON. Secretary: BILL WILLIAMS.
VICTORIA GROUND, STOKE-ON-TRENT ST4 4EG. Tel: 44660.
Stoke City Development Office: Tel: 45840.

Stoke City F.C. match-day magazine edited and published by Dudley Kernick, Stoke City Promotions.
Printed by Hemmings & Capey (Leicester) Ltd., Ireton Ave., Leicester.

Harry's Hype

...rry Redknapp

Good evening, and welcome to Dean Cou... I am writing these notes prior to the Exete... Birmingham games, but certainly a... Saturday's game with Bradford City, I... there is every reason to be quietly confi... that we can more than hold our own in... first ever season of Second Division footb... I must give a special mentions to J... Smeulders, who came into the team a... Gerry Peyton suffered an injury. 'The Bear'... he is nicknamed by the players, was du... play at Canterbury for Poole Town where... plays on a non contract basis. But he step... into the game with Bradford City and finis... the day with the Man of the Match Aw... from our sponsor The Evening Echo.

Not only have we made a good start on... field, but we have in my opinion made a g... step forward by attaining the finest trai... facilities in this area, thanks to Bournemo... Sports Club who have allowed us to use t... newly acquired ground at Bournemo... International Airport. The facilities there... first class and hopefully it is an arrangem... that will last for many years. It certainly... gesture that I very much appreciate.

Finally, the atmosphere against Bradford... was first class, the way you got behind... team for 90 minutes made all the differe... Let's have the same support from you ton... and I'll promise the same commitment f... the players.

...C Bournemouth

Dean Court Ground Bournemouth (0202) 35381

Directors: ...olan (Chairman), ...ard (Vice Chairman), ...anaging and Secretary), ...p, T. E. A. Morey, ...ley, G. P. Pound, ... Barton, G. Hayward

Manager: ...rry Redknapp

...tant Manager: ...mmy Gabriel

Coaching Staff: Keith Williams, Terry Shanahan

Trainer/Physiotherapist: John Kirk

Administration Staff: Keith MacAlister (Ass. Sec.), Jenny Swift, Justin West

Lottery Staff: Arthur White, Harry Woodman, Andree Snooks, Lisa Swift

Groundsman: J. Harriss

Club Chaplain: Alan Fisher

Club Doctor: Dr. K. East

Club Scout: Maurice Ennals

Match Magazine Designed and Pr... Panbourne Press, Pan Hou... Poole, Dorset. Tel: Parkstone 740559-732152-...

ON THE BALL WITH LAWRIE

All the talk since last Saturday's victory over Bristol Rovers in the fourth round has been about the F.A. Cup, since that victory put us nearer another trip to Wembley. The excitement around The Dell on Monday as 12.30 p.m. approached was, I am sure, similar to many factories and offices around the area. And as the draw was made the delight when we were drawn out for a home tie was then tempered with caution when we were followed out of the bag by Everton, who themselves must feel that lady luck has deserted them in this year's competition, for after meeting last year's finalists, Arsenal, and the League Champions Liverpool they have to travel to another First Division side. It will however be a different tie from our first two where we had to be careful not to under estimate the opposition which on paper we should have beaten and I was pleased that our attitude in both games had been right as both Bristol Rovers and Chelsea gave us very hard games for the full ninety minutes. The Everton tie however will be a different proposition as they are one of the top First Division sides and the game at Goodison early in the season proved that we must get a result at The Dell. Although not many clubs taste the enjoyment of a Wembley Cup Final victory today's visitors Sunderland, went all the way in 1973 upsetting the odds by defeating Leeds in the Final. Being a Geordie I well remember shouting myself hoarse at Wembley and shedding a tear or two when Bob Stokoe ran on to the pitch at the end to embrace his victorous players, one of whom, Dave Watson, is of course playing his part in our recent succesful run which has seen us suffer only one defeat in the last fourteen matches. Since Sunderland lost in the F.A. Cup to Birmingham, they now are left with concentrating on gaining League points. Both Ken Knighton and Frank Clarke won promotion for Sunderland in the first season and our now intent on consolidating their position in the First Division. Meanwhile we need to gain maximum points from today's game and again next Saturday to maintain our challenge for a EUFA Cup place. If we are to capitalise on our two last away League games, where we managed two 3-0 victories at both Leeds and Birmingham, and with six out of the top seven clubs at home today we must make sure of taking maximum points. So let's really get behind the lads again today, as knowing Sunderland supporters although they will be in a minority they are certain to make themselves heard. On that note I would like to mention that the ...

SOUTHAMPTO... Football Club L...

The Dell, Milton Road... Southampton, SO9 4X...
Tel: 39444
Booking Office 39633...
Commercial Office 366...

President: H.G. B...
Vice President: E.C. ...
Chairman: A.A. W...
Dir...
John ...
Sir George Meyrick ...
B.G.W. Bowyer ...
F.G.L. Askha...
E.T...

M...
Lawrie McM...
Asst. M...
John M...
Commercial M...
Malco...
Club Se...
Brian ...
Hon. Orthopaedic S...
R.K. Jackso...
Club ...
Dr. C. L...

Club Magazine Pro...
Editor: Malcolm ...
whom all corresp...
should be a...

J.B. Shears & ...
Kempshott, Basingsto...
Individual contributions m...
Matchday Magazi...
necessarily reflect the vie...

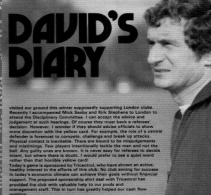

There can be few more attractive fixtures this season at Luton than today's long awaited return with Watford. Our visitors have a far more settled look about them now Graham Taylor has succeeded in selling several players who helped provide them with two tremendous seasons. It will be a close game, and the importance of the result cannot be overlooked by either team. With five games remaining, we feel we can still edge our way to the top.

Graham and I will insist that our teams stick to their footballing principles. We have not achieved our results by strong arm tactics. We hope the terrace supporters will get behind the teams but not over-react. It is vitally important that both sets of supporters uphold the good names of our clubs. We must remain a fine example to some of those idiots who have

DAVID'S DIARY

visited our ground this winter supposedly supporting London clubs. Recently I accompanied Mick Saxby and Kirk Stephens to London to attend the Disciplinary Committee. I can accept the advice and judgement at such hearings. Of course they must back a referees' decision. However, I wonder if they should advise officials to show more discretion with the yellow card. For example, the role of a central defender is foremost to compete, challenge and break up attacks. Physical contact is inevitable. There are bound to be misjudgements and mistimings. Few players intentionally tackle the man and not the ball. Any guilty ones are known. It is never easy for referees to decide intent, but where there is doubt, I would prefer to see a quiet word rather than that horrible yellow card!

Today's game is sponsored by Tricentrol, who have shown an active, healthy interest in the efforts of this club. No club aiming for success in today's economic climate can achieve their goals without financial support. The proposed sponsorship shirt deal with Tricentrol has provided the club with valuable help to our pools and management staff. This in turn has greatly helped our cash flow position.

Our fans have made us feel very proud recently with the support they have been giving the team. Win, lose or draw, the present players are giving 100 per cent and their reactions to your vocal backing was evident against Preston, Cardiff and QPR. Keep the cheers going, and let us hope that we see an excellent game of ...

BOS... CHA...

... the match all you Pompey fans have no doubt ... waiting on since the League Cup draw was ... and I myself always thought that Cup-ties ... under the 'lights, with a big crowd present, ...elf to a more exciting game.

...t's game against Leicester in the League Cup ... back many memories — some good, some ... of the tussles Liverpool had with them in the ...ixties. For a while they proved to be a bit of a ... Team, in fact Leicester knocked us out of the ... FA Cup in the semi-final only to be beaten ...elves by Manchester United in the Final. ...ver, it was they who were beaten on our way ...ning the Cup in 1965, and not that I'm one for ...titions, but a victory tonight would finally cast ...oubt from my mind about bogeys. Leicester ...always been an attractive footballing outfit and ...players of the calibre of Weller, Birchinall, ...ington, Sammels and current international ... Whitworth they are not far short of being a ...in the land again. In fact when the season ... last year they looked more like championship ...al than eventual relegation candidates, but ...ll is like this. Even in the Cup-ties last year, ... First Division clubs fell to the less fashionable ... and we will be doing our utmost to add yet ...r scalp tonight.

Ian St John

Don't forget what happened last season

Whenever I think of Brighton, I used to think about an 8-2 defeat by Bristol Rovers and then an inglorious F.A. Cup exit to a non-league side.

In case you happened to be on another planet at the time, they were the kind of results Peter Taylor and I got when we first went to manage Brighton after leaving Derby.

They have come a long way since those days (perhaps they have not got a good manager).

But in case anybody is in any doubt of what they are capable of doing to us, I suggest they recall last season's game here when they beat us 1-0 after we had gone more than 50 matches unbeaten at home.

They come here today after we've had the disappointment of losing at Ipswich, having played extremely well and been very unfortunate.

But that is behind us now and our disappointments just seem to come as more of a jolt simply because we have not been used to having many over the last few years. I hope it stays that way.

MAN OF THE MATCH AWARD
(For the Davarro Cup)
Bristol City (Home) Gary Mills
Arsenal (Home) Martin O'Neill
Leicester City (Away) Kenny Burns
Middlesbrough (Home) Kenny Burns

Brian Clough

BRIAN CLOUG...

CITY COMMENT

BUSY PERIOD

It has been a busy time for us just recently with tonight's match against Middlesbrough our third important League game in the space of ten days in which time we have also paid a short visit to Kuwait for a game against their national team.

Our trip to the Middle East last week went very well indeed and we returned for the match with Coventry on Saturday after a nice break from our normal routine.

We visited Kuwait a couple of years ago and last week we again received a very enthusiastic welcome from a country that takes its football very seriously indeed. Kuwait are obviously not a world power in the game but in the Middle East they have a good reputation at international level and they have never been beaten by Saudi Arabia who of course are putting so much money into their game at the moment.

It was important that we produced a good performance because we were really flying the flag for the English game and I was delighted with the way the team played.

We had to play well to win 2-1 after being a goal down at half time and I think all the players felt the benefit of sampling the different atmosphere and conditions we met.

USEFUL PLAYERS

Temperatures were in the eighties for the match which was played in a very good stadium on a grass pitch. Kuwait had one or two very useful players and there was a great deal of interest in the match because of their World Cup qualifying match against Bahrain last weekend.

Several British coaches are working in the country at the moment including Peter McParland the former Villa, Wolves and Irish winger and Graham Williams who played for West Bromwich Albion and Wales a few years ago so I was pleased that we gave a good account of ourselves and of English soccer generally for their sakes.

Two years ago when we were last in the country, Steve Sims had his first match in the senior side and in last week's match we were able to try out Jon Sammels playing in the back four alongside the centre half. I think Jon enjoyed the switch and he came through it very well and this is one of the advantages of a few days away like this, it gives you the chance to try out new ideas.

During our stay we were met by the British Ambassador and his wife and spent some time with one of the local sheikhs who looked after us very well indeed. All in all the trip did us a lot of good and obviously was good for team spirit.

THE DIFFERENCE

It was nice to be able to train in temperatures around the eighties two-thirds of the way through our own season and we certainly noticed the difference when we got back to train on a wet and windy winter's morning back home after our few days in the sun.

Tonight's match against Middlesbrough completes our hectic recent spell and we will be looking for two points this evening against a side who, like ourselves, are looking towards Europe.

•*Turn to the 'City Viewpoint' page for action pictures of City in Kuwait.*

JIMMY BLOOMFIELD

Aberdeen

1971/72 – Mexico 70 still looms in a minimalist look, featuring minimal action against Airdrie.

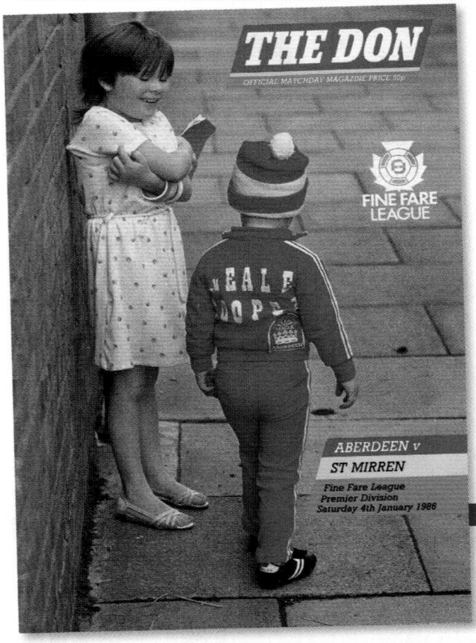

1985/86 – An evocative slice of documentary action on the streets of the Granite City.

1970/71 – Terrific Space Age football-and-floodlight art, playing with the effect of lighting from above. See how the lights pick up the motif. Great work.

1963/64 – The epitome of Scottish 60s taste in typesetting, with lost letterhead fonts, a laurel wreath crest and a perfect unity of conservative design.

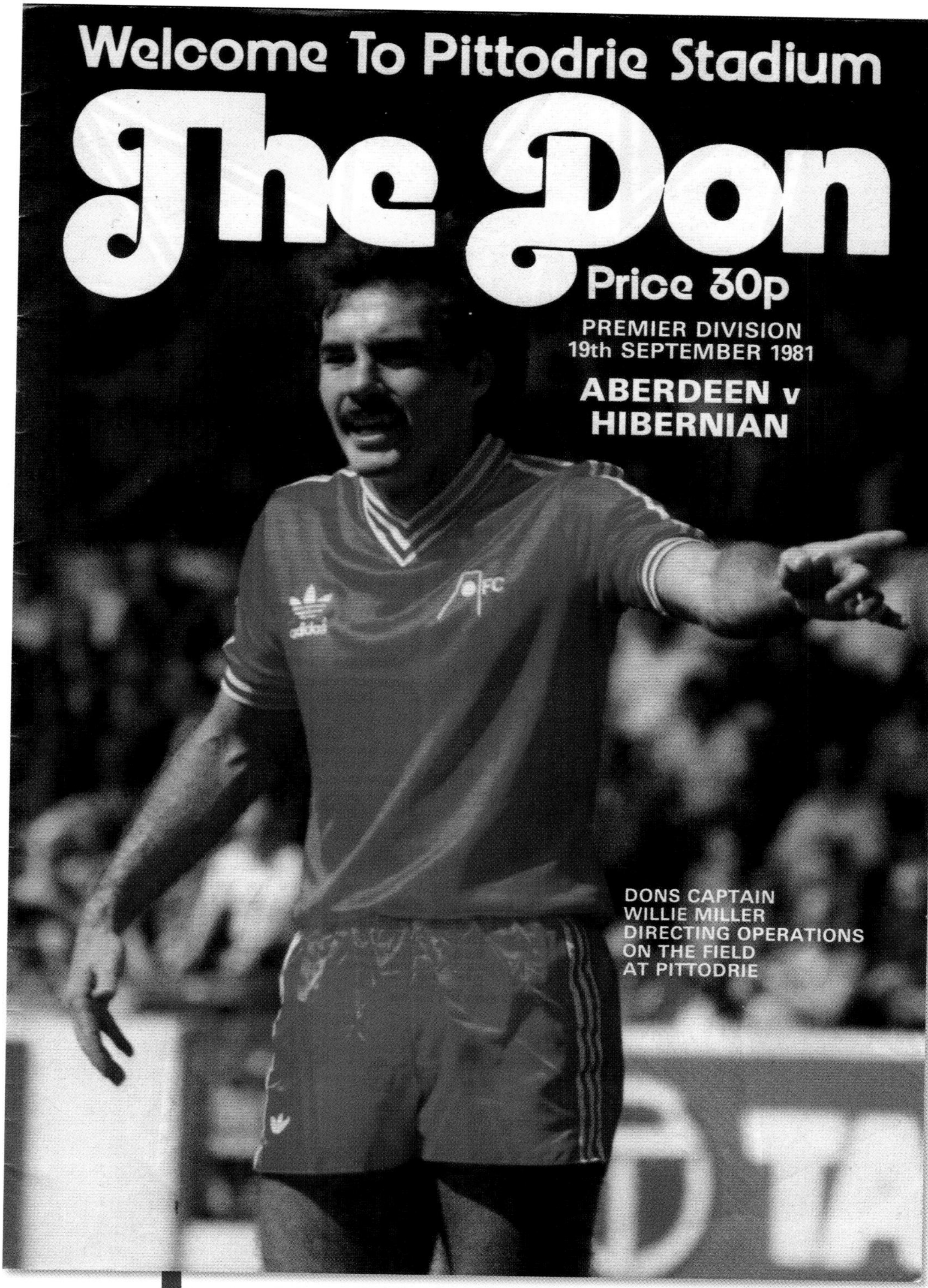

1981/82 – Skipper Willie Miller at the height of the Dons' might. Aberdeen won the Scottish 'Premier Division' in 1979/80, 1983/84 and 1984/85 and were runners-up in 1980/81 and 1981/82, lifting the Scottish Cup this season and in three of their next four attempts. Maybe consider bringing back this font, this badge, this kit... this team?

1968/69 – In all seriousness, this could be a programme from 1928, never mind '68. The Celtic cross, Olde Scottish type and production values are positively medieval.

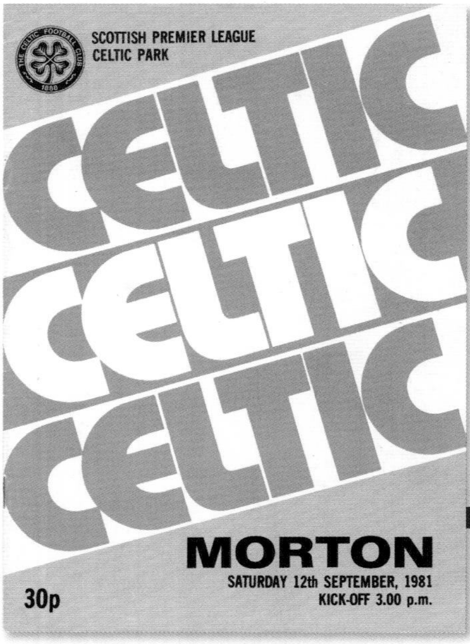

1981/82 – We get the feeling this might be a Celtic home programme. Shouty styling designed to intimidate the 34 visitors from Greenock.

1969/70 – Wow, Euro campaigns really brought the very best out of Celtic. Love the updatable panel showing the home and oppo kits, and the dress-pattern chic. A fave.

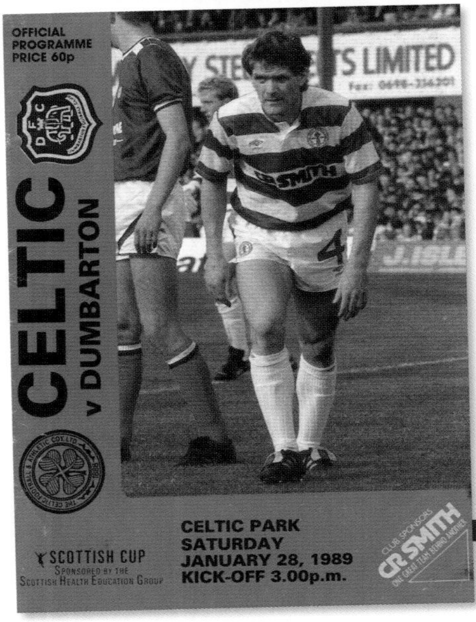

1988/89 – The sidelong look: Roy Aitken attempts to sneak unseen into the Dundee penalty box.

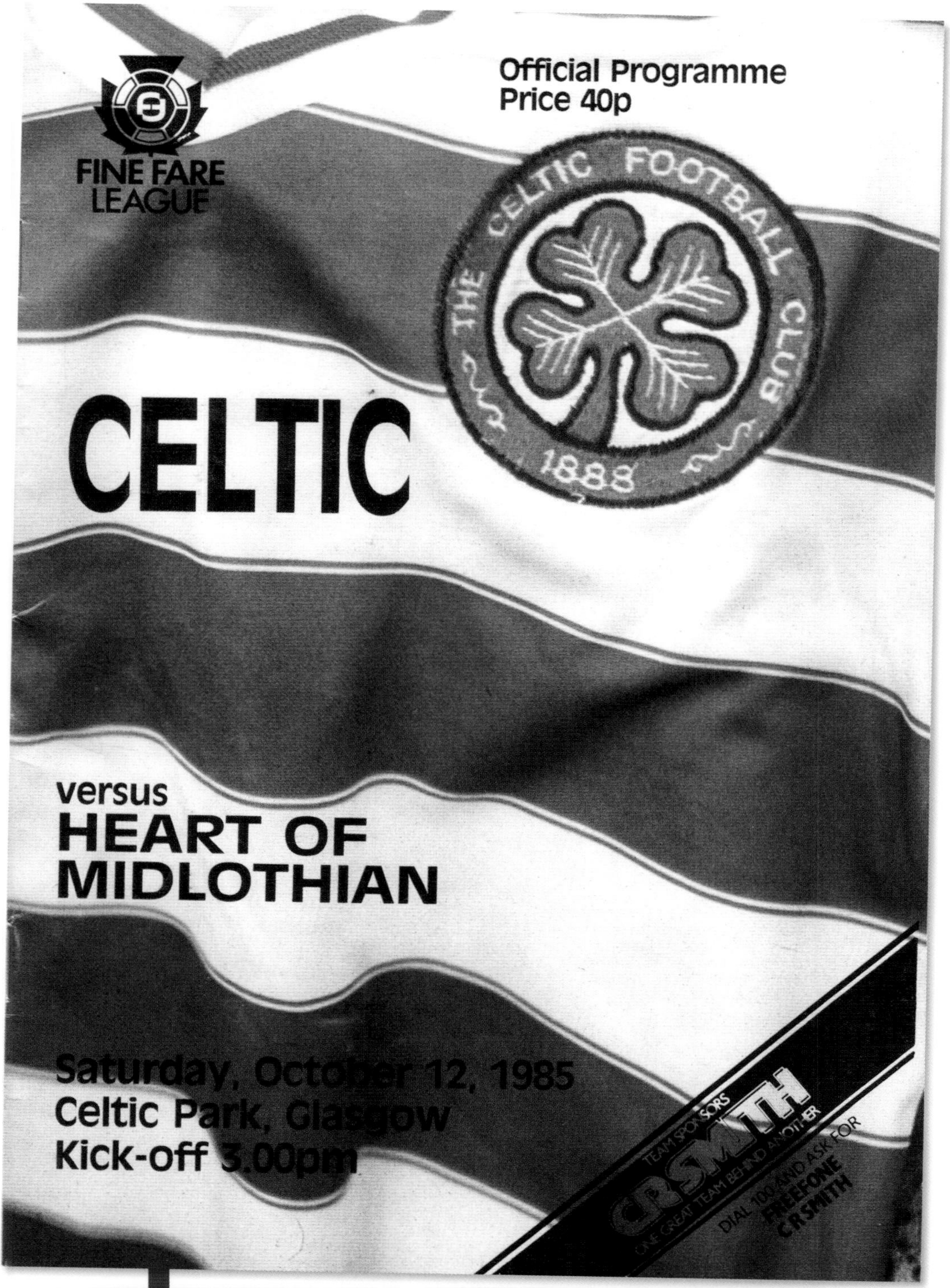

1985/86 – The way to do it. Incredible how this deceptively simple, iconic concept was never envisioned before, and unfathomable why it hasn't been reused to death ever since. The ultimate solution to the problem of how to reflect the shirt design and badge on the prog cover. An entirely suitable public image for yet another championship season.

Dundee

1972/73 – Almost unchanged since '66 – the old cover ad and the shirt badge's flourishes deemed too 'flash' – this tight little design is a model of icy conservatism.

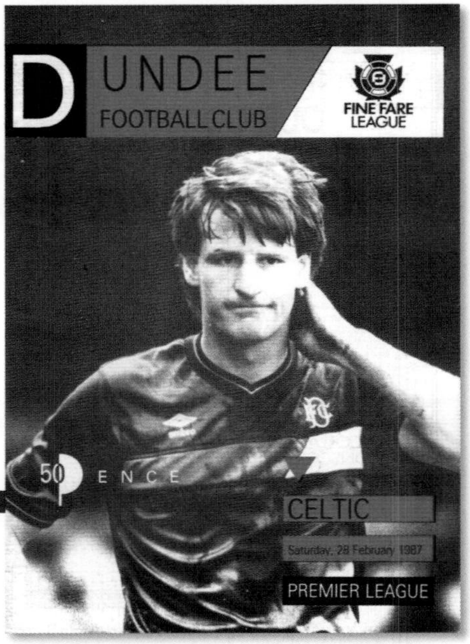

1986/87 – If only the budget had run to a colour cover, you'd see that the red-and-white banner here perfectly echoes the shirt design. Neat compromise.

1974/75 – Another modest success, this time featuring an illustration made on an etching toy. Resembles a book of disappointing football short stories.

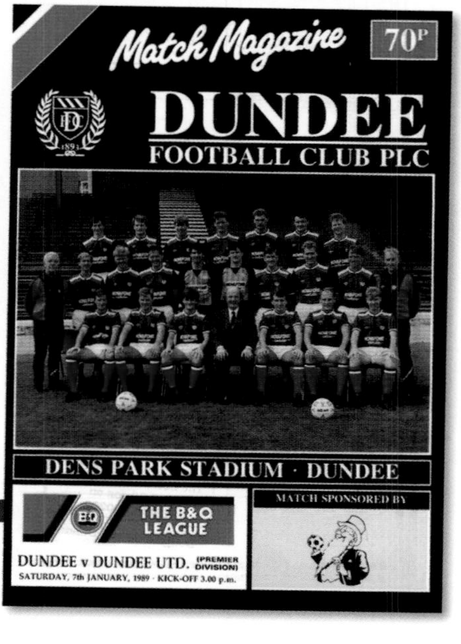

1975-76 – After the self-restricted privations of the Fine Fare era, the B&Q League signalled a DIY splash of colour – right in the middle of a run of seven derby defeats.

Dundee United

1971/72 – So soon after the Terrors' colour-switch from all white to shocking orange, fans and designers alike were still coming to terms with the upheaval.

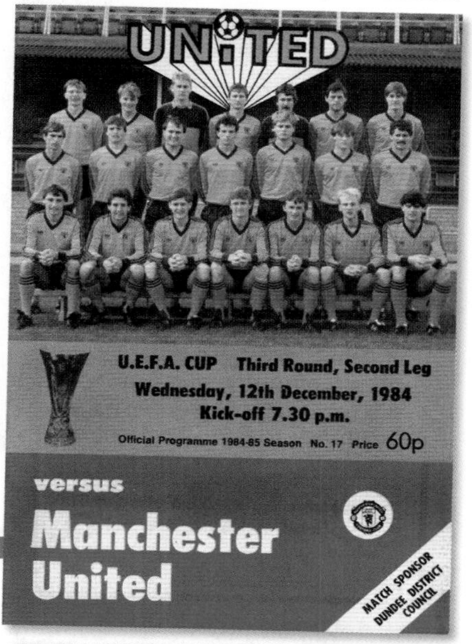

1984/85 – We like High School perspective and little footballs for dots on 'i's. After a worthy draw at Old Trafford, Tannadice was to witness a slim 2-3 defeat.

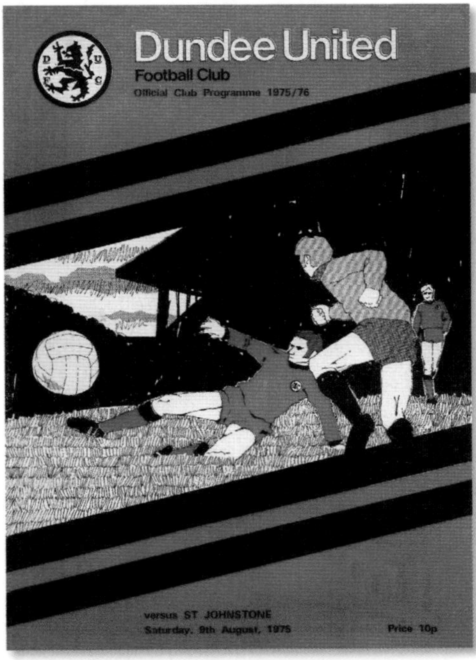

1975/76 – A cracking illustrated cover. Having thus raised our expectations, resembles a Penguin book of even more disappointing football short stories.

1967/68 – "A hectic moment at Ibrox as Mackay gathers with Ferguson rushing in."

Heart Of Midlothian

1963/64 – Local colour: The Forth Bridge from the cockpit of a low-flying 707.

1987/88 – The 'Heart' badge as a wedding cake, all neatly cut up ready for guests' goodie bags. The Royal Mile's brick mosaic is notoriously hard to capture in icing.

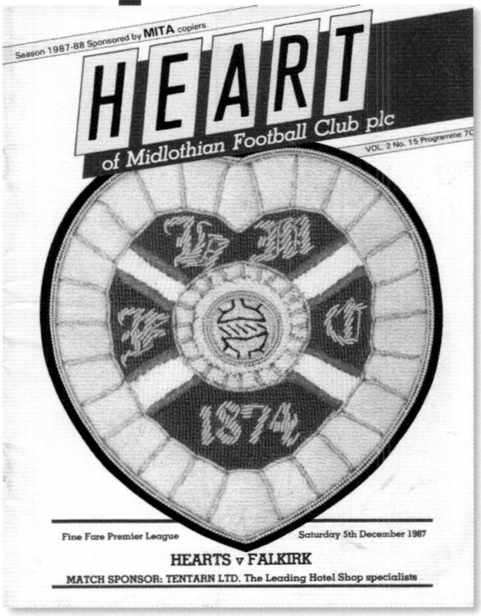

1970/71 – A football prog from the 70s masquerading as a teen mag from the 40s. The Social Club News section featured a swirl of chaperoned tea-dance shindigs.

1980/81 – Full colour is allowed into the maroon half of Edinburgh for the first time. We kid you not.

Hibernian

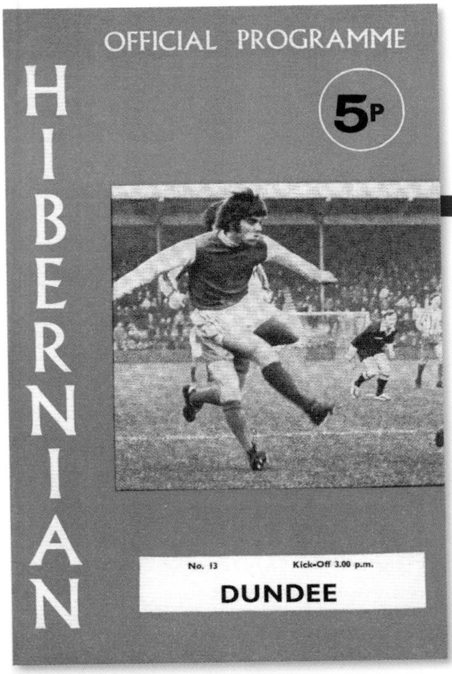

1971/72 – Canny Scottish minimalism in action. Not a wasted word, not a spare ounce of flesh on this strictly vanilla option.

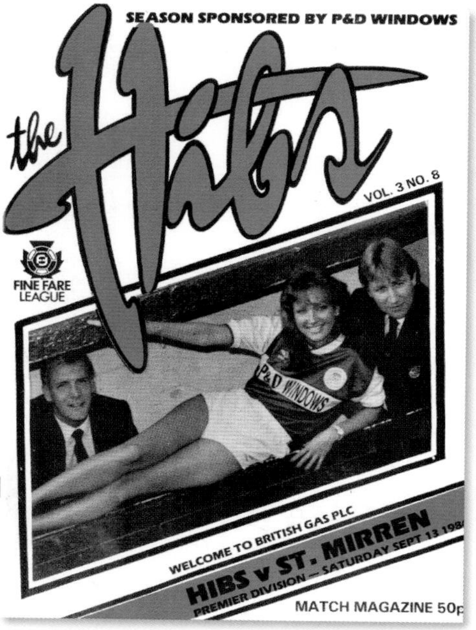

1986/87 – The arrowhead on the 's' shows the way for production values. Cheap, from two-colour cover and Kajagoogoo font to love interest in the dugout with Alan Rough.

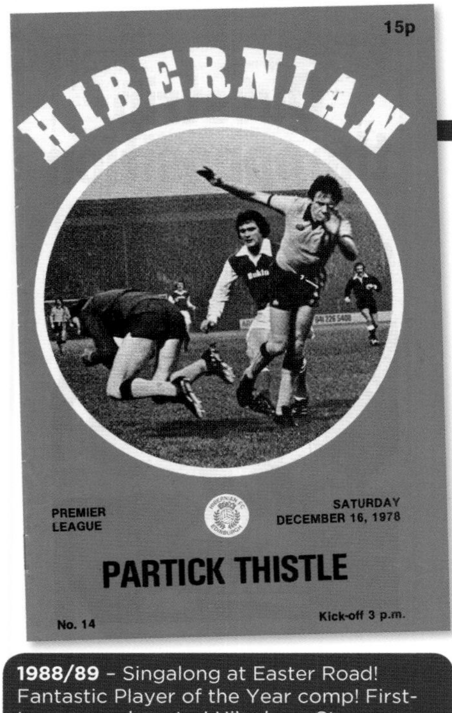

1978/79 – A programme 10 years out of date ushers in the age of commercialism with Britain's first shirt sponsorship deal.

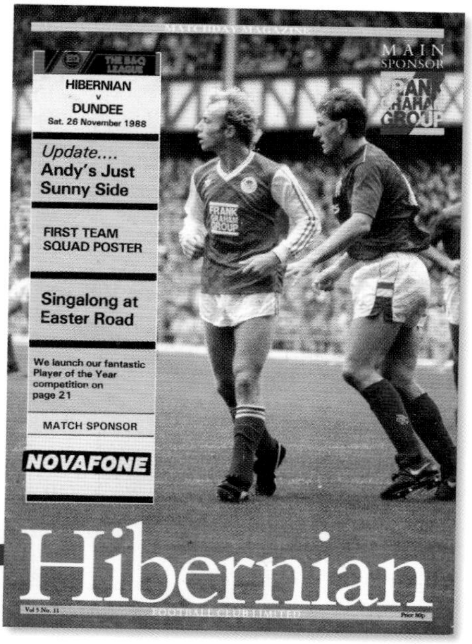

1988/89 – Singalong at Easter Road! Fantastic Player of the Year comp! First-team squad poster! Hibs hero Steve Archibald in front of Ibrox's Archibald Leitch stand!

Rangers

1966/67 – Sheer class, this fan's eye view of Ibrox, complete with besuited supporters, vintage motor and fluffy cloud enveloping the hallowed scene.

1972/73 – Handsome bit of design – red, white and blue through and through, with Euro silverware safe in the trophy cabinet.

1980/81 – Great Gatsby font. Great Umbro kit. Great Scott! Blue socks?

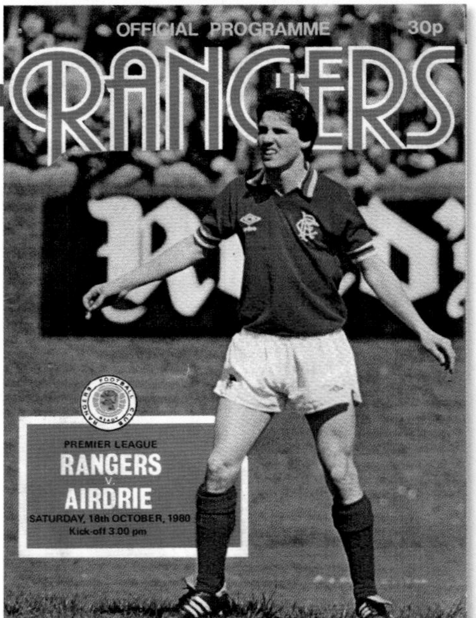

1975/76 – Spoiler alert: Big Martin Is So Happy because Rangers won the Scottish League last season, reminding everyone else by means of a big flag.

1985/86 – The Leader: new player-boss Graeme Souness arrives at Ibrox from Sampdoria in time for the end of the season, spurring waves of positivism. On the final day, the Gers beat Motherwell to win a last-gasp place in Europe, while Celtic win the League title. Souey was red carded on his debut in August, but went on to lead Rangers to their first championship in nine years.

Authors

Gary Silke and Derek Hammond are the authors of *Got, Not Got: The A-Z of Lost Football Culture, Treasures & Pleasures* (2011); *The Lost World of Football* (2013); *What A Shot! Your Snaps of the Lost World of Football* (2013) and *Shirt Tales & Short Stories: The Lost World of Football Kit* (2014). They have also produced an expanding set of club editions, which currently includes: *Got, Not Got: The Lost World of Chelsea, Coventry City, Derby County, Ipswich Town, Leeds United, Leicester City, Liverpool, Manchester City, Manchester United, Newcastle United, Norwich City, Southampton, Tottenham Hotspur* and *West Ham United.*

Acknowledgments

Thanks to all the contributors who have been up in their lofts, under the bed, in the airing cupboard and even into the airtight glass-fronted collectables vault in their personal spare-room shrines, all digging for their favourite and memorable programmes. Sorry if we couldn't squeeze all of them in.

Martin Bennett, Pete Berkowitz, Allen Brydges, SN Chang, Ian Davidson, Neville Evans, Gavin Haigh, John Hammond, Graham Marsden, Steve Marsh, Simon Shakeshaft, John Wilkinson and Andrea Yeo.

Picture Credits

Neville Chadwick Photography: cover, p6
Miles McClagan (twitter: Miles McClagan @TheSkyStrikers)

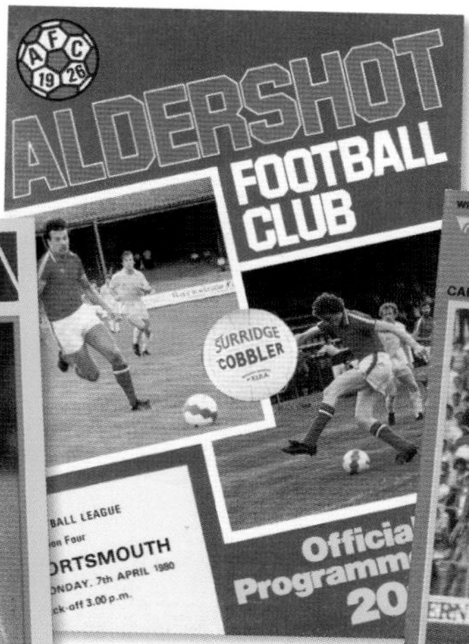

Critical Acclaim for *The Lost World of Football*

"Wonder at the unreconstructed non-PC days when Manchester City bikinis were on sale in the Maine Road club shop, when a top-selling football annual promoted Park Drive cigarettes, and when Coventry City invited their more photogenic female fans to be 'our girl of the match' in the programme. Just as *Got, Not Got* invited the reader on an irresistible meander down Memory Lane, *The Lost World Of Football* is no easier to put down."

Backpass

"The authors have put so much into this book – it's a mixture of remarkable photographs, toys, stickers, club icons, and not forgetting the writing – it's beautiful!"

Andy Jacobs, *talkSPORT*

"A hugely evocative pictorial memorial to the innocence of a game before it became a business. Each page filled with the iconic paraphernalia of a homespun fandom that shaped a generation's adolescence but allowed us the space to make our own dreams."

The Morning Star

"This book is superb."

Steve Anglesey, *The Mirror*

"Should you yearn for the days of petrol station freebies and naff endorsements (Trevor Brooking patio doors, anyone?), you'll love this celebration of clutter and culture. Packed with evocative pictures, younger readers can rejoice in the fact that they've never received Kevin Keegan slippers in their stocking. Great fun."

FourFourTwo

"Brilliant!"

Sport magazine

"There's a whole series of books called Got, Not Got: brilliant books looking back at old football memorabilia."

James Brown, *talkSPORT*

"The original *Got, Not Got* was a masterpiece, so the pressure was really on to come up with the goods yet again. Would there possibly be enough to fill another book? The answer is of course, yes. Not just a small yes, but a rather large one – and also a bunch of club-specific volumes and a further gem in the guise of *What a Shot: Your Snaps of the Lost World of Football.* A truly beautiful thing, a phrase which neatly sums up the *Lost World of Football.*"

Fly Me To The Moon fanzine

"The book is superb – an actual step up, if possible, on *Got, Not Got.* Got it, love it... lost about five hours at the weekend!"

In Bed With Maradona

"It's the football book equivalent of *The Godfather II* or *Toy Story 2* – the same, but arguably even better than the original *Got, Not Got*. On every page, there was something to remember or something I'd never heard of but wish I'd owned back in the day. On every page a gasp or a titter. Lavishly illustrated, brilliantly written, *The Lost World of Football* is a thoroughly engrossing read from cover to shining cover."

Hopping Around Hampshire blog

"*The Lost World of Football* is a must-have for fans, a sought-after stocking filler."

Mirror.co.uk

Critical Acclaim for *Shirt Tales & Short Stories* and *What a Shot!*

"Well written and beautifully illustrated, this book is going to ruin many Christmas mornings [for fans' wives and girlfriends!] – it's a cracking stocking filler."
Paul Hawksbee, *talkSPORT*

"Those witty *Lost World* chaps have come up with another winner with an unashamed stroll down the Memory Lane of footie kits. Great anecdotes, and is well worth the cash!"
Sunday Mirror

"*1000 Football Shirts* and *Shirt Tales & Short Stories*: two excellent books on soccer uniforms hit the market in the past year. *Shirt Tales & Short Stories* tells the story behind 60 classic British kit designs. Can't decide which book to get? Easy: Get both!"
ESPN

"If you have any interest in football kits whatsoever, this is an absolute must! Covering English clubs from Arsenal to Wolves, it also features a selection of Scottish teams and a page for each of the home nations. As well as the shirts themselves, scattered throughout the book are kit adverts from the 70s, 80s and 90s as well as shots of the kits in use from the time."
The Football Attic

"Love *Shirt Tales & Short Stories*. Great book!"
Hummel UK

"It looks fantastic. Nothing less than you'd expect from the *Got, Not Got* team. The A5-sized volume crams in photos, ads and illustrations of kits for the country's leading clubs. Double page spread per club, it's vibrant and exciting in its design and looks packed with facts and opinion and gives a real flavour of football kits from the past. Home kits, away kits, rare kits, beautiful kits and ugly kits – they're all here including some I'd never seen before. There are also articles on the major kit manufacturers from the past – all presented in Derek and Gary's irreverent but loving style! Another superb read!"
Kit guru John Devlin, author of *True Colours*

"*Shirt Tales & Short Stories*: the very best form of football nostalgia."
Vi-Tippa magazine, Sweden

"*What A Shot!* is heaven on earth washed out colour snaps from a pre-digital age, windows back to a world that is literally a millennium ago. On the pitch at Ayresome Park to in the stands at old Filbert Street. An overgrown Valley to photos of the old Stretford End. An old 1970s coach outside the offices at Elland Road. Inflatable bananas at Maine Road. Neglected terraces at Workington. Or fan pictures posing with Steve Bull. You will live the football dream again with these two incredible collections."
Fly Me to the Moon

"Celebrating the lost art of imperfection! The mainly blurred book consists of pictures that fans took with proper cameras in football stadiums 30 or 40 years ago. They're mostly terrible, but impressively so. I love this book!"
Stay-at-Home Indie Pop blog

"*What a Shot!* is another lovely thing to hold and to browse. Drop a few hints and you might get both this and *The Lost World of Football* for Christmas!"
Hopping Around Hampshire blog

"When *What A Shot!* landed in my lap, I thought I'd gone to retro heaven – a book of pure photo-based gold. It's a compilation of photos from the authors alongside a host of those sent in from Mr J Public – and by god if it isn't one of the best collections of football photos known to man, then I don't know what is!"
The Football Attic